Ubi Deus Dixit

Reconstructions in Lutheran Doctrinal Theology

This series will explore what contemporary theology in the tradition of Luther "should believe, teach and confess" about the God of the gospel. The series will critically engage, explore, and freshly formulate a wide range of topics in dogmatic theology. Every study will ground itself in the doctrinal tradition stemming from Luther's Reformation theology and accordingly will be explicitly focused on the knowledge of God given to faith by the Holy Spirit in Christ according to Luther's pregnant formulation *vera theologia et cognitio Dei sunt in Christo crucifixo*. The studies will articulate the content of faith in formulations which as such propose to be binding upon the contemporary community of faith.

Series Editor:
Paul R. Hinlicky

Editorial Board:
Matthew Burdette
Jennifer Hockenbery
Lois E. Malcolm
Derek Nelson
Piotr J. Malysz

"Not every theologian is conversant in multiple disciplines. But Duane Larson explores science, law, scripture, philosophy, and even economics to reclaim a right understanding of the well-known but often misunderstood doctrine of Two Kingdoms."

—PETER W. MARTY,
publisher, *The Christian Century*

"Duane Larson's rehabilitation of Luther's insight on the Two Kingdoms is timely, subtle, useful and sprightly. Eschewing (all-too-common) extremes of theocratic ambition and political passivity, Larson shows us how political theology belongs in the murky middle. Agamben, Žižek, and other unlikely interlocutors with Martin Luther stimulate insight and upend bromides. Its nuanced readings of Scripture, engagement with natural law, and attention to secular realities make this book a must-read for anyone interested in the urgent question of the Christian's political existence today."

—DEREK NELSON,
Professor of Religion, Wabash College, Indiana

"Rev. Dr. Larson speaks powerfully to the urgencies the Christian religion faces in the current fractious times. Drawing from the wisdom found in philosophy, honest consideration of the Lutheran experiences vis-à-vis power and church, and with deep appreciation of the Lutheran eschatological imagination, Larson unfolds the promise of Luther's doctrine of the two kingdoms as a hopeful apocalyptic vision with roots in the proclamation of the Apostle Paul. The engagingly written work with original theological analysis and arguments both educates and empowers its readers."

—KIRSI STJERNA,
First Lutheran, Los Angeles/Southwest California Synod Professor of Lutheran History and Theology, California Lutheran University

"Lutheran political theology must retrieve and reinterpret the foundational insights of Luther's two kingdoms. Duane Larson brilliantly overcomes misunderstandings in a constructive project that restores to central place the living word of God. The Gospel of Jesus Christ contends with the principalities and powers under a theology of the cross, on the right, and reimagined divine sovereignty under natural law, on the left. A tour de force!"

—CRAIG L. NESSAN,
William D. Streng Professor for the Education and Renewal of the Church,
Wartburg Theological Seminary, Iowa

Ubi Deus Dixit

Where God Has Spoken:
The Lutheran Doctrine of Two Kingdoms

Duane Larson

CASCADE *Books* · Eugene, Oregon

UBI DEUS DIXIT
Where God Has Spoken: The Lutheran Doctrine of Two Kingdoms

Copyright © 2025 Duane Larson. All rights reserved. Except for brief quotations in critical publications or reviews, no part of this book may be reproduced in any manner without prior written permission from the publisher. Write: Permissions, Wipf and Stock Publishers, 199 W. 8th Ave., Suite 3, Eugene, OR 97401.

Cascade Books
An Imprint of Wipf and Stock Publishers
199 W. 8th Ave., Suite 3
Eugene, OR 97401

www.wipfandstock.com

PAPERBACK ISBN: 978-1-6667-1451-7
HARDCOVER ISBN: 978-1-6667-1452-4
EBOOK ISBN: 978-1-6667-1453-1

Cataloguing-in-Publication data:

Names: Larson, Duane [author].

Title: Ubi Deus dixit : where God has spoken: the Lutheran doctrine of two kingdoms / by Duane Larson.

Description: Eugene, OR: Cascade Books, 2025 | Series: Reconstructions in Lutheran Doctrinal Theology | Includes bibliographical references and index.

Identifiers: ISBN 978-1-6667-1451-7 (paperback) | ISBN 978-1-6667-1452-4 (hardcover) | ISBN 978-1-6667-1453-1 (ebook)

Subjects: LCSH: Two kingdoms (Lutheran theology). | Lutheran Church—Doctrines. | Church and state—Lutheran Church. | Christianity and culture.

Classification: BV630.3 L37 2025 (paperback) | BV630.3 (ebook)

VERSION NUMBER 06/12/25

In Loving Memory of Joen

Contents

General Introduction to Reconstruction in Lutheran Doctrinal Theology, by Paul Hinlicky | ix

Acknowledgments | xv

List of Abbreviations | xvii

Introduction | xix

1. The Problems of the Two Kingdoms Doctrine | 1
2. Two Kingdoms Texts and Challenges | 38
3. Natural Law in the Temporal Realm | 73
4. Sovereignty and the State | 109
5. Paul's Eschatological Politics | 145
6. A Future for the Doctrine of Two Kingdoms? | 180

Bibliography | 223

Index | 233

Reconstruction in Lutheran Doctrinal Theology

Editor in Chief: Paul Hinlicky

Associate Editors: Derek Nelson, Lois Malcolm,
Jennifer Hockenbery, Piotr Malysz, Matthew Burdette

General Introduction

THE PRINCETON PHILOSOPHER OF RELIGION Jeffrey Stout reflected not long ago on the sorry fate of Christian theology since Barth. He wrote of a doubly cruel loss: both of audience and of theme. Fear of the future, or fear of being left behind by it, cannot but sap theological nerve in a culture for which History-Written-by-Winners is the de facto deity. This failure of nerve must threaten all the more where and when theology still arises in faith alone at the improbable word of the resurrection-vindication of the crucified Jesus. All this points to a crossroads at which the tradition of Christian theology stemming from Luther in particular stands. It does not take much effort or insight to observe how Lutheran theology today either dwindles into irrelevance as the mere defense of an ever-shrinking piece of ecclesiastical turf or dissipates into revisions increasingly distant from, if not antagonistic to, its source. Consequently, it takes *courage* to venture the relevance of this tradition of Christian theology and to pursue its reconstruction in forms that are fresh yet recognizable developments of core affirmations going back to its genesis.

This series of books, therefore, boldly explores what contemporary theology in the tradition of Luther "should believe, teach and confess" (as *The Book of Concord* once admonished) about the God of the gospel. The studies focus explicitly on the knowledge of God in Christ given to faith by the Holy Spirit according to Luther's pregnant formulation, *vera theologia et cognitio Dei in Christo crucifixo sunt* ("true theology and knowledge of

God are in Christ crucified"). At the same time, the studies do not ignore, mischaracterize, oversimplify, or otherwise run roughshod over the context in which retrieval takes place. The "theological production of doctrine" (C. Helmer) articulating the knowledge of God is consequently an enormous challenge today after the cultural "death of God" announced by Nietzsche's Zarathustra at the turn of the twentieth century. A century later, the ripple effects—varied and far-reaching—of Zarathustra's discovery have hardly subsided. Not only courage, then, but also *insight* into the dramatically transformed spiritual context of "post-Christendom" in the contemporary West is requisite to the theological task today.

With courage renewed, this is a challenge which theology in Luther's tradition can and must undertake in that it has no other claim but that it knows God in the Christ who was once for all truly "crucified, dead and buried"—knowing Creator, and so also creation, only in him, with him, and through him. The theocentric focus on knowledge of God by way of the scandalous "monstrosity" (Hegel) of Christ *crucified*, the Son of God *incarnate*, for the interpretation of topics in doctrinal theology thus demands *critical* retrieval; critical *retrieval* in turn effects a contemporary *pruning* of an overgrown tradition and of necessity entails disciplined experimentation.

A few words by way of introduction to these claims! Lutheran theology flourished in the time of Christendom when Christian theology, including Lutheran theology, undertook the task of promulgating a comprehensive worldview. But Christendom slowly withered under a variety of assaults for this overreach during the Enlightenment. It was buried in the ashes of the twentieth-century experience of Hitler, Hiroshima, and Stalin, moral catastrophes that were perpetrated on the soil of Christian civilizations. Only in retrospect can it be seen how much the enlistment of Lutheran theology in the project of Christendom blunted its critical edge and explosive testimony to the God of the gospel. So nostalgia for those so-called "glory days" of Lutheran theology should also be buried. Let the dead bury the dead.

As may be seen in the twenty-eighth article of the Augsburg Confession, the Lutheran Reformation challenged the medieval understanding of Christendom as the political polity of the Christian people under the governing alliance of pope and emperor. Yet as a "magisterial" Reformation, it conceived of itself as the proper renewal of the polity of Christendom, although historically this tended, without pope, to a new "Caesaropapism." The church became an instrument of the emergent modern nation-state, a "people's church" as opposed to a "confessing church." So a root issue of ecclesial self-understanding was posed during the German church struggle in the 1930s. But with the post-war collapse of Christendom, whether in Protestant or Catholic iteration, the Lutheran version of, and lingering aspirations for, a renewed alliance of throne and altar has become an albatross around the necks of all who would continue Christian theology with insight drawn from Luther. Thus the task undertaken in this series turns upon a core assumption about the contemporary cultural-spiritual context of *post-Christendom* in Europe and North America, an unprecedented situation which both elicits and requires theological renovation.

Today we reckon with the rise of the natural sciences but also with the conceits of Enlightenment modernity, which ideologically justified extractive colonialism with the racialism of white supremacy, exploitative forms of industrial capitalism, murderous forms of socialism, total warfare, and now the threats of economic and/or ecological collapse. The list of disasters on the soil of Christendom could be multiplied, while the real, but tottering achievements of the modern order are today staggering under these accumulated pressures and in danger of disintegration. We enter into a multipolar world no longer dominated by one superpower; willingly or not, we become data sources for the control, manipulation, and prediction of surveillance capitalism, whether in alliance with the national security state pretending to defend "democracy" on one side, or, on the other side, with emergent autocracies, bold and powerful, which disdain any very pretense of "democracy."

The forms of Lutheran theology inherited from the passing era of modernity, then, have become not only dysfunctional, but deservingly discredited along with dying Christendom itself. Lutheran theology in the epoch of emergent modernity had oscillated between "modernist" forms of accommodation to rising secularist ideologies and "fundamentalist" forms of resistance to them. Both of these strategies are today in disrepute because each in its own way sought the rehabilitation of the political order of Christendom. Persisting in these lost causes only inhibits theology from facing up to present and future dangers, seeking and finding salutary ways forward.

As Dietrich Bonhoeffer saw from his prison cell, the polity of the Christians, *corpus christianum*, has now dissolved into its components, the body of Christ and "this world," indifferent to "Christ existing as community," if not hostile—yet astonishingly loved by God! The studies in this series take for granted this contemporary cultural-spiritual context and see no particular need to advocate, especially in our Euro-American post-Christendom, the need for a new synthesis. Instead contributions stipulate each respective author's understanding of this context and proceed to the critical and constructive task of the production of doctrinal articulations of Christian faith's knowledge of God. To be sure, authors will understand this context and the path forward in varying, perhaps even *contrary* ways. But we have sought some measure of coherence for the series by asking authors to give attention to one another's work in constructive dialogue, patient elaboration, and charitable critique.

The series attends to the challenges of the world's plurality and multipolarity in two ways. First, the notion of what constitutes legitimate subject matter of dogmatic reflection has been opened up. Thus books in this series critically engage, explore, and freshly formulate traditional topics in dogmatic theology but also some newer ones. Second, the theological tradition stemming from Luther is not the exclusive preserve of nominal "Lutherans," but bears from its origins an ecumenical intention, appeal, and to some extent influence. Accordingly this series has deliberately enlisted authors beyond the boundaries of denominational Lutheranism who intend in their own fashion to continue what Luther started. Thus, while every study grounds itself in the doctrinal tradition stemming from Luther's Reformation theology, each proceeds as a critical development of it.

The series has not solicited theologians from the Two/Thirds world, though we think our series will be a richly informative for those who find the complexities and partisanships in current Western theology baffling. The rising generation will happily see a flowering of indigenous Lutheran theologies across the globe which wrestle with problems not identical to the Euro-American context of the demise of Christendom. Perhaps our wrestling in the series can serve as a cautionary tale in certain respects for global partners in the Lutheran theological tradition. Perhaps these new Lutheran theologies will shed light in turn upon our own Euro-American perplexities.

The situation of post-Christendom, in parallel to "postmodernism" but not identical with it, thus forces a winnowing so that what is essential for theology as a discipline is clarified as knowledge of the God of the gospel such that other dimensions of Christian doctrine are clearly developed as corollaries of the saving, therefore essential, knowledge of God. In arguing cognitive claims about God, the studies articulate the content of faith in formulations which as such propose to be binding upon the contemporary community of faith in that they are integral to the gospel of God which authors and authorizes Christian faith, community, and mission. Such proposed formulations neither repudiate nor repeat formulations of the past but seek freshly to articulate their pertinent content, rationale, and relevance.

This series originated after the publication by Cascade Press of Paul Hinlicky's *Lutheran Theology: A Critical Introduction*, when Cascade queried whether he would be willing to edit a series of books on Lutheran theology. Hinlicky gathered together theological colleagues, most of whom had worked with him on the *Oxford Encyclopedia of Martin Luther*, to form an editorial advisory group. He also recruited an editor who would reflect the series's ecumenical orientation. The group brainstormed prospective authors and topics and began solicitation of interest. The response has been overwhelming as the series launches with thirty some authors with topics under contract to appear over the course of the next seven years. We have deliberately sought out a rich mix of senior and junior scholars from a variety of backgrounds holding to various positions within contemporary systematic theology, experimentalist *and* retrievalist, deliberately breaching denominational walls and crossing old battle-lines.

Systematic theology is, even at best, an ambiguous good, reflecting our status as wayfarers on a pilgrim way. In a better world yet to come, we would not labor to articulate the knowledge of God, but simply worship the God of the gospel who in the cross of Christ has sought and found *us*, and so come to *know* us. But here and now, between the already of the resurrection-vindication of the Crucified and the not yet of his final victory for us and for all, we write *about* the God whom *we know as knowing us* that we may serve *intelligently in this fateful interim time*. Such is our task, neither hankering after the fleshpots of Egypt nor storming the kingdom to take it by force. In the end (pun intended), true theological statements are doxological, finding their correction and vindication in the great doxology of the creation rescued and fulfilled at the Pauline "redemption of our bodies." In this confidence we offer this series to the glory of God and for the edification of the Body of Christ in its mission to the world.

February, 2025

Paul R. Hinlicky with Matthew Burdette, Jennifer Hockenbery, Lois Malcolm, Peter Malysz, and Derek Nelson

Acknowledgments

THE WRITING OF ANY BOOK is a journey full of discovery for the author. A writer may begin the trip with a clear goal in mind and a fairly forthright map for getting there. But rarely, if ever, is the trip one of simple expectations met. The traveler discovers road reconstruction, detours, and unanticipated delays, as well as fascinating attractions that even the most current GPS guided maps will not include. And if the journey is by foot, the road often becomes a trail and the trail often grows weathered, not often trod, and so faint. Then some local comes to me from who knows where, with her walking stick and happy dog, and she tells me where the trail picks up clearly again and updates me about its condition. Her guidance is but for a portion of the trail. But it is enough for the time. As for the time that remains, surety grows that others will show up just when most needed.

Writing this book has been like that. I began the project with what I had thought was a clear sense of tactics and strategy. That mental map proved insufficient. The hike would take much longer than first expected. Not long after the formal start on the trailhead, a horrid diagnosis required that my primary duty be as caregiver for my terminally ill spouse. Then, though I had anticipated it for months, her death brought me grief that blocked most thought and action. Only the loving support of friends would nurture me back into a writing mode. They are so many, but of them I happily shout out to all the members of Christ the King Lutheran Church in Houston; my friend and pastor Peter Marty; dear neighbors Kim and Jennifer, who insistently made sure I was doing okay; and beloved bringer of new life, Anne McIntosh. With many more, they were and continue to be encouragers on my journey of "thinking faith."

Then there are those who read and commented on portions of this book while it was in process. Such a rocky trail I made them walk with their reading of my cumbersome drafts! Yet they responded patiently with good questions, conceptual clarifications, and constructive suggestions for turning esoteric scholarly writing into something somewhat more legible. Where my obtuseness still prevails, that's on me alone. They include Phil Baker, Rick Rouse, Kirsi Stjerna, and Peter Pettit. For expert guidance on the legal material that was almost all new to me, I thank Russell Post. For his superb close reading and detailed responses at every step, I thank my editor, Paul Hinlicky. I am sure I severely tested his patience over these years, especially over the final stretch, but, nevertheless, he persisted. No writer could have a more knowledgeable, expectant, and properly challenging editor than Paul. Finally, I thank those too many to name who have cheered me on during this hike and have professed their eagerness to welcome the book. To echo faintly Marx's famous line, every writer writes more for the sake of a better future than simply to understand the past. And every prospective reader reads with the hope of constructive insight for self and society. Our steps forward and our pauses to reflect are all about wanting to make things better, no matter how long it takes for words to seed and strengthen Christ's Beloved Community. I am grateful that my work here has not been dictated by loneliness, but suffused with friendship, which is the seed of justice in any government.

List of Abbreviations

Luther and Lutheranism:

BOC	The Book of Concord
LW	Luther's Works (American Edition)
WA	Weimar Ausgabe of Luther's Writings
AC	The Augsburg Confession
Ap	Apology to the Augsburg Confession
FC	Formula of Concord

By Giorgio Agamben:

CC	The Coming Community
CK	The Church and the Kingdom
HS	Homo Sacer
KG	The Kingdom and the Garden
P	Potentialities
SE	State of Exception
SoL	The Sacrament of Language
TR	The Time That Remains

By Dietrich Bonhoeffer:

DBWE	Dietrich Bonhoeffer's Works in English

Introduction

"There is a Christianity that has forgotten that the Lord commands, 'Follow me!' and has fitted itself out religiously as a mystery cult, has struck the alliance of throne and altar, and has sunk into middle-class mentality."[1]

I WANT TO RE-INTRODUCE people of Christian conviction and people friendly to the former to what has been called the Doctrine of Two Kingdoms. I want to do this from within the Lutheran tradition in which it was nurtured and became normative for faith and life, though also with favor to its "original intent" when authored by Augustine. I also want to begin a "re-construction" (presuming a deconstruction) of the doctrine. For understandable reasons, the doctrine has been de facto dismissed even by Lutherans in official or "thought influencer" capacities. The reasons include missteps even soon after the doctrine's encoding. Misinterpretation abounded. Therefore misapplication abounded too; the most egregious misinterpretation and misuse being Hitler's co-option and commandeering of the doctrine so to fuse religiosity with loyalty to him and his Reich. I understate in saying that much human emotion and theological-political substance must be addressed if the doctrine is to be reclaimed and rethought while maintaining the integrity of original intent.

Why do I want to do this? Please allow me to offer a personal and theological answer. I am not sure what Ernst Käsemann in the above quote meant by "middle-class mentality." The cultic attitude of whatever narrower sociological category he was referring to is now mainstreamed and normalized beyond class specification. But his remark still sticks. I am struck by how resonant his recognition of the alliance of cult, throne, and altar is with the state of Christianity today around the world. I've witnessed firsthand this alliance in South Africa and Namibia. In the morning people in impressive

1. Käsemann, *Church Conflicts*, 78.

numbers would receive Holy Communion in a Lutheran congregation. In the afternoon I recognized many of them eagerly participating in an open-air prosperity gospel church that strangely fused biblical literalism and an evidently pneumatic spiritualism with confident pride. I personally respect sincere piety and expressive worship. But something also seemed amiss to my confessedly faulty eyes, as if an addition to or replacement of something essential to Christian faith was slipped in by a performative worship leader beneath intended spectacle. I've seen similar scenes in venues of different accents—Russian, Polish, El Salvadoran, Peruvian, British, even Southern California Surfer Dude—where presider intent and behavioral consequences were very similar. It was as if what Slavoj Žižek has called the machinery of language was machination. Surely sincerity of piety was present. But because I respect piety, I questioned what appeared to be performance and posturing. The same question more dramatically came to mind with a remembrance of Sinclair Lewis[2] when I witnessed a cloudy storm of American flags occluding the lone cross in a Texan megachurch. That not-beatific stage setting was accompanied by rising decibels of patriotic music in concert with a video of F-15s flying over the Washington Monument.

Each and every one of these scenes to differing degrees cast unreflectively a confusion of national patrimony with religious liturgy, an alliance of throne and altar. And if they were done with precise forethought, so much, frankly, for the worse. For then performativity transcended conviction. The machinery of language was machination. The machination is to con-fuse the "kingdom" of this world with the Kingdom of our God, something that Christ abjured. Yet so it goes.

The reader may be discomforted by my words. So am I. Am I already too harsh? Too honest? Too partisan? We live in fractious times when the line "Question Authority" has moved off of car bumpers to plant deep in human psyches. The radically populist hermeneutics of suspicion is fully ingrained now in our faith lives and our political lives. Faith and politics seem to be so almost fatally intertwined. It used to be that God and government were not allowed even once a year at the family table. Now the perseverating discussion is either 24/7 or fear of an anxiety attack disables all, even urgent, conversation. Either way, it is soul-killing.

It is a sad day when we no longer take a self-identified Christian at face value. We feel like we must ask for credentials. "Your papers, please!" Faced by manipulative spectacle anywhere on our small and fragile planet, and with ears tuned to insistent "disinformation," I return to Käsemann ruminating on the short time and distance from the Third Reich to the 1980s.

---

2. Lewis, *It Can't Happen Here*.

His words still fit in the 2020s. "It seems as if I exaggerate, though these days we are careful to protect ourselves from strong language so as not to disturb objectivity with rhetoric. But must we not seriously reflect on whether the Nazi period and the horror of the concentration camps, rather than being an exception and, as it were, an accident in our history, actually initiated an epoch of worldwide barbarism to which we are more and more exposed?"[3]

"Epoch" is a long period to have to endure painful societal fracture. "Spectacle" is a descriptor for the tactic of anesthetizing a public to the pain wrought and yet to be brought by the strategist. The tactic is not always and only spectacle. But it is favored by governments, corporate interests, powerful princes and priests, and old-fashioned authoritarians who would arrogate ever more social and financial capital to themselves no matter how already behemoth-sized their portfolios. Control must always grow. It is not just an Orwellian trope to assert that concupiscence is buried beneath the multiple layers of spectacular and banal disingenuities carefully gamed out. They are the myths carefully constructed over very long terms by the self-centering powers and principalities so to sustain themselves in self-righteousness and so that the truth of their and our corruption, fallibility, and weakness may never be exposed. This is a basic truth that pervades all our philosophy and theology about religion and civil government. And what pervades we prefer to evade.

As Käsemann stated, Bultmann was wrong to preach that it is the Bible (alone?) to be demythologized. Oh, of course the Bible has its time-terms and also still exotic imagery. Bultmann sought with good intent to release the biblical terms from their bondage to history. He thereby hoped to give us the interpretive lenses so to relate biblical truths better to our notions of ourselves. But he did not realize that our notions themselves of ourselves already are as mythical as we think Scripture is. I'd say indeed it is simply us and our ideological constructions that must be demythologized and Scripture's eschatological and apocalyptic terms are perfectly sufficient in doing just so. The human self is the problem. Wherever we go, there we are. It is not the Bible but our social-political being that must be demythologized. Scripture, to overly summarize, always stated that our problem was us and that the answer is "let go and let God," an apt translation of Luther's "sin boldly. Believe more boldly in Christ and rejoice in him."[4] It takes a power other and greater than ourselves to liberate us. It also takes a revelation, an apocalypse, from a qualitatively different time, eschatological time, for us to hear and see rightly what has already been done for us.

3. Käsemann, *Church Conflict*, 79.
4. LW 48:282.

Yes, we do need still to understand the Bible's terms and worldviews, freeing them, as it were, so to find ourselves relatable to them. We also recognize that we must be freed from our own captivity to myths we have constructed to salve our anxiety as heirs of modernity's turn to the self, inadvertently charging us to control our universes. The varied witnesses of the Hebrew and Christian Scriptures always were and are allied so to reveal our Potemkin villages of piety and civility for what they really are: attempts at individual and nationalistic self-justification with warrants to do harm so to stay at the top.

The myth that is now our priority for demythologizing therefore is that God intends that all government should serve God and that only the godly should serve government. Neither the Bible nor the Great Tradition of Christianity ever said this as a doctrinal or dogmatic norm. Yet, we Christians to a great or lesser extent have elided faith in God with faith in government.

Which brings me to the point of this book. Given the situation first stated above, one might presume that this book is about the new "cult," as many journalists name it, of Christian Nationalism, the new conjoining of "throne and altar." Though I will reference it, this book is *not* about Christian Nationalism. It is about the Lutheran iteration of the Doctrine of Two Kingdoms. Many responsible thinkers have addressed the exigent challenge of Christian Nationalism. I recommend them.[5] The Two Kingdoms doctrine, however, gets at the root of the perverted politics of a fused church and state. Or, I should say, severe misinterpretation and misuse of the doctrine—singularly practiced in Hitler's absorption of the church into the fascist state populated by proudly "true" *Deutsche Christen*—is the cause of nationalism newly amuck.

The Two Kingdoms doctrine has been in place as guidance since at least Augustine articulated it in the fourth century. Its foundations are biblical. The doctrine is a synthesis of Jesus' responding to Pilate that Jesus' kingdom is "not from this world" and both Paul and Peter counselling their Christian readers and hearers to respect and obey the governing authorities because God instituted them for the good of human beings.[6] The doctrine's Lutheran bases are stated in the Augsburg Confession (AC) and the Apology to the Augsburg Confession (Ap), Articles 16 and 28, and the Formula of Concord (FC), Article 10. All are what Lutherans regard as their doctrinal beliefs, known as "Confessions," and are set forth in The Book of Concord (BOC).

---

5. See, e.g., Tyler, *How to End Christian Nationalism*; Du Mez, *Jesus and John Wayne*; Ingersoll, *Building God's Kingdom*; Hedges, *American Fascists*; Whitehead and Perry, *Taking America Back for God*; Gagne, *American Evangelicals*.

6. John 18:36; Rom 13:7; 1 Pet 2:13.

Succinctly put, the doctrine states that the church had its own specific "realm" and duties and civil government its own. Priests and prelates should stay in their lane and civil government officials in theirs. They also should stay in communication with each other, ensuring that the prescribed duties of each are performed, because both realms must work together complementarily for the good of everybody, whether religious or not. The distinction between the spiritual and secular, also, was and is not of "equals." Christians are to serve everyone else with peaceableness, humility, and love, and not at all with any sense of colonialist ambition or superiority. Christians also know that the spiritual eschatological realm in which actually and wonderfully we nest infinitely transcends the material secular temporal realm in which we live, move, and enact our being. Any alliance of throne and altar, any confusion and collusion, of state and church contradicts the distinctive integrity that God gave to the spiritual and temporal kingdoms.

I argue that if the doctrine of Two Kingdom had been considered and followed more seriously after the first generation of reformers in general and Lutheranism in particular, we might not have wholly avoided the threats of this present day, but the threats we now face might have been more moderated. Theological, philosophical, and political "mistakes were made" by the church and the state. They led to the unintended consequence of religiously supported fascism we face today.

Mistakes include not having read Paul as the apocalyptic theologian he was, stirred by an eschatological vision that the early church fathers and mothers after him shared. Though Augustine, Luther, and more were given the vision and voice, only recently have philosophers and theologians caught on again. Indeed, only now have we come around to understanding and interpreting the Two Kingdoms doctrine itself in terms of eschatology and apocalypticism. It makes a world of difference. Another mistake is the seeming absence of the Theology of the Cross in Luther's articulation of the Two Kingdoms and most interpretation and application since of the doctrine. More depth and breadth about the Theology of the Cross itself and its application, too, makes a world of difference. Finally, as for this brief catalog of mistakes requiring more immediate attention, it has always struck me as curious that "two-kingdoms" thinking has only been done from theology's side, without attention to the temporal side from which the philosophers wave at us. What is the point of insisting on the "Two" when we do not respect the partner, especially the philosopher of law? The oversight appears gross when one discovers as I have that Western philosophy and law have so distanced themselves from concepts that Luther believed were essential for two-kingdoms thinking. Two of these essential concepts are natural law and human/political sovereignty. These concepts are all but lost in philosophy and legal practice.

If a two-kingdoms conceptuality for political theology is to work, it must be reconstructed so to redress all these problems from eschatology and apocalyptic language up to contemporary legal theory. This book is an attempt at such redress. I want to reclaim the Doctrine of Two Kingdoms as viable and indeed necessary for the faithful Christian's life with and in service to the neighbor. In character with the goal of this whole series in reconstructions of Lutheran doctrines and practices, I've sought to engage "secular domain" disciplines like philosophy, law, and even cosmology to establish at least the main fundaments for a revivified doctrine. Other problems of severe misinterpretation will be assayed too. Singularly helpful in this project is the work of Italian philosopher Giorgio Agamben. He is among the "postmodern" philosophers today who have made thick analysis of the human animal/culture/politics their life's work. Considered a public intellectual in Italy, Agamben is not well known in the United States and hardly known at all among most theologians. But it is not because of his novel alterity that I feature him. Agamben has made a huge impact on Pauline scholarship, his self-differentiation from the church notwithstanding. After being encouraged to read his groundbreaking book *The Time That Remains*, I realized that his career-long exegesis of what he calls *Homo Sacer* (the "sacred human") in the political terms of the day is required reading.

Reading Agamben suggested to me not only that a rereading of Two Kingdoms *eschatologically and apocalyptically* is necessary. Other ruminations about (1) the original gift (!) of language as communion between the divine and the human and then (2) the practical use of language as intended toward the prospect of the original "sacramental" gift of language literally, struck me as opportune prospects for rethinking natural law and sovereignty. Because these two important concepts in "original" two-kingdoms thinking have been swept aside by the pragmatic positivism of those who define and administer law today, there is return again to the legalization of privileged supremacy for some people in religion and government and dismissal of the moral/spiritual priority of servanthood for the many in religion and government. Agamben's thought about language in tandem with the Theology of the Cross with a return to eschatology and the right churchly use of apocalyptic can enable a meaningful and useful recovery of the Doctrine of Two Kingdoms. But a caveat is in order. My resourcing of Agamben does not imply that I consider him to be a *souverain cause célèbre* for theology. He might appreciate that, but I do not believe he would approve it. He does provide iron on which to sharpen theological thought. But as is the character of antifoundationalist postmodern philosophy, the intention always is to prompt, to deconstruct, and to prompt again. No philosophical modality is more dedicated to *semper reformanda*. And being in the thick of similar conversation among many philosophers, some of whom I also will introduce, Agamben reminds us of the kind of community of mutual exhortation and consolation that we all must be as would-be thoughtful Christians of conviction, humility, and generosity. And so I pose doctrinal reconstruction with due temerity and tentativeness.

For Whom Is This Book and Its Itinerary

This book is intended for students of theology, clergy, colleague academic theologians, and adults who have interest in the state of religion, law, and politics in America and the world generally insofar as the enmeshment of "throne and altar" has been socially incarnated on a global scale. For those who have not read formal theology, some chapters will be easier to follow than others. But with some willpower and patience, every one of the intended readership can get the gist of the more challenging chapters.

With this Introduction, I identified the Doctrine of Two Kingdoms and the current contextual situation in which we read it (or do not). In chapter 1, I will explore in more detail the problems that have derailed the doctrine unto the present day. Having presented the most apparent problems, the next question is whether this doctrine is worth saving. Can we renovate it, commend it, and use it? Obviously, I think so. But how? The answer entails assaying the doctrine's history of reception and then cues—though they cannot be exhaustively explored—for the doctrine's re-employment today.

Thus, chapter 2 takes a detailed look at the doctrine itself and the circumstances before and around its incorporation into the Lutheran "canon." This includes brief reference to Augustine. My resourcing of Augustine here underscores that my appeal to Two Kingdoms is not so parochial as merely some *reine Lehre* (pure doctrine) of a precious Lutheranism. I mean this to be an ecumenical and catholic argument pertaining to the Great Tradition which has further positive relevance for a humane and inclusive politics. In sum, with chapter 2 I mean to be descriptive and somewhat introductory. It is also the kind of chapter that can be read on its own and useful for the new student of Lutheranism or a study group.

With chapters 3 and 4, I address two problems that I identify as the most severe ones posed by political philosophy, with some attention also to epistemology. The Two Kingdoms doctrine can only make sense if what it conceives to be true of the temporal realm is in fact so. For that reason I turn to the temporal to track its own history of two major concepts. The first is natural law, with its subset of higher law. The second is sovereignty. It is not an overstatement to say that Lutherans presumed in their formulation of the Two Kingdoms Doctrine that the religious understanding of natural law and sovereignty was in full accord with the secular understanding. Natural law and sovereignty each were authoritative norms for government and the practice of law through three centuries after Luther. But, of course, the philosophical worldview itself evolved. The common understanding and commitment to natural law held from Cicero through Luther and the humanists changed formidably beginning with the Enlightenment. It finally was abandoned (I argue) after the linguistic positivism of the twentieth century met the legal doctrine of constitutional "originalism" in the twenty-first.[7] I begin referencing Agamben in this chapter.

Furthermore, it wasn't just a surprise occasion of narcissistic power grabbing that erupted in Hitler and Stalin and more in echo of tyrants long before. The understandings of sovereignty held by Luther and even Pope Leo X were fairly similar, but finally not so at all with Hitler. Hitler was stoked by his huge narcissistic ambition. He depended also on the new political philosophy of Carl Schmitt (who himself resourced Luther) to justify his power lust and turn people's faith toward his fascist leadership. About Hitler and his coterie we also see the postmodern identification of "spectacle" and the "machinery of language" on full display. So we have this major question facing any attempt to rehabilitate the Two Kingdoms Doctrine today. That question is whether the doctrine's presumptions of the import of natural law and sovereignty have any correlation with whatever has replaced them in secular civil society today. Or is there any replacement? Having explored in some depth the (d)evolution of the concepts of natural law and sovereignty from Cicero through Bentham, Kant, and more, I will land on the consensus around the work of philosopher of law and attorney H. L. A Hart as a possible correlate for two-kingdoms thinking as nuanced also by Luther's Theology of the Cross.

With chapter 5, I make a significant turn. Here—finally!—I explore the relevant biblical texts that have funded two-kingdoms thinking. I have restrained from discussing this earlier in the book, as I fancied keeping the book itself on a mostly historical track. By waiting to introduce and interpret the relevant biblical texts until this chapter, I view them through the lenses of contemporary New Testament scholars and philosophers. Here again, I discuss Agamben's unique and significant influence and promise for political theologizing. In particular, I unpack Agamben's exegesis of Rom 13 and related Scripture texts regarding his seminal idea of "messianic time."

---

7. Cf. Gienapp, *Against Constitutional Originalism*.

I then turn briefly to eschatology and contemporary science to underscore the "reality" of multidimensional space, hinted at also by Agamben, for understanding Two Kingdoms as a proposal of metaphysics.

Finally, in chapter 6, I interpret anew what the doctrine could offer government as a protocol for the making of public policy. At greater length I suggest what the church's "practical" work in its own realm must attend to. The church must reclaim its role of being "spiritual first" so that Christians may better serve the good of the political order. To the reader this may seem rather obvious. But were it so, I argue that such obviousness is lost to the secular citizen who bemoans Christian attempts to colonize government today. How to be church in the world also includes comment about the Theology of the Cross as an ethic as well as method. The Theology of the Cross is a form of "knowing" and so of "doing," and therefore must be integral for renewed two-kingdoms thinking. I trust the "eschatological epistemic" implication of this revised interpretation of two-kingdoms thinking makes clear the urgency of the church's work to attend to the deeper spiritual sensibility of faith. Only faith first can sufficiently fuel the church's work of love in the temporal arena.

As I said above, we live in fractious times. We had a brief moment of hope when "the end of history" came to Francis Fukuyama's eyes and ours with the collapse of Soviet authoritarianism. That was short lived, another illusion in humankind's long history of self-deception. Now we fear another prospect of authoritarianism clothed even more intently by religious fabrications. The Doctrine of Two Kingdoms, however, when read with eschatologically opened eyes and heard in the liberating apocalyptic timbre of the gospel, in-spires with that hope which comes only from God's eternity into our time. The doctrine has been and can be arcane, which dismissal thereby may constitute the worst misinterpretation and misuse. My prayer is that despite my own at times too-technical and infelicitous language, we might get a teasingly better view of possible politics *and* that our spiritual homes however temporal would indeed in-spire and ex-cite us, breathe hope into us and thus charge us out of ourselves for love of the world that God so loves. Ultimately—which means not a distant end, but means the most meaningful "now time," which is eschatological, which is *right now*—God intends that everyone know the messianic beauty in which we all already are embraced. In this human hope the theopolitics of Two Kingdoms correlates perfectly with the gospel of Jesus Christ.

All Saints Day 2024

1

The Problems of the Two Kingdoms Doctrine

"O God of light and love. . . . Inspire us, we pray . . . that we may rejoice with courage, confidence, and faith in the Word made flesh, and may be led to establish that city which has justice for its foundation and love for its law; through Jesus Christ, the light of the world, who lives and reigns with you and the Holy Spirit, one God, now and forever. Amen."[1]

UBI DEUS DIXIT. "Where God has spoken." This Latin phrase appears in innumerable theological writings throughout the history of Christianity. Students of theology may recognize, too, that to open a book with the phrase alludes to Karl Barth's famous phrase of *Deus dixit*. He used the term to update a classic argument for the reality of God. Simply to utter the word "God" who is "wholly other" can only be done, Barth argued, if the wholly other God provides the word about and from God. Much has been said for and against Barth's early argument. Barth's argument was far more nuanced than many readers since have recognized. Instead, at the "popular" level, evangelical Protestant Christians took Barth's theologically powerful assertion about revelation as simplistic support for strictly literal biblical interpretation and conservative civil government. In strict biblical literalism "days" in Gen 1 are composed of twenty-four hours and in Rev 22 people who are blessed wear actual robes before the return of Christ. In between them, every word is as specifically referential to mundane reality.

1. From the daily Collect of the Episcopal Church in the Unites States, Prayer for the Feast Day of William Temple, Archbishop of Canterbury, Nov. 6, 1944.

The assertion as to "where God has spoken" then became separated from the theological and philosophical framings of Barth and others. It became a punctuation mark for declarative sentences endorsing literalism like "God said it in the Bible. Believe it or be damned."

Reading the Bible as simple referential secular language about how God made and intends the world to function set off the next firework. Because "God said" certain things in the Bible about how Christians should relate to government and the world, the argument goes, we must then do exactly what God "says." We must "exercise dominion" over the creation (Gen 1:28). Because government is "instituted by God" we must "be subject to the governing authorities" (Rom 13:1) and "accept the authority of every human institution" (1 Pet 2:13–14). But how then do we reconcile the difference between exercising dominion and being subject to the authorities?

One answer is that Christians should withdraw from all involvement with government and respect authorities from afar. Obey. Maybe vote. But never otherwise involve yourself with political matters. A major problem with worldly withdrawal, of course, is unless one defines one's neighbor very strictly as "close by," a Christian cannot take seriously Christ's command to love actively all people without paying at least some attention to the politics of doing so. Though we believe that Christ's kingdom is of a different order, unless one can live wholly "off the grid," it is impossible not to be affected to some degree and necessarily so by civil government. No danger to government or faith is presented by religious separatists. Some of what they present to helter-skelter civilization is hospitable and spiritually refreshing in brief doses, however untenable the full-time lifestyle is for most people. Retreats to monasteries and visits with Amish friends can be restorative and good for the soul.

Another answer is that Christians should become the governing authorities. This is a long-practiced answer, but threatens the health and stability of church and society. "Governance by Christians" is the agenda argued and realized today after decades of planning by conservative evangelical leaders. We know the movement as Christian Nationalism. Christian Nationalists take the verses I have cited seriously and literally. They also have tapped into some of the doctrines of traditional mainline Protestantism[2] in an attempt to add more intellectual heft to their theological and political position. Theirs actually is not a new disposition. Variants of the enmeshment of Christian faith and pride of culture were precursors to cultural supremacy and nationalism (which I define as exclusivistic patriotism beyond due pride in one's nation) since Constantine made an empire out of

---

2. E.g., the so-called "doctrine of the Lesser Magisteria," which I discuss in ch. 2.

faith. Nationalism took a formal and initial theologically unintended form in 1648 when the Peace of Westphalia aligned a ruler's dominion with its ruler's personal faith. Identifiable nationalism emerged in the nineteenth century as a concept for a cultural-linguistic community. Nationalism assumed a demonic figuration when Hitler's Reich took control of the government, assigned "Christian" as a predicate to nationalism, and took control of the German church. Cooperative (and co-opted) citizens then proudly wore the identity of "Deutsche Christen." There are differences between then and now. But they do not change the substance of the matter. The modern evolutionary emergent of Christian Nationalism, like religious and political authoritarianism, is now a clear and present danger to democratic political systems and to Christian faith itself, as well as to all religion.

But as I stated in the introduction, this book is not primarily about Christian Nationalism. Rather, I address the Doctrine of Two Kingdoms, its meaning, its misinterpretations, and its misuse. Its misinterpretation just might be at the root of today's varied reconstructions of Christian faith as authoritarian, nationalistic, militaristic, and triumphalist, familiar qualifiers all. When Jesus told Pilate that Jesus' kingdom was "not of this world," he put into opposition his rule and Roman rule. When both Paul and Peter not long later wrote that Christians should obey the earthly authorities, they were both distinguishing Roman rule from God's rule *and* saying that to obey the authorities was also to obey God, because God instituted them. What interpreters overlooked (at best) when later interpreting all three of Jesus, Paul, and Peter, not to mention John the Divine's excoriation of the Roman governing authorities in his Apocalypse (the book of Revelation), is that there still was the absolute distinction between the kingdoms such that they could not and should not be fused in the minds of mortals *and* that God's reign in Christ would become the final and consummate rule of peace "over-ruling" all else. In other words, the superlative eschatological rule and presence of God transcends and will transcend at the last all other regimes, and whatever Jesus and all the New Testament witness said about such things must be read eschatologically. In sum, the kingdoms relate, but one is greater than the other, and so long as history abides, so also Christians must abide temporal governments. And we must abide so long as those temporal governments do not defy God's good will for all people. Until God's reign comes in full—and it will!—politics and religion relate. But they must not ever be confused, and cannot ever be fully separated. Further, the purposes of one must always cohere with the purposes of the other even as we confess that the spiritual kingdom is not only different from but also greater than the temporal kingdom.

This is the stuff of the Doctrine of Two Kingdoms. The concept first appeared in Augustine's typology of the reign of Christ vs. the reign of the devil (*regnum Christi vs. regnum diaboli*). Its material content, however, was more described in Augustine's imagery of the City of God and the City of Man. About a thousand years later Martin Luther recast Augustine's terms as the duality of the spiritual kingdom and the temporal kingdom, each of which God charged to function differently and to be administered differently. In effect, Luther used Augustine's formal title of "Two Kingdoms" and material content from Augustine's great work, *The City of God*, to fill out Luther's and the reformers' view as to how religion and government should work and relate. At the same time, Luther still recognized that these two theo-political figurations were involved in the greater apocalyptic combat of Christ and the Satan. The largest spiritual imagination contextualizes the theo-political model of Two Kingdoms within that apocalyptic fight. But the administration of the spiritual kingdom over which God in Christ reigns is not in conflict with the administration of the temporal realm in which God is hidden. In this latter and lesser relationship with distinction of spiritual and temporal domains we are called to discern and practice faith and politics, each of which have their own integrity and are neither to be enmeshed nor separate.

As noted, with the spiritual domain is its eschatological qualification, which is actually a removal of all qualifications. By "eschatology" tradition has normally meant "last things." Last things were and still are thought of as at the end of history's arrow of time. But this purely temporal understanding of eschatology is insufficient. It does not cohere with the extradimensionality of spirit. "Eschatological" also refers to ultimacy, even literally to the "ultimate word," the most meaningful word, the "Last Word" which rules all words in "all worlds" as the very eternal Word of God. This is the primary meaning I intend hereafter. It is also the way in which most theology since the turn from modernity has understood it.

The eschatological horizon and its attendant apocalyptic language (as compared to simple referential secular language) for Paul, early subsequent theologians, and Luther in their reading of him cannot be overstated. But with the Enlightenment, Christians largely lost their eschatological imagination. No matter the goodness of the Enlightenment's recharged humanism and the rise of the natural sciences, its leading philosophers quarantined Christian faith from publicly approved pure and practical reason. Religion was in effect reduced to private piety, and even that was stripped of eschatological sensitivity. With this, political and legal philosophy also diminished the stature of such theretofore important concepts as "natural law" and "sovereignty." That was fateful because the reformers identified natural law and personal human sovereignty as the correlates in the temporal kingdom to the important dicta of the spiritual kingdom.

Describing why and how Two Kingdoms thinking and non-thinking had some role in ushering in the phenomenon of Christian Nationalism is, of course, a water-under-the-bridge enterprise. The salient question is what to do now. Can the doctrine be reclaimed? Should it be? If so, given real changes in understanding of philosophy and law as well as theology, what adjustments in interpretation of the doctrine need to be made? The questions are neither small nor minor. Reclamation projects inevitably affect their whole neighborhood and environment. Luther himself came to see the relationship of the spiritual kingdom and the temporal kingdom as a trope for his whole theology. He thought it was a kind of Theory of Everything (TOE). That implies an uncomfortable question for us who think ourselves still to be "good" Lutherans or whatever other Christian denominational identity we might claim. If we have gotten this doctrine wrong or abandoned it after so long mistreating it, what else must we change in our regard of church and state and even faith in general?

Contemporary philosophy and contemporary biblical scholarship now agree on something we had not recognized in our reading of Paul, of Luther, and the Doctrine of Two Kingdoms. Scholarship holds now that Luther's thought was situated in Pauline eschatology with apocalyptic language befitting the eschatology. To read Romans with apocalyptic imagination makes a universe of difference. In sum, for at least two centuries since the Enlightenment and likely more we had "read" the Two Kingdoms as if they were statically dualistic, as if the spiritual kingdom were a private place for faith and piety on the same plane as the temporal kingdom's place of coordinated public life. We supposed that when the private and the public were kept so, then private and public were at their best. Much criticism was leveled at the very idea of Luther's Two Kingdoms when read this way. Thinking this way indeed enabled Nazism's rise and takeover of the church. If the doctrine were meant to be read this way, the criticism and practical abandonment were deserved.

But if Paul and Luther (and so many in between) are read apocalyptically, with a certain kind of eschatology that we believe they had in mind, we find that faith cannot restrain from life in the temporal world, *and* we will be congenial with the world's pluralism. We also find that the eschatology of any of the "Dominionist" versions of Christianity with their own idiosyncratic and literalistic apocalyptic language is so wrong as merely to be secular itself. Eschatology is *not* about the end of one lateral temporal arrow of time, though the narrower arrow of time we know and experience does end. Eschatology is about the transcendence of God already present to, with, in, through, and infinitely greater than our temporality. And apocalyptic is the spiritually-charged imaginative and still reality-referential language that bespeaks the revelation of the kingdom already come and coming more. To read Paul and Luther (and Calvin et al.) apocalyptically is to discover that we are called to bring our faith into the world as spirit-inspired poets of the most positive vision. We are also called not to "conquer" secularity. God's spiritual order and the secular are not in conflict. God made them both. However, God's spiritual order and God's temporal order are in conflict with the Satan's—the Liar's—kingdom, all that opposes God and God's loving intentions. The spiritual already quietly works in the secular because the secular has already been caught up in the higher dimension of spirit. Augustine called the secular the "staging ground" for the spiritual, just as history is caught up already in the universe's higher dimensions. A proper eschatology acknowledges this and a proper apocalyptical language testifies to it. A large problem, however, has been the loss of that sensitivity in Christianity itself. The loss, in turn, has distorted the interpretation and use of the Two Kingdoms doctrine.

There are other problems that must be addressed regarding the Two Kingdoms doctrine. On the theological side is the apparent absence of the Theology of the Cross. This is surprising because Luther regarded it as central to his method. I also argue that certain philosophical basics that were subscribed to by theologians and philosophers alike, like natural law and sovereignty, were integral to the doctrine if it were to "work." But along history's way, those two assumptions virtually disappeared in the formal thought and administration of the temporal kingdom's work. On what basis is law and governmental institution to be respected by Christians and secularists alike if their presumed fundaments are no longer assumed as *the* fundamental criteria for moral fairness? Thought must be given, too, to what constitutes "right thinking," insofar, as I will argue, Immanuel Kant quarantined theology, with all religious sentiment, from what he regarded as truly reasonable. So, unique to this treatment of two-kingdoms thinking, I will consider them too and what must be considered as acceptable replacement criteria for a workable "postmodern" appropriation of the doctrine. Nevertheless, let me be clear, the recovery of eschatology and "humane" apocalyptic is utterly necessary to understand and practice the Doctrine of Two Kingdoms rightly, and so then to rethink the qualities and quantities of natural rights, sovereignty, and religious thinking as all together is necessary for a robust praxis of two-kingdoms imagination.

To return to the doctrine itself, what Luther called the "temporal kingdom" does not conflict with the "spiritual kingdom." Indeed, both are related positively and negatively. Evil personified insinuates itself into the relationship of the kingdoms and is so arrogant as to define itself as a kingdom-pretender with a stranglehold on the secular. Evil finally will be spiritually and temporally crushed. But evil is not the nature of the temporal kingdom. We even hold that God is "hidden" in the temporal domain. It is made by God, providentially cared for by God, and God will see via human hands and hearts to its good, notwithstanding that sin has its temporal successes, too. In this way the "theo-political" intent of the two-kingdoms nomenclature is sustained. What we call "church" and what we call "state" then, again, are neither in conflict nor enmeshed. They have their domains and their responsibilities. They are distinct but not separate. They relate but they respect difference. They mutually exhort when their duties and boundaries are not respected. Given the proper eschatological imagination with its aptly apocalyptic language, regularly being reminded of what is real and what ruses require unmasking, Christians are gracious toward and loving of the temporal where Christian faith lives and serves.

Note that I used the past tense four paragraphs above. I observed that the Lutheran tradition "has held" to this Doctrine of Two Kingdoms. Many Lutherans have concluded even in print that this doctrine has become irrelevant and embarrassing. I agree that Lutheran malpractice of the doctrine and its co-option is shameful. Lutherans still misinterpret the doctrine and Paul's exhortation in Rom 13 as a command to keep faith private but otherwise support the governing authorities in all ways. We know how Hitler's regime seized on this for support of its fascism and extermination of all things "not Christian." We know, too, how reputable twentieth-century theologians like Reinhold Niebuhr misunderstood the doctrine along similar lines and so railed for destruction of the doctrine. Today criticisms are leveled at the doctrine substantively and on nomenclature, as if there are no other suitable titles by which to teach the doctrine, or as if the enumeration of "two" somehow defies confession of God's "one" kingdom. Some expressions of Lutheranism just find the whole doctrine impractical because everything about the faith is univocally about justice anyway.[3] Yet

---

3. The Evangelical Lutheran Church in America's first public draft of a social statement on how Christians should relate to civic government, while full of well-considered and aptly-offered policy, relegates "Two Kingdoms" to a footnote, simply saying that the phrase is not suitable for the current day (ECLA, *Draft*, 16n11). There is no citation in the social statement of the confessional texts that led to the doctrine. Nor is there any reference to the standard biblical guidance in Rom 13 or 2 Pet that have resourced Christian understanding of spiritual and temporal authorities since the first century. It is but a draft, but it exposes the de facto thinking about the doctrine within church leadership. While passive aggressive, it is still another form of denunciation of the doctrine like that issued by a Norwegian Lutheran paper in 2002. See Nygren, "Luther's Doctrine."

these Lutheran detractors can't formally claim that the doctrine is defunct because its fundaments are stated in articles 16 and 28 of the Augsburg Confession (AC), which every Lutheran candidate for pastoral or diaconal ministry must vow as authoritative for their faith and life.

Some leading contemporary Lutherans, nevertheless, have spoken clearly to the necessity of a robust use of the Two Kingdoms doctrine. Ulrich Duchrow, for example, devoted his career to explicating and applying the doctrine. He was among the first to chastise earlier twentieth-century theologians for their misinterpretation of it as prescribing a private vs. public schema, faith being private and the public sheerly obedient to government.[4] Anders Nygren did similarly before him. This, of course, is well after Bonhoeffer's own self-sacrificing reclamation of the doctrine. Yet many in leadership counsel de facto disregard of the doctrine. They do not understand that they place themselves in a position similar to sincere but sincerely naive Christians of the early twentieth century. These current advocates create conditions that will disable them from trenchant criticism of the new *Deutsche Christen*. Instead, with eyes open to weaknesses of the Doctrine of Two Kingdoms, I advocate for reclaiming and adapting it. I finally want to commend it as a necessary tool to redress the anti-ecumenical anarchy and illiberal arrogance that Christian Nationalism is foisting on the church catholic and all government. I want to rethink and cheer anew Two Kingdoms as an ecumenical Augustinian political theology for church and culture.

In sum, I offer the prospect that a reiteration of a classic Christian doctrine can help us out of our mainline religion ennui about church and politics. It can and should refreshingly re-engage the cultivated despisers of religion who have so suffered under the weight of religiopolitical ideology. I want to reclaim and amplify again the original Pauline insight in Rom 13:1–7 that respecting and obeying the sovereign does *not* mean never to resist the malpractice of religious or political authority. It *does* mean that justice and goodwill are always expected to characterize a legitimate sovereign, because legitimacy is about more than being lawful and what is lawful is not always legitimate. What the "subject" of the sixteenth century (become "citizen" formally in the eighteenth century) and the "sovereign" both should be about is the point of the Two Kingdoms doctrine. If read and heard rightly, institutions of faith and civil order each will stay in their collaborative rather than confused realms. It is to these two realms, two

---

4. Duchrow, *Two Kingdoms and Lutheran Churches*. Cf. also Duchrow et al., *Liberating Lutheran Theology*; Schelia, "'Zwei-Reiche-Lehre.'"

kingdoms, two jurisdictions, to which and where God has spoken. *Ubi Deus dixit*.

Defining Terms

The Lutheran Doctrine of Two Kingdoms essentially states that God rules over two domains in different ways. The primary institutional actors in the spiritual and temporal kingdoms are, respectively, the church and the state.[5] The primary claim of this doctrine is this: that God works salvation, the eternal joy of all persons and their liberation for neighborly service through the church, on one hand, this being the "kingdom on the right," and that God invisibly works for the welfare of all people, not just Christians, through the rulers of the world, this being in Lutheranspeak the "kingdom on the left," the temporal kingdom. For the spiritual kingdom, God established the church and its primary identity markers, (1) the proclamation and teaching of the gospel and (2) the right administration of the sacraments. For the temporal kingdom, God established civic government. Its function is to ensure security and prospects for thriving for its citizens, using the power of law and order to do so as necessary. This includes the temporal order's duty to provide for the space and protection of the spiritual kingdom, too. Writ large, this means that the state should ensure religious freedom. Authorities in the respective domains were not to usurp authority in the other's domain, though holding the other in the other's domain accountable for doing their own job is a duty, when necessary, too.

This arrangement worked for a time. Around the world, though, and over the centuries, the more generalized phrase of "religion and politics" has become compounded with additional political and emotional meaning. It now complicates our conversations in church and in government beyond the awkward chat at the Thanksgiving dinner table. To get better clarity about how our conversation could and should go, we need to return to primary definitions.

Start with "politics." The word comes from the Greek *polis*, literally meaning "city," where many "politicians" (pols) bump up against each other. "Politics" is what the many people do and must do to have an orderly and mostly satisfying life together that does not transgress their individual freedoms and dignity. "Politics" is not a dirty word. It is a necessary thing

---

5. While I by convention will regularly use this terminology, I also suggest that the two-kingdom typology could also apply to how any religion and government most positively could relate. The details of such an ideal are too many and complicated for this study.

and a good thing if we do it well. The only alternative to any politics is to live entirely alone and entirely self-sufficiently. Even to have only family members around requires politics, and so also a way to manage the family, which is called a household, literally, an economy, the "rule of the household" (*oiko-nomos*).

The word "religion" has some similarity to politics because "religion" is about connectedness, too. "Religion" comes from *re-ligio*. *Ligio* is like ligament. It is what connects. *Religio* is to reconnect to oneself, to others, to everything. Religion is about "total connection," which would mean connection also to what one understands to be one's god. Religion is about the fullness of relationship, fuller even than the formal relationships assumed in politics, because religion adds transcendence to the material mundanity of politics. If one seeks wholeness of connection in one's life, religion necessarily and positively must include politics. I'll explore more than the semantics soon. For now, one should be able to begin to see how important, and how urgent, for us a positive relation between religion and politics should be, like God and government, distinct, and not mutually invasive, but not separate either.

I also must make a case for the word "and" in the phrase "religion and politics" too. We could respect the word "and" here far more than we do, when with "religion" and "politics," "and" is the most weight-bearing, most heavily trafficked, and most compact grammatical bridge ever built. Usually "and" denotes connection and differentiation at the same time. Often what is connected by "and" is desirable, like "pie and ice-cream" or "sunny and warm." Sometimes "and" connects complementary opposites, like "yin and yang." "And" can extend an argument or a disjointed stream of consciousness, like an infinitely long Joycean sentence. "And" also can present to us two utter contraries that we would rather not encounter, like "good and evil" or "heaven and hell." We cannot live without "and," *and* we often would rather not suffer the weight it bears. But we must.

The phrase "religion and politics" does that; two words, the former with ultimate significance and the latter important but formally penultimate. "Religion and politics" are the bread and butter of public life. The phrase served well enough for people to find healthy ways of living together. It served well because there appeared a more than majoritarian consensus and trust in the name and being of God. It served well, too, because the evolution of human rights into constitutional polities was clearly on the trajectory from peoples' forced obeisance to autocracy to the mostly free consensus on some sort of democracy.

But now, after the passing of the Western hegemony called "Christendom," for which we do have some cause for gratitude, secularity has attenuated and pluralized the notion of "God" even in what have been monotheistic societies. But now, there is hot debate as to whether all human rights were God-created or human-devised. But now, people argue whether "higher" or "natural" law were both only useful evolved fictions. But now, again in fateful repetition of history, government of and by the people is compromised by the powers and principalities of economic greed, ethnic supremacies, nationalisms, and narcissistic grandiosity. But now, the acidic gel of postmodernity (its foundation ironically paved by Kant's separation of reason into apposite categories of pure and practical) denies the existence even of objective truth.[6] But now, the "epistemic operating system," that is, "our social rules for turning disagreement into knowledge,"[7] lacks its maintenance personnel trained in critical reflection and understanding of delicate social systems. But now, an atheistic notion of secularity strives to regulate common public discourse and in so doing drives "religious" consciences into their own civil wars between revanchist fundamentalism and progressive spirituality. Our present state of religion in, at least, the United States, is pretty bad when Christians are wary of Christians.

The theological renovation we need requires more than rehashing old tropes. It requires actively affirming other disciplines as allies, like philosophy, economics, political science, psychology, sociology, the physical sciences, and more along with their own discrete themes and proposed solutions. This is standard procedure for doing academic theology. Yet the interdisciplinarity regularly needs refreshing for a general public unaccustomed to such integration. It is right to point to this holistic agenda. For, finally, Two Kingdoms was not just a discrete theme in Luther's larger project. Indeed, after one studies all his writing, one discovers that Two Kingdoms is an apt cipher for Luther's worldview. Everything about all the world and all one's faith is caught up in Luther's sense of the Two Kingdoms.

The doctrine's title is synthetic. "Two Kingdoms" does not appear by this name in the Lutheran Confessions, to which Lutheran pastors and deacons vow subscription at their ordinations. But its content is iterated in AC 16 and 28. These articles outline what authorities in the spiritual and temporal (civil) realms are to do respectively. The authorities' role in each is primarily to attend to the security and good function of their respective kingdom and also to ensure by advice and consent the integrity of the other" kingdom. Religious authority is to ensure religious integrity in its domain. Religious authority is *not* to export doctrine or practice from its domain

---

6. Consider Jeffrey Stout's analysis a generation ago, but still pulsing with right insight, in his *Flight from Authority*. The concern is addressed anew and translucently in Rauch, *Constitution of Knowledge*.

7. Rauch, *Constitution of Knowledge*, 15.

into the temporal domain. Conversely, the political authority must neither import religious policy and practice into the political, nor establish policy in the religious domain that would supplant or compromise religious freedom, faith, doctrine, and practices. Authorities of both domains are to respect the integrity and difference of each other, maintain their own boundaries, and work complementarily together for the good of all.

Implications of Polarity

The two-kingdoms model of the relation between God and government does not side with religiosity or secularity insofar as either or both are led by aspirations of domination or negation. Where these aspiration abide there is a selective biblical literalism on the side of religiosity that is mirrored by a concrete operationalism on the side of secularity. This is because it has been proven difficult for people to respect, much less understand, the mutuality intended in the relationship of the domains. Instead, literalistic interpretation, religious or secular, that includes the absence of eschatological imagination insists on an a-mutuality. This only increases societal fracture. The typology I identify here of these two poles is heuristic. It may not apply in all respects to self-identified biblical literalists. But it is close enough to make the point that for biblical literalists—being the extreme of religiosity—God speaks with one voice and one content to all people notwithstanding their individual, social, or cultural differences. The literalist pole thus also directly aligns its concept of God and God's will with government. It emphasizes one biblical image of God's kingdom and believes that government should be conformed to that image.

On the other hand, the pole of secularity with regard to the relationship of religion and government is but the flip side of the same coin. Having no other understanding of religious and biblical language other than the literalistic—that is, thinking mainly in a concrete operational mode—adherents to a secularism freed of even a hint of religiosity. Adherents to secularism (distinct from secularity), as Charles Taylor observes, exceed their own liberalism by exorcising spiritual convictions from the public square of what had been a hospitable *fraternité*.[8] Today's Jacobins are ready to "tax the churches" whenever spiritual conviction is a stated premise for a proposed resolution. This applies to as reasoned a theological proposal as it does to a bizarre Q-anon story or anti-evolutionist preaching from Genesis. The latter's literalism and antiscience is taken by secularists as representative of the whole of Christian theology. Today's committed *laïque* tolerates religion

8. Taylor, "Meaning of Secularism."

only when it is locked in the closet. It is tolerance neither of religion nor of free exercise, a compromised constitutionalism indeed.

The Doctrine of Two Kingdoms does not trade in the above coinage. The doctrine differentiates itself from both by designating religion with its own specific "realm" and duties, and temporal government with its own. Priests and prelates should stay in their lane, and civil government officials in theirs. They also should stay in communication with each other, ensuring that the prescribed duties of each are performed, because both realms must work together complementarily for the good of everybody, whether religious or not. The distinction between the spiritual and secular, also, was and is not of "equals." Christians are to serve everyone else with peaceableness, humility, and love, and not at all with any sense of colonialist ambition or superiority. But they—we—also know that the spiritual eschatological realm that courses through our own bodies and minds is infinitely larger than the material secular temporal one in which we also live, move, and enact our being. Any alliance of throne and altar, state and church, contradicts this spiritual predisposition and, ironically, prioritizes the temporal kingdom's secular terms to warrant its faithless behavior. And any great divorce between government and religion tends to inscribe a Hobbesian cynicism upon a nation's once soft heart. Politicians and preachers who have no memory of America as a shining light to all nations now speak of the nation as a garbage can full of the world's deplorables. *Liberté, fraternité, egalité* indeed. What weird mirrors of each other's deficits are the literalistic theocrats and secularists, qualified totalitarians both.

I argue that if the doctrine of Two Kingdom had been considered and followed more seriously after the first generation of reformers in general and Lutheranism in particular, we might not have wholly avoided the threats of this present day, but the threats we now face could well have been more moderated. Theological and political "mistakes were made" by the church and the state, that led at least in part to unintended consequences of religiously supported fascism and secularism's antipathy to all religion we face today. The mistakes include (until recently) not having read Paul as the apocalyptic theologian he was, stirred by an eschatological vision that the early church fathers and mothers after him also shared, keenly described with the right apocalyptic imagination of Augustine, retrieved again by Luther.

The Doctrine of Two Kingdoms, if briefly, once satisfactorily guided the public life of a society riven by the Reformation. How would the "church" and temporal government manage the new relationship in the Protestant regions that once held the church as the ultimate governing authority, or vice versa? For the reformers, that depended on what and where God "spoke," *ubi Deus dixit*, which was in one way to the spiritual order and in another way to the temporal order, that is, the governing authorities. A clear difference as to interests and purpose of the differently charged "institutions" of God was recognized and acknowledged. Yet they were and are also charged to cooperate for the good of all while respecting each other's integrity. Cooperation also becomes more difficult when severe difference is internal to each kingdom and not just between the kingdoms, as when Christians like literalistic Dominionists within the spiritual kingdom hold to a "flat" eschatology and seek to dominate a temporal government that no longer functions on the classic premises of natural law and sovereignty. The overall absence of the classic premises eschatological, apocalyptic, natural law, and human sovereignty is the complex obstacle to a return to two-kingdoms thinking.

More Than Separation of Church and State

So here *we* are. I write from the so-called declining mainline. I write as a Christian, attentive to the Great Tradition, committed to the classic creeds; catholic, and so ecumenical, and so also "generously orthodox"; and so also again with respect for and to my Abrahamic religious relatives, broader religious traditions, and society at large, because all of them are my neighbors to whom my life is ordered for love and service. And all this because I am an Augustinian Lutheran whose core baptized identity is one of being loved by God and so released from myself to work boldly while sometimes foolishly for the common cause of the world's good.

The doctrine provides useful principles for banal political life (political banality is a good goal to strive for!). We would do so much better in our churchly and social polity if we could keep these criteria in mind. But obviously we haven't, and we don't. There are so many rocks on this road that make us stumble. And there are adversaries on this road with other purposes than to grow in faith and to mature as fellow different human beings alongside us. Knowing that there is a dotted line dividing the road into lanes, each going in the same direction, makes the travel smoother and the negotiation of traffic more effective. Let's proceed for a bit with this "road analogy," mindful that analogies have limits.

One lane is for the church, the "spiritual" lane. The other for government. We can and do cross over to the other lane and back again. When doing so we adjust our driving. We ensure that there is enough space between cars to change lanes and we signal before we do. A foot will brake or accelerate. Our hands grasp the wheel or hit cruise control as eyes look well ahead and check mirrors regularly. All depends on the particular situation at hand, always, ideally, following the formal and informal rules of the road. Maybe the Two Kingdoms principle is like that one-way road of two lanes.

I know of freeways with twelve lanes going the same direction. That can be scary. Yet, thousands of people do just fine with it every day, millions every year. It might be scary at first for the novice. But the rules and good driving practices are just the same as the simple two lane. The complications today of our religious and political lives may seem like the large freeway now, compounded by noise and sometimes confusing signs. Travel by these lanes, however many there are along with megachurch buses, tractor-trailers, fast cars, and old slow vehicles with tail pipes hanging by a wire still—all smaller metaphors for the panoply of churches that make up Christianity—is still better than trying to get somewhere quickly on the smaller road where cars, buses, motorbikes, bicycles, donkey-carts, oxen, and free-ranging cattle make up their own lanes. It should be needless to say, but it needs saying anyway, that insisting on one's own rules and ignoring the common rules results in collisions and crashes. People get hurt. Further, hurting people hurt people.

Our situation today is more like the busy two-lanes having become many mega-congested lanes compacted into the two, what with postmodern skeptics, ideological secularists, and literalistic univocalists shouting out their rules. But in the Great Tradition of what had also been called mainline Christianity we have had two lanes going the same direction. They handled the traffic well. With some re-education and patience, and some road reconstruction, we can use those lanes again in much the same way that the evangelical pastor serving as a state legislator tried. And we can do better yet by reassessing, reframing, and reclaiming what Augustinian Lutheranism has known as the Doctrine of Two Kingdoms.

Do we have a shared covenant as to the rules of the road today? Do we have agreed understanding not only of the common good and how to achieve it, but, also, and perhaps more importantly, agreement about the *origin* of the common good? What is the common good? Beyond the experience of injustice and oppression that motivated individuals to ally against tyranny and eventually write a Magna Carta, whence the very claim of universal human rights?

The claim today is quite unexpectedly questioned. "Liberal" theologians often grant that a dogmatic secularism underlies religious right's suspicion of what it perceives as postmodernity. However, the religious right's suspicion is not of postmodernity per se, but of modernism's atheistic DNA leftovers in postmodernity. This is something that the populist audience does not appreciate when it asserts still that all practices of the spiritual realm still should be kept away from the public, like keeping Harry Potter under the stairs. Actually, postmodernity levels the playing field and invites all voices back into the public square. But modernity, pretending to be other than it is, still has its foothold and its insistent memes, as in textualist court chambers and literalist church theaters. Postmodernity really has not yet trickled down to dissolve the modernist fundaments of law and religion amongst presumably liberal populists, while their conservative mirrors still insist on posting the Ten Commandments in public schools to be taught "textually."

And so the great debate which shouts today's great divorce: either God is exiled to the strictly privatized spiritual realm or God should dominate the public and the private. Two Kingdoms then serves as correction to the modernist excesses of the religious right and to modernity's progressive priests and prophets. Two-kingdoms thinking framed postmodernly returns to "original intent" *and* contemporary contextuality transcends the divorcing implication of dialectical debate to recover the vision of unity with difference. The Two Kingdoms "distinction with connection" grew from the happy agreement that God created both domains, that God celebrates the integrity of both domains, and that God desires to and will grow in happy, while differentiated, relationship with both domains. Christians understood this in such a way as to look forward to the arrival of the book of Revelation's heavenly Jerusalem, Augustine's coming City of God, Josiah Royce's and Martin Luther King Jr.'s actualization of the Beloved Community, the consummation of the marriage of the spiritual and temporal kingdoms. After Christendom, ideologically dogmatic secularity's dominance of public speech and (shallow) thinking disallows such reasoning in our public discourse. There is substance here for conservative complaint. It is a datum for intellectual compassion while still rejecting the offensive reactivity of Christian Nationalism.

This also ups the ante for a reclamation and renovation of the Two Kingdoms doctrine. It must woo back from the precipice of anarchy the disenchanted congregations of the body politic. The doctrine can recall the reactive fusers of the civil and spiritual and the equally reactive practical atheists to a more solid common ground of mutual affirmation of dignity more than deplorability. What we commonly hold to is the basic dignity of every human being, no matter their religious predications. As far as we can empirically measure, every faith tradition holds to this principle. It is the root of the Golden Rule, to treat the neighbor as we would treat ourselves. It is universal. Everyone is a neighbor. The MAGA neighbor who plows the snow from my driveway and warmly engages in conversation without the compulsion to proselytize by the neighborhood mailbox already knows how to begin to bridge and respect differences. And so, being universal, the language, action, and produced policy that seek to hold and build the common good through law must be done so in and with language and spirit based on the shared commitment to ensuring the freedom and dignity of every individual. This includes acting for the safety, peace, and enablement of attaining material prosperity for all whenever and wherever possible, which is also not to tolerate intolerance.

The same applies to when government would insert itself into leadership functions and declarations in spiritual communities. What God speaks for the common good may apply in part to a religious institution. Sexual boundary violations and financial mismanagement are as important to prevent and as subject to civil punishment as in the religious arena. Matters which are specifically of spiritual import, however, including doctrines and practices, require the acuity of recognized trained and called leaders for and from those communities' traditions. God intends that individual human beings receive from God in this "kingdom" all that they need for their faith in God's accompaniment and eternal destiny, including garnering and gaining here the resources needed for mutual care and consolation of others. This will help individuals more skillfully and courageously to serve in society at large. But it isn't the kind of word or help or mentoring that government officials as such should or can provide. The point here is that these "lanes" are compromised when any driver in one lane commandeers the other lane, too. This would be like a driver not quite completely crossing over into the other lane and then even changing speeds, thereby obstructing both lanes and preventing traffic in both from traveling safely. That's when collisions and worse happen.

The discernment of differentiated but mutually accountable jurisdictions, what I summarize as the Two Kingdoms practice, benefits society as a pragmatic operational good. Another benefit is that the doctrine is intellectually as well as spiritually hospitable. It graciously invites a variety of people into the conversation. Though perhaps the doctrine's authorship and dissemination have a history of being delivered as if "from on high," the antiparochialism at its heart commends its utility as welcoming of deep and expansive consideration from many people and intellectual and practical disciplines. Indeed, as I hope will be made clear in the course of this book, given that the Doctrine of Two Kingdoms originates from an Augustinian concern for the *common*wealth, Two-Kingdoms talk necessarily presumes that God speaks, while we acknowledge our "past tense" experience of God even presently, *and* that the principle intends common conversation. In the most precise and gracious way, the Doctrine of Two Kingdoms is a catholic doctrine that intends practice now without being autocratic or authoritarian.

Positively Secular

By now it should be clear that with the Lutheran Doctrine of Two Kingdoms the "and" of "religion and politics" does not sequester God to the left side of "and." God acts not just in religion. God also works within the administrations of government. This does not mean that government is or should be "godly." Government is not and is not designed to be an expression in the terms and content of a particular religion. If anything—and this is admittedly a surprising but necessary claim—God works in government in a "secular" manner. God is secular. And secularity requires "God" while God hides in the secular.

Now that I have provoked, I'll explain. To affirm secularity and God, and to state with tongue not in cheek that "God is secular," is not to surrender to the dogmatic secularism of post-Christendom. Rather, it is to argue that a two-kingdoms or "two-jurisdictions" model for how God and government relate frees us from popular misunderstandings with their legalistic oversimplifications of the meanings both of "God" and "secularity." With refreshed understanding of these terms, we could step back toward a healthier body politic. As I already have noted, I construe "secularity" itself as a healthy (!) term drawn from Augustine's political theology. I anticipate that conversation here by noting that for him, the "secular" was not opposed to God or empty of God. It was, rather, that space that awaited God's manifestation and in which God works invisibly. The secular realm has even been called a staging area for the holy. There is much promise here already for resolving our rhetoric of dogmatic secularity.

As for the popular misunderstanding of "God" in our speech and social practices, a longer word here is appropriate. God is one. The one God through the positive functions of government serves the needs of humanity beyond religion. Through government, God cares too for those who do not believe in God. Not to so care would be impossible for God and is logically impossible for the most complete definition of "god." It is a kind of ontological argument, after all, that Barth proposed.[9] If God is that greater than which nothing else can be conceived, then only ontology, a claim about reality, can ground the claim of "*Deus dixit*," that God has spoken and acted, and still does. Whatever the character of the ontology, even were it of a Jungian archetypalism expressed in symbolic terms and imagery (and so for

9. Barth, *Anselm*.

theologians, Tillichian), there is still a referenced "whom" or "which" there; the Ground of Being, the source from which all comes into being; on which all depends; toward which all returns, in which all—all—is united.

That there is a "whom or which" there, however opaque, implies a "where" whence God speaks and acts. Perhaps the "where" is as omnipresent as the trope of "place" or "space" is today in postmodern expression. Augustine spoke of this holy origin and destination for humanity with his declaration of the heart as restless until it rests in God, the graced beginning of faith's movement (*initium fidei*) from and unto God. Luther spoke similarly of what it means to have a god: that which a person cherishes above all else moves and guides one's life. For some people "god" might thus be a refrigerator, or a sailboat, or a high-capacity automatic weapon. For others God is the ineffable mystery somehow also disclosed in Jesus Christ. For both Augustine and Luther, the question of God and, we infer, God behind the question is a universal ferment. By being just so, the question and God behind the question evoke God-talk. They call forth theology. Theology, thus, is evoked by God. This means, too, that theology is a recursive reflection upon God and God-talk. It is therefore necessarily humble and critical, as theology. Further, while it is inspired by God (*initium fidei*), theology is judged by God. When theology would address human life together, thus being political, it is then doubly accountable and doubly subject to judgment by God and our public. The supreme origin and court, however, of course, is God, because God!

Wherever theological reflection begins, whether a traditional creedal locus or as an existential situation like religion and government, the very fact of its being *theo*-logy means that God is both hidden behind the reflective impulse and eager to help. Wherever we start in doing theology, God already has a place for faith to find it, which is to say that in that place faith is already funded and has been so funded even before our knowing it. John Webster, appropriately, gives this argument about God's self-revelation and God's knowledge of God's own self a Trinitarian grounding. Webster thereby amplifies Karl Barth's regal opening of *Deus dixit* in his *Church Dogmatics* II.1. "The Holy Trinity is the ontological principle of Christian systematic theology." That is, the divine Word (the second person of the Trinity), communicated through the prophets, the apostles with the illumination of the Spirit is communicated to all true believers. This is the "objective cognitive principle for systematic theology." The subjective cognitive principle is the "redeemed intelligence of the saints" (believers). These principles of systematic theology will and must undergird, I will trust, this attempt at a systematic doctrinal theology gone constructive.[10]

Formal theology recognizes a caveat in Webster's improvement on Barth. Concomitant with the innate intellectual hospitality of the Two Kingdoms doctrine is the required principle of humility when speaking of God speaking. It is impossible for humans to speak truly of God unless God subjects God's self to be a real object of human knowledge. The thing about God however is that "God" always includes God's presence. Just as it is rude to speak of another person in the third person as if that person is not there when she or he is right at your shoulder, to speak about God "objectively" is also rude . . . and weird. For us to talk about "God" means that God is present to enable our talk about (and to) God. So, with theology, which we are doing and will do here, to speak about God as the willing object of our knowledge, is also to concede and be humbly aware always that theology *about* God arises from and is judged—these days the word is "curated"—by theology *of* God. God theologizes about us! *Deus dixit*! And our speech is owned in some respect always by God being there before we are. Theology about God arises from God and is judged by God's theology about us. Fundamentalists prone to speak authoritatively and inhospitably out of their hats should beware. Liberal churches who remain silent when they should speak should beware, too.

The rules, such as they are, of postmodernity allow that one must start somewhere and then state one's case in as pragmatically effective and internally coherent and warranted a manner as possible.[11] We'll start with such allowance, because we must start somewhere, and the point of this book is to consider the reconstruction of a theme that is much more urgent than interminably arguing about foundations and method. Yes, history up until the most recent second before these words are pondered is full of examples of talk about God that could not possibly be about God, so false, destructive vile, and psychotic these predicates have shown themselves to be. But if there has been and is speech that for the time being seems, well, to be pointing to the holy, we presume something grounding it that transcends even the most beautiful genius of human imagination. *Deus dixit*. And if reasonable doubt, as opposed to today's populistic reactivity and willful doubt, should whisper still into one's ear the intimately familiar question of "What if it isn't so?," then we in both faithful and scientific diligence must align with Jeremiah's

---

10. Webster, "Principles," 56.

11. George Lindbeck's *Nature of Doctrine* still exercises major influence. It has informed practical ecumenical rapprochement at high dialogue levels and influenced catechetical curricula at the most common pedagogical levels, even if not so acknowledged a generation later.

spiritual pragmatism: "As for the prophet who prophesies peace, when the word of that prophet comes true, then it will be known that the Lord has truly sent the prophet" (Jer 28:9).

What Is "Politics"?

Having entered further into the politics of divine speech, we must be clearer yet about the word "politics." According to a now classic text on the administration of large organizations, "politics" is the art of moving an organization forward in its mission while giving and maintaining a sense of meaning in all the organization's members without having abundant resources for doing so.[12] What I have hinted at several times already I make explicit here. The definition of politics I will follow is *the common search for the common good in the form of a concrete polity*.[13] Luther assumed a concrete polity in his day of princes and priests in their own emerging domains within an empire. Within that specific structure he argued on theological and practical grounds for providing the best care possible for the common good, including a relatively free church system, health care, education, and a welfare system. Concrete polities can change and differ. When today within the American dominant two-party system we argue and "do" politics, the presumption to which we give lip service, but now practice little, is that we attempt to be nonpartisan in our seeking the best for all and still insist that our polity must include the voices of those who "lost" in the most recent election. Respectful debate, then, is core to what we regard as healthy political and divine speech.

A correlative definition of politics centers on power as the right and capacity coercively to govern. While not primary for Luther, this was in his mind too when he spoke regularly of temporal authority as having "the power of the sword." But he still put this definition in service to the first, as the role of governmental power was for him to preserve and advance the safety, health, and opportunity for economic success of the governed. Moreover, Luther's readiness to support such use of power reveals a problem with two-kingdoms thinking.

The problem is that violent power as such is mistakenly identified as a divinely authorized and normative tool. In the spiritual realm, orderly life together is sustained by the Spirit's noncoercive persuasion. Coercive

---

12. A paraphrase of the definition given by Bolman and Deal, *Reframing Organizations*, 195.

13. "Concrete polity" is the suitable abstract term for "organization" no matter how really "organized" it is.

power for the civil realm is rightly understood as an emergency necessity given the widespread (to understate it) reality of sin. But sin's amplification of violence as a controlling mechanism in the civil order must not be abetted or outrightly affirmed as now normative. On the other hand, that coercion must be used as an emergency measure to protect citizens and society should not be demonized either. Yet, also, when the state maintains a monopoly on the means of coercion as a purported necessary order (*Notordnung*), trouble happens. Many contemporary writers fault Luther on just this point, that he would call for moderation by the princes when enforcing the law, but appeared to identify God's creative will with the overuse of force, as in the Peasants' Revolt. The state potentially is given therefore a "can't win—damned if it does, damned if it doesn't" vocation. Because it possesses the power of the sword, there is a latent danger of demonizing the state. And being mindful of the danger of demonizing the state, Christians can be prone to renege on their responsibility to speak against the state's irresponsible use of coercion when that does happen. Bonhoeffer warned against both tendencies in his radio address when Hitler came to power. "Silence in the face of evil is itself evil." Bonhoeffer could discern the difference between appropriate and vile state use of coercion. In that, he was able robustly to access two-kingdoms thinking when he spoke to his situation. But the problem of Luther's endorsement of violence still obtains and continues to challenge efforts to own the Two Kingdoms doctrine.[14] Augustine's skepticism about the coercive role of the state is also at the heart of his two-kingdoms distinction, a reservation that Luther appears to lack.

We also have come to understand the attractiveness of political power in a third way. It can amplify the personal freedom of the person who has it, often at the expense of others, in a zero-sum game. Such familiarity with venality gave rise to the jocular perversion of the Golden Rule, that those who have the gold are those who get to rule. It is a paradigmatic understatement to note that the desire for power looms large in politics. Power lust has become the transcending motivation for politicians to put selves and party above the common good. Just to keep one's position within a given political group one must do what one is told, even if already one's position has been secured by electoral gerrymandering. Follow the talking point of the

---

14. For example, see Stringfellow, *Conscience and Obedience*, 67. About the civil order and violence, he writes, "It is, to my mind, not so much that the ideas about legitimacy or order are false, in a dogmatic sense, but that they are too abstract, too small or too narrow to accommodate the gospel, too convenient to emperors and officials, too simplistic and too misleading for the faithful. I am unable to circumvent, for example, the incongruity of Luther's tolerance of tyranny because that saves order when the order that is enforced, in fact, is disorder."

day against the opposition above all else. If you do that, you'll get and keep privileges that otherwise are not available to most citizens. In other words, the third definition of politics, and far from my preferred meaning, is the practice of gaining and keeping partisan hegemony. Inevitably, these definitions merge into an ugly dance trio. Still, my primary intention is to speak of politics as the usually "secular" advancement of what I believe theology to be about in a larger way: the pursuit of the common good. I will try to be more reserved in the use of the second and third definitions.

The common search for the common good within a concrete polity—i.e., the proper function of politics—seems to have waning support today when political parties seek hegemony above all else. It is so easy now to default to the third definition, particular when critical theory reads the struggle for power even into the hard sciences. It does not take long at all to see the signs, banners, and flags rippling with righteous indignation about God having been exiled from the classroom and nation. All this is effectively to shout that it is up to the populists now to get God back in by rewriting law so to reinstate lost privilege. The loud voice of self-projection through a microphone into a 1932 German public square repeats now as feigned and digitized virtue transmitted at the speed of light around the world. Claimants to thrones who "know" where God isn't also do know that millions of people within days will consume hours upon hours of fear-inducing propaganda.

If Christian hegemonists are claiming the day by exercising politics as power, they are premature. There are those still who intuit that there is a space and place of God where God can be heard inflecting grace and grace's corrections through all spaces and places. There are hearts still sparked by inspiration for aspiration. Hearts still beat with Augustine's rhythm seeking home's rest. Even where there is absence of God's talk in this world's spaces, the silence stimulates desire to find and hear it. Given the would-be faithful Christian's inarticulate urge again to encounter the Holy, the absence of the churchly word—the ignoring of the primal *Deus dixit*—gives the question of God and government existential import for individual persons and politics as such. But if the question of God and government is ignored or quashed, particularly by those of us who desire to be God's people, if the church does not so know and so speak God-Christ into the present political moment, politics will grow larger and shallower for lack of theological soul. Reciprocally, if the politics of a day don't inspire work toward the common good, then government is not catalyzing the healthy debate of the "why" to which both church and culture should be responding in healthy conversation. In other words, I'm signaling that a return (again?) to the affective sense, proclamation, and sacramental administration of the *spiritual* is the paramount obligation of religious communities *so that* our politics will be concretely and powerfully practiced and further stimulating of, at least, creative philosophical and policy reflection.

This is also to say that we must first speak and be about who Jesus Christ is for us today in the spiritual domain we inhabit. It is commonplace however for many religious leaders to default to the term "justice" as the church's priority. I will hazard a charge of heresy from fellow progressives here by my saying that priority is misplaced. The church's priority is to steward the spiritual mysteries that in turn will inspire and shape acts for justice. This does not deny or demean the requirement of justice. Micah 6 absolutely is Christian policy, as well as a good meme. But justice without spirit, like works without faith, enervates like a subjective wish-dream. Faith *will* produce works, as Being *will* Act. The latter does not happen without the former. Spirit will mean justice. But not to give any voice to Spirit, perhaps out of sympathy for and desire to connect with today's Jacobins, quiets Being and Act. The perdurance of justice requires prayer and the transcendent power of love that comes with it. The care and feeding of faith that is to be active in love in the world is the primary and urgent—given its paucity—order of business in "God's righthand" spiritual kingdom. "Justice" is the first adjective for describing the point of government in the grammar of "God's lefthand" kingdom. For the righthand kingdom, however, Christ is the Friend-Brother-Fellow Human-Teacher-Lord we are intended to meet in the spiritual space. This is why Paul exhorts that "we preach Christ and Christ crucified; . . . Christ the power of God and the wisdom of God."[15] If you want church to be about justice, then first expect Christ to meet you and feed you there. *Then* you will receive power for justice, because, for Christians, Jesus Christ *is* justice *par excellence*. As Paul puts it, Christ is the "justice/righteousness" of God, given to us in faith (Rom 3).

According to the terms of justice in the temporal domain, the justice/righteousness of God is a gift the citizens of the spiritual domain do not deserve. Thank God for the grace and mercy meant to be known fully in the spiritual kingdom! The justice of the temporal domain, meted to the purported deserving as it is, can never be the model of the perfect good nor the sufficient model of "each to their own" (*suum cuique*). Compared to the spiritual domain, temporal justice is necessary but not perfect, given the universal character of sin. Given the difference and tension between the promised presence and perfection of justice in Christ and the imperfect anticipatory justice of the civil order, the Christian's call rings even more urgently to work with government and beside government for justice. We

---

15. 1 Cor 1:23–24.

need daily to draw from their peculiar resources to do just this, to do justice however imperfectly, which is also to do politics. The personal and communal life of prayer, which includes being spoken to by God, precedes and propels good politics, just as politics must inform in part that for which we pray.

So what, again, is politics? It is the imperfect work of justice in the temporal realm that to be sustained must be inspired by the better experience of justice, mercy, and grace in the spiritual realm.

The Political Is Theological

The situation today is theologically urgent too, obviously, because we will reflect on words about God and words purportedly from God. For God to be God means that God is always urgent. Anytime God is spoken of as an object becomes a moment when God presides as subject. This makes all speech of God a matter of urgency. "Theology" literally means words or thoughts about "God" and, simultaneously, words of or from God, words first owned and so said by God.[16] I've already remarked that real theology can't happen without God's self-revelation and, that said, theology is always subject to God's judgment on our doing of theology.

There is also a horizontal-anthropological axis to theology. All speech is inherently political because it is communication between at least two people. The praxis of theology is likewise. Theology, technically speaking, is inherently political because the audience of God's address is plural. Indeed, even God's being is political in the perfect manner! Father, Son, and Holy Spirit "get along" eternally, without which perfect mutuality creation itself would fracture. God the Beloved Community in the Spirit begets Church and World, so to expand our joy with concrete community in our time. One hopes that the church would attend more consciously to its bearing the divine image of happy "political" relationship and thereby show the world some hope as well.

The primary implication of the above is that politics is inherently theological.[17] This is simply true and will never be otherwise. Religion and faith

---

16. The Greek components of the word "theology" simultaneously constitute "objective genitive" and "subjective genitive" cases. And, as we shall see, since God is God and no other, the case is made for the subjective genitive as having full priority. There can be no true words about God without God "being there" to give them in the first place. Otherwise, the logic goes, the human speakers would be making themselves "as God." It's an interesting logical taunt buried in the "serpent's" temptation of original humanity.

17. This is a foundational premise now in philosophy since Marx, if not Nietzsche,

always have had their effects on politics, and politics always have implied a religious quest. The identification of the God of Israel in the Hebrew Scriptures always included the question of in whom one believes. This often, especially under the prophets, included the at least tacit denunciation of following other political leaders who opposed the God of Abraham, Isaac, and Joseph. The critique of other empires in the Hebrew Scriptures morphed into criticism of all empire in the New Testament. Current New Testament interpretation strongly denounces empire and emperors. Anticolonialist interpretation especially of the Gospels either urges Christians to maintain a faith "not of this world" or to engage the world directly and deeply with a thoroughgoingly peaceable politics, notwithstanding the impetuosities of Herods, Caesars, and contemporary autocrats. Whatever the case (including the now minority liberation theology resort to violence), theology has a political character and consequence. And where religion was ostensibly rejected, as in the utopian (and dystopian) literature of the nineteenth and twentieth centuries, politics were and are still motivated by inchoate religious impulses. This explains the twentieth-century phenomena of political religions including Nazism, Marxism-Leninism, Shinto-Fascism, and other fascisms.

The internal psychic drivers of religious dispositions impel the political, too. Faith, distinct from "theology," has within it the practical if not formal verbal necessity to have a moral effect on the world. Formally and ethically, communal religious faith (and what religious faith could not be communal?) has a necessary practical relationship with political orders. To express the matter at the most mundane level, the most reclusive of monastics had to relate at least minimally to a very "other" world for their economic (and so political) sustenance. As a professor of mine liked to say, even Simon Stylites needed someone to hand over a peanut butter sandwich to him there on his odd tower. That required a series of economic and so political transactions from laborer to producer to marketer to consumer, however piously and generously the transactions were conducted. The thought of idiosyncratic Stylites and all the politics necessary to satisfy his peculiar solitude came to my mind again decades later when I noted that one Trappist monk's place setting in his abbey's refectory was distinguished by a bottle of Tabasco sauce. No other of the thirty place settings around the room were so marked. That required a slight adjustment of the usual rules, a modest act of charity. But, nonetheless, it was political. Like each of us, even the most evidently sacrificial human beings among us are peculiar and

---

and carried forward robustly in contemporary philosophers like Adorno, Benjamin, and Agamben.

mutually oriented. Rules and knowing when, how, and how much to break the rules all are basic elements of enabling a community—a *polis*—to thrive. This is the positive aspect of politics. Politics is the art of compassionate community that requires more practical sagacity as well as compassion as the community grows. And so the apostles appointed deacons.

Imagining the Doctrine's Use

Just what might a renewed use of the two-kingdoms principle look like in our public life today? I can imagine a few examples as clues presently and will amplify on them later. I can imagine that a high school football coach would be free to host public prayer on the field after a game. But just as prayer is not to be coerced in the classroom, so also every possible guardrail against coercion would be emplaced and consciously followed. Such guardrails would include the coach's clear example of graciousness to those players who choose not to participate in prayer. Graciousness would be educative, too. It would entail school administrators sponsoring events that teach and welcome full discussion about what the First Amendment implies for such practices as prayer on the field. The Supreme Court in Kennedy v. Bremerton School District was correct in allowing for the coach's practice. But the Court erred by not adequately exploring the meaning and practice of coercion in its decision. The decision was merely absolutist about the free exercise clause, giving little regard to the role of the establishment clause and, per the Two Kingdoms doctrine (were Christians to affirm and apply it), imposed prayer on reluctant persons, thereby transgressing into the spiritual kingdom where temporal authorities are not to exercise rule. Did God speak there on the football field or at the Supreme Court? The Two Kingdom principles for discernment might yield an answer more on one side than the other. This is not to say that God didn't speak at all, but human discernment of where, how, and to what end God spoke needs further formation.

Or for a final example, flip the setting back to the politician who publicly shares his belief that he or she, like Moses, is personally appointed by God for such service. Again, there is no constitutional or biblical injunction against bringing one's values to one's legislative activity. Indeed, the vocation Christians are given in the spiritual domain charges Christians to do so. As a Lutheran Christian, I believe that by and in my baptism God has personally appointed me to advocate for and live a life of justice for the neighbor and to oppose all principalities and powers that defy God. But one wonders what "personally appointed" means. Practical atheistic secularism might impute "hearing voices" to such a claim, thereby dismissing a politician's credibility. But how would claiming a divine appointment differ from a Pauline Christian affirming that "Jesus Christ, living in me, is my justice"? Not to respect the belief means delegitimizing all religious vocations and a good many civil ones as well. A postmodern Christian cannot gainsay anyone's adoption of at least part of the biblical story as one's own narrative.

The question is a hermeneutical and ecumenical one that an insistently secularist public cannot understand. But it is a serious question for serious political theology. The problem is amplified if the belief in a personal divine call further self-identifies as Christian Nationalist. This scenario invites too many further questions than can be addressed here. But I will focus on one, since divine grace and its complement of human intellectual hospitality in a pluralistic civil order have been mentioned severally already as part and parcel of two-kingdoms thinking. One of many differences between the Augustinian Lutheran impulse and a self-identified Christian Nationalist[18] is in our understanding of required hospitality to the "other." Hospitality is a bottom-line mandate for persons of spiritual and temporal life. In the civil domain, hospitality[19] is a logically necessary practice for any pluralistic society to survive; it is of the character of the "natural law" of the Golden Rule. This is a basic theological observation. Owning one's believed call to live one's Christian faith in service to the civil order is one matter on which we must agree. Claiming that the same claim entails its domineering imposition over all other claims in the civil order is another.[20] If a party intends to establish one set of religious convictions over and against other religious convictions in the temporal political space, it can only follow that the intent will transgress the spiritual kingdom's rule of hospitality embedded in Christ's two great commandments and the temporal kingdom's natural law of the Golden Rule, not to mention the legal rubric of the first amendment. Of course, "nationalism" brings its own train of problems into the mix. Sans that term (for now), I believe the principle of Two Kingdoms also can aide the most conservative of Christians in the difficult task of parsing and performing one's vocation in the temporal arena. On this point, the degree

---

18. Appropriate debate is waged also as to whether "Christian" should/could be used as an adjective. Insofar as an adjective would give greater normativity to what is predicated, on the basis of the first commandment alone I would argue not.

19. I prefer "hospitality" to the more commonly used word in civic life of "tolerance."

20. As is the case with the so-called "Seven Mountains Mandate" of the New Apostolic Reformation movement. A leading proponent of this form of Christian Dominionism is Lance Wallnau, highly networked and influential among current extreme conservatives. See Johnson and Wallnau, *Invading Babylon*. In response, among many, see Marshall, "Destroying Arguments"; Aho, "Christian Dominionism."

of theological sensitivity required to do so must be accompanied by faithful patience of those already practiced in ecumenical habits.

Other Challenges to the Doctrine

There are other less abstract challenges to address. When aggregated, as they have been over time, they evoke agreement to a general motion to suspend the Doctrine of Two Kingdoms on charges of its being abstractly impertinent, practically irrelevant, and even outrightly destructive. First, on the large social scale, people respond more to personal stories and concreteness than to abstract theories. This is why politics and religion "tactically" are advised first to appeal to people's feelings. People generally have difficulty understanding and living with nuance and ambiguity, especially when a policy means to guide a complex multicultural society of varied values. Recognizing this, opportunistic religious and political leaders keen on personal power play on the common person's need for clarity. Simplism serves the autocrat's ambitions. It is not a stretch to imagine a leader who in cultlike manner says, "I'm appointed by God. God has given us the words that I am uniquely equipped to understand so we can have the happy life God wants for us. So just follow me and my teaching!" The words ring similarly through the ages whether spoken by a church prince or a fabulist fascist. This first challenge can be met finally only with clear and direct words. Clear and direct words must be the filtrate of the abstract thinking necessary for correct understanding. We cannot avoid abstract thinking, but yet with it we must find responsible and practically clear expression. We must always work toward that goal and know that revision will always be necessary.

A second challenge is a formality, but must be asked and answered at some length. This is the question of how a principle or conviction becomes a "doctrine." It is an interesting story how the teaching of Two Kingdoms gained "doctrinal" status for Lutherans. Two Kingdoms did not attain status in print as a doctrine until 1933. The title reappeared in 1938 and has remained so since.[21] Of course, that a teaching may long be accepted, even for four centuries, before being named as a doctrine does not necessarily denude it of its authority. Consult a historian about historiography. Not everything is recognized immediately for what it truly is. One can reasonably imagine that even in their mythological innocence Adam and Eve consulted

---

21. Westhelle writes that Franz Lau and Harald Diem were the first to ascribe the status of doctrine to the accepted teaching of the *Zweireichslehre*. See his "God and Justice."

at length before deciding what to name a platypus. The greater question, anyway, is the degree of a proposition's authority.

In public consciousness doctrine and dogma are often conflated, though they are very different. By definition, doctrine is one matter and dogma another. Dogma is teaching that has been ecumenically established. The Great Tradition in Christianity receives as dogma, that is, as high formal authority, such teachings as the primacy of Holy Scripture, God, Trinity, the simultaneous divinity and humanity of Jesus Christ, the nature of sin, the crucifixion and resurrection of Christ and thereby the redemption of humanity, the Holy Spirit as the Christian's advocate and guide, the church as the body of Christ charged to serve the world, God's rule manifest over all the universe, made clear in the new time to come, and more. The primary dogmas are, as it were, bulleted in the ecumenical creeds and to be taught with diligence. Yet, with all their authority, dogmas are subject to or normed by (*norma normata*) the Word, Christ Incarnate and Risen, ruling his body the Church with and through the Holy Spirit. Without Christ as the norm over the Bible, even the Bible has no authority. Christ is the un-normed norm (*norma normans sed non normata*). Even the ecumenically affirmed and historically authorized dogmas are normed.

Doctrines are different. Like dogmas, they are normed norms, too. But they are "less normative" than dogma. They are, as it were, "normed normed norms" with lesser scope. They may derive from ecumenical theological scholarship but have not been "voted on" by any formal ecumenical assembly. Or they may derive from a founder's and/or founder's movement of new interpretation of Scripture and dogma. I concur with the suggestion made two generations ago that doctrine is a proposal of dogma to the church catholic.[22] I'll emphasize "proposal." That is, doctrine is a teaching or way of understanding a *locus* of theology *proposed* as a definitive understanding of what the church teaches and has always taught. For that proposal to happen, it usually, though not prescriptively, already has a status of normativity within the proposing group's authoritative texts. But it also stands to reason that a *proposal* of dogma can only last so long. If the potential partner refuses for centuries to accept a proposal of dogma as dogma, eventually the proposer must abandon all hope for a wedding. Maybe "Two Kingdoms" should be abandoned as a doctrine, though seriously to do that would entail a formal revision of the pertinent confessions in the Book of Concord (BC), as well as a stated non-acceptance of Luther's above cited texts about so-called Two Kingdoms.

---

22. Gritsch and Jenson, *Lutheranism*, 3.

This then leads to this formal and practical problem. Persons ordained as Ministers of Word and Sacrament or Ministers of Word and Service (pastors and deacons respectively) in most expressions of Lutheranism vow to teach according to the Holy Scriptures and to Lutheranism's authoritative texts in the BC beginning with the AC. The *principles* for a Two Kingdoms doctrine are included in the BC, as are references to some of Luther's teaching on civil authority.[23] But a formal naming of "the Two Kingdoms" as a titled doctrine is not. Indeed, I take the references in the BC to mean Luther's and Melanchthon's work. But these works themselves were not "final" and were subject to ongoing reinterpretation. In short, we have particular doctrinal content without a formal, though synthetic, title. The character of this doctrine's "adoption" is an open question that goes beyond the BC's own normativity but is yet dutifully respectful of that normativity.

We obey and think anew within a tradition that with its own history of textual evolution displays its innate commitment to always reforming, *semper reformanda*. The sublety of this, indeed, the implicit mandate to reflect critically and constructively, is also at the center of the tradition. The challenge has always been that it will be difficult for the concrete operational mind to ask about the relevance of a doctrine like Two Kingdoms when the political contexts are ever shifting. Though simple in its bases, the doctrine is nuanced, and time only adds to nuance (like interpretation of the US Constitution). A practiced prosecuting attorney (like a Calvin?) will ask the Lutheran just where the text says that "Two Kingdoms" is formally a doctrine.[24] The Lutheran must answer that the doctrine is a synthesis and a trajectory of careful thinking. Today the jury looks like it would favor the prosecutor over the defenders of the doctrine. It is difficult, but possible, not only to defend but to promote this doctrine over the populist short-term and unnuanced preferences of "common sense" that fail to account for our deep pluralism and post-Christendom secularity. After all, the non-understanding secular press and public was greatly surprised when a conservative Lutheran leader appealed to the doctrine to state clearly that

---

23. See Apology (Ap) to the Augsburg Confession 16 on Political Order and its footnoted references to various of Luther's and Melanchthon's publications.

24. I also recognize that the "Calvinist" prosecutor also has an explicit naming and explication specifically of the Two Kingdoms doctrine in her own tradition that is far more operationalized than the Lutheran version. But it also became fodder for a two-kingdoms collapse into Dominionism that classic Reformed Christians would not recognize. I'm not interested in exegeting that matter here. If interested, one can begin to study the Reformed track of the Two Kingdoms doctrine by reading book 4 of Calvin's *Institutes of the Christian Religion*, beginning with ch. 7 and with particular attention to ch. 20.

any person who advocated white supremacy is a heretic and should be excommunicated.[25]

A third challenge is the matter of naming itself, as every act of naming includes exclusion and can change over time from its initial intended meaning to a much different public ascribed meaning centuries later. So far I have listed nuance and a certain malleability of doctrine as challenges in assessing and reclaiming Two Kingdoms. But there are also linguistic difficulties with the word "Kingdoms." First, it implies a separateness between religion and worldly government that the doctrine itself actually resists. Second, with the seeming separateness, two "kingdoms" hearkens to a dualistic vision of the universe in which an absolute chasm stands between the spiritual and the material. Finally, the term suffers anthropocentric and sexist connotations. With "king" there is the image of an old, white, bearded man presiding over the cosmos from his big chair in heaven and similarly bearded white men issuing dicta from their own earthbound chairs about said divine patriarchy while consuming copious amounts of wine and throwing turkey bones to the dogs. That the longest reigning ruler in the history of the United Kingdom was a woman doesn't matter here. The image has been stuck on us by centuries upon centuries of male supremacy that wonderful stories of feminist empires will not soon overcome in our storehouse of archetypes.

Further, reasonable people object to "Two Kingdoms" because Scripture and tradition speak of *one* kingdom, the kingdom of God. Why should or would we speak of two when the Bible and Jesus himself speak of the one kingdom of God? Yet Jesus and the Christian tradition since evidently were comfortable referring to the "kingdom of this world," the "worldly kingdom," the "temporal kingdom," and so on. The tradition also refers to the reign or kingdom of the devil, which inserts a third and very conflicting domain into the metaphysical imagery. Clearly there is no standardized language about the differing and conflicting arenas within God's interests. But there should be, finally, no difficulty for the faithful Christian theologian to sustain Two Kingdoms while affirming above all that they are one under God. One kingdom may have plural and dissimilar jurisdictions, just as a nation has different states where even the ontological commitments are strikingly different.

In sum, an ongoing objection to the doctrine's title is that it is time bound and gender bound. Could there be other reasons to drop the title? Are there better options that do not echo patriarchy or oppressive political systems? "Two Realms," "Twofold Reign," and "Two Domains" have been suggested. Many theologians use "Two Ways" of God's governing or God's

---

25. Jenkins and McFarlan Miller, "Lutheran Church-Missouri Synod."

"two hands," a trope also used by Luther. I respect the reasoning and the varied uses. In respect of broader conventional use, I'll mostly use "Two Kingdoms," but will use other synonyms to sustain an expansive interpretation.

"Kingdom" Detail

More must be said about terminology. It is better to deal with it now than to cloud other conversation later. Luther's use of "kingdoms" has posed a question for some because Luther himself was inconsistent about its meaning on one hand, and popularly misunderstood about where he was clear about his meaning. He was not always careful with his terms. About where he was clear and his reading public unclear, Luther did not mean to advance "two-kingdoms language" in the Manichean manner that misinterpreters of Augustine imputed to him. The specific terms of "Two Kingdoms" for Augustine was about the conflict between Satan and Christ. In no way did Luther mean this; we've seen already that he transposed two kingdoms into the keys of "spiritual" and "temporal." And with "spiritual kingdom," he associated only Christ and church. Luther's "dualism," based on Scripture, is the division between believers and nonbelievers. Therefore "God has ordained two governments: the spiritual, by which the Holy Spirit produces Christians and righteous people under Christ; and the temporal, which restrains the un-Christian and wicked so that—no thanks to them—they are obliged to keep still and to maintain an outward peace."[26] Having recognized this, we also affirm that the Doctrine of Two Kingdoms envisions a positive relationship between temporal government and the spiritual kingdom, while Christ's reign is in the larger conflict with Satan's reign. The temporal realm is not sequestered from that tension.

Luther also confuses readers with his use of "governments" as seeming synonyms for "kingdoms." This raises an important point in that Luther means by the former term a functional description and by the latter an ontological stipulation. I think this distinction has been lost to many interpreters. The difference is that, as Luther says, God rules over two kingdoms (*zwei Reiche*) by two modes of government or ways of ruling (*zwei Regimente*). The two terms are complementary while nonidentical. They are terms necessary for understanding the "place" and "position descriptions" pertinent to each place.

The deliberate designations of "kingdom" and "government" suggest also why it may not be helpful to suggest simpler and more congenial terms for contemporary ears. Luther indeed indicates both a "spatial" and

26. Luther, "Temporal Authority," in LW 45:91.

a "process" meaning whereby neither "kingdom" nor "government" can be collapsed with the other. He also means to identify two spheres that are distinct but not separate. "Kingdom" is not only a "way" of exercising rule. It is its own ontological place, while "government" is both functional and nominative. I land on the accented distinction, that "government" refers more to function. In short, the two kingdoms are assigned governing structures appropriate to each. Neither "kingdom" should be reduced to their functional meanings.

I also agree that "kingdom" as a geographical or spatial reference in common speech poses problems. How does one recognize the boundaries? How can we see where the spiritual kingdom ends and the earthly or temporal kingdom begins? But fully forsaking a metaphysical and metaphorical sense of "kingdom" forecloses the sense of place and space that Luther intends. God, after all, *is* at home throughout Luther's universe. Further, knowing and striving for one's "place" is among the most powerful drivers of human being and self-understanding. "Home" is not wherever the Christian is as if there is no "special" space for Christians. But Christians do know home is where Christ accompanies them and that is about more than how one feels. I choose "kingdom" because it has ontology and a kind of "geography" to it, and because Christians don't give up on Christ as Lord of all space and time.

This is a major supposition to which I will return with Giorgio Agamben's notion of "messianic time." Agamben proposes, via a strict linguistic analysis of Paul's epistles, an understanding of temporality that honors the human need and sense for "place and space." Further, Agamben aligns well with current cosmological theory (discussed in chapter 6). To maintain the very possibility of such dialogue is necessary for full and coherent systematic thought. In such light, one should not overly equate "government," that is, the mode or way or keeping order, with "kingdom," or finally dispense with the term or idea of "kingdom" altogether.[27] "Kingdom" in my understanding

---

27. This is my quibble with Craig L. Nessan's treatment of Two Kingdoms in his excellent introduction to Lutheran ethics, *Free in Deed*. There he reframes the Two Kingdoms as "God's Two Strategies." This naming helps to correct the dualism and patriarchy that characterized poor interpretation and application of the doctrine particularly over the nineteenth and twentieth centuries. It also assures the role of the one sovereign God over and against pretenders in church and state who tend to accentuate their own authority. Nessan acknowledges that "two strategies" might compromise the ontological status of "place" as intimated in the terminology of "kingdoms." "Place" is real because God is the manifold and power of all; without God, no place and no ontology. So I take Nessan's terminology of "two strategies" as an accent on God's purposes without negating "spaces" for such purposes (p. 61). He chooses instead to speak of God's "two strategies" to counter the "kingdom of Satan" and bring forth "the one kingdom of God." But the spiritual and temporal markers still exist. One strategy applies

will serve too as an analogy for temporal and transtemporal dimensions in cosmology.

With *two* kingdoms and *two* governments (*zwei Reiche* and *zwei Regimente*) then as dialectically definitive, all in the shorthand of "Two Kingdoms," I turn to the *zwei*, the two, to state another essential caution. "Two" does *not* imply dualism, though there are real boundaries between the space of faith where conscience lives freely and the space of public life where law is required to maintain life enhancing order. Luther writes that such boundaries, however ambiguously discerned, are as real as the physical border "between Leipzig and Wittenberg."[28] Yet by their distinction they are also unified by God who draws the distinction. God makes the distinction and does so by keeping the spaces next to each other; "neighbors," as it were. By and through their contiguity the spaces mutually inform. The border is permeable. Princes and bishops do their jobs in their own spaces, but they do not do so insulated from each other. Nor do they cross over and do the other's job. They do their own jobs better when they communicate well with each other. There are real borders, but—a wonderful qualification!—the borders are crossable. Sometimes they have crossing guards.

But the two kingdoms are not contiguously related only in a social sense. One of Luther's strongest gifts was to see and understand human character. We individually are both strong and flawed, faithful and cowardly, loving and selfish, trusting and anxious, humble and proud, self-confident and self-righteous. We each are saint and sinner. Perhaps because Luther knew this so well about himself he knew it in all of us human beings striving toward personhood. The personal extends into the social and the social infuses the personal. The chaos of our public life together finds itself within the human spirit too just as do the dynamics of heroism and cowardice. The essential dynamics of personal and social identity are no different, though more complex to discern now with communication at the speed of light, than they were by paper nailed on a church door. In other words, Luther saw that the same dotted line that differentiates the spiritual and public/historical spaces runs right through every individual Christian, as it has since the fall and will until God's two spheres become one. Until then, the two kingdoms abide at large and in the individual heart, and both require

---

to a spiritual space that includes and transcends the public space we know as history, and the second strategy applies to just that historical space. Nessan agrees finally that "spatiality" is still required for understanding, and that, as the reader will see in ch. 5, spatiality commands an important part of this study. Nessan is integral to the rescue of the Two Kingdoms doctrine today.

28. Luther, "Temporal Authority," in LW 45:116.

their proper oversight: the exercise of the law on the left and the Spirit of Christ on the right. Both are moved by love.

Summary

I've rehearsed a number of problems about the Augustinian Lutheran Doctrine of Two Kingdoms. They include ambiguities about the terminology of "kingdom" itself. Before modernity, kingdoms were understood readily as the domains of rulers with chartable boundaries and unique characteristics. People also readily understood the meaning of "kingdom" when it referred to spiritual space. That God has a kingdom was as little questioned as a temporal king or, more problematically, the pope, having a kingdom. Since modernity—which is to say the ascendancy of the interpreting human subject over theretofore received truth—kingdom language came to be thought both antique and laden with unacceptable metaphysical connotations. Add enumeration to the metaphysical and political implications, then the Reformation Doctrine of Two Kingdoms gets severely misunderstood, misused, and finally discounted. "Two" then mistakenly denoted absolute separation between personal piety and public policy. Worse yet, the former became hostage to the latter. Secular authoritarianism commandeered the church. But merely to turn the table and allow zealous religious authoritarians to commandeer the political order instead is as malign and misusing of the doctrine.

With respect for postmodernity, my intent is to recover the proper originally intended meaning of the political theology of Two Kingdoms. It means to honor both spiritual and temporal realities, coordinating them as distinct but related. To do this "postmodernly," it is necessary to recognize too how different the understanding of the temporal world is today. From the Reformation era to the early Enlightenment, the concepts of natural law and sovereignty were nigh universally accepted and lauded. They were the counterparts in the temporal domain to which the theology of the Two Kingdoms doctrine explicitly related. But now those concepts are practically, if not formally, absent. Consideration of the why of their absence assumes a major portion of this project. If the doctrine is to be useful again, we must ask what "new" philosophical correlates we might include for the temporal jurisdiction. Much of this book will consider just that, with ample help from philosophy.

But absence of central notions and mistakes of interpretation are not peculiar only to the temporal kingdom. The spiritual kingdom has suffered its philosophical and theological misunderstandings, too. I argue that a misbegotten form of biblical interpretation—literalism without eschatological imagination—compromised our own piety and led us into a conflictive ideation of faith vs. politics, in which either pole must dominate the other or they withdraw from any mutuality. Recovery of an eschatological spirituality that is also profoundly based in reality, aided by the work of postmodern philosophers and contemporary Pauline scholars, will help us to rethink, respect, and positively re-employ the doctrine, having re-coordinated it also with new understandings of natural law and sovereignty.

Thus the overall aim of the following pages. Before taking up that task, though, now in chapter 2 I turn to the textual content itself of what came to be called the Doctrine of Two Kingdoms.

2

Two Kingdoms Texts and Challenges

"I need to enter a house whose insides are bigger than its outsides.
I could be changed in a house like that."[1]

WITH THIS CHAPTER I examine the Lutheran movement's initial articulation of the Two Kingdoms doctrine. I start with the doctrine's original iteration in the constituting theological documents of the new Lutheran movement in 1530: the Augsburg Confession (AC) and the Apology (Ap) to the Augsburg Confession.[2]

Philip Melanchthon authored the AC and Ap. In hiding at the Wartburg castle from his enemies, Luther still was in touch with and advised Melanchthon. But Luther was not the only influencer. Other colleagues in the movement also vetted the text. This makes it all the more notable that there was little debate among the reformers about AC 16 and 28. The Wittenberg theologians and their colleagues from other territories clearly affirmed civic government, punishment of lawbreakers, just war, military service, fair economy, property possession, marriage (!), and condemned the idea that true Christian faith required abandonment of responsible citizenship.

In Article 28, the Lutheran reformers worked hard to clarify the source and scope of the authority of the church and bishops. There was to be a clear separation of "the spiritual and the secular." Both the spiritual and secular

---

1. Barnett, "Poetic Space."

2. I suggest it would be more useful for readers who are unfamiliar with the confessional texts that I will reference here to have a copy of the Book of Concord (BC) alongside them than for me to quote them at length.

authorities are to "be honored as the highest gifts of God on earth."[3] The spiritual authorities must stick to ensuring the integrity of the church in its administration of Word and Sacrament (see AC 5 and 7). The church as a spiritual institution therefore must demure from all formal and direct action in lawmaking or any other matters of public order and secular authority. Though the church as such is not to so act, individuals whether baptized or not nevertheless are encouraged to engage in society as responsible caregiving citizens (Gen 1:26–28). Note that the emphasis in Article 28 appears to be on the separation of powers and the delimitation of bishops' behaviors. We have here the substance already of the Two Kingdoms doctrine. Necessary nuance will become apparent later, particularly regarding the question of if and when the boundaries between the authorities should be broken and how. This will become clear in the discussion in the Formula of Concord (FC) of when to declare a "state of confession."

As for the civic authorities, they always must administer justice "for the sake of maintaining public peace," even if against their own wills. True leadership requires self-sacrifice, for the duty to ensure justice and peace itself is and must be greater than any honor of office of either bishops or princes. It is also evident that the reformers were concerned more with curtailing the authority of the bishops than the princes, given how much bishops cosplaying as princes interfered in the civil order that bishops and their consequent overbearing impact on the lives of local parishes. The reformers were all in for good order and mutual loving regard within and between congregations regarding ordinances, ceremonies, and other local communal activity. But they held Christian freedom highest, bidding bishops to relax unreasonable burdens that do more harm to conscience than good. In current parlance, we'd say that the reformers disdained distant autocracy and lauded the wise pastoral care that can issue only from the close knowledge of one's congregational members.[4]

As a themed "doctrine," it is fair to say that the title of Two Kingdoms is incipient. The idea of Two Kingdoms (or any synonym) is in the confessional texts while a formal doctrinal name is not. Nor does the title show up elsewhere beyond the confessional texts. As I noted in chapter 1, it appears that the term "doctrine" was not even attributed to this locus until the twentieth century. Still, the energy invested especially in and around Article 28, with which the Roman Catholic representation at Augsburg quite disagreed (for obvious reasons), shows that the reformers were so keen on this essential distinction between the exercises of spiritual and civil authorities that

---

3. AC 28:18.
4. See especially AC 28:69–78.

the conviction was well-nigh doctrinal. Like the older adage of *lex orandi, lex credendi*—that the rule of prayer become the rule of belief, in essence meaning that practice becomes doctrine—here we see that an expression of confessional conviction against the opposing party is de facto a proposal of doctrine. Thus I will follow the convention of using "doctrine" as our *signum* of a particular conviction and practice since Lutheranism's start. Long held common beliefs need not have names until such a time as focused attention on them is necessary, which commonly happens when faced by doctrinal alternatives that challenge one's very being.

Other published treatises—we can call them "background texts"— supported the reformers' arguments they presented to the emperor and pope in the AC. For example, Ap 16:2 alludes to Luther's *On Temporal Authority* of 1528, as well as other theologians' interpretive work on the matter. They are referenced with exemplary subtlety: "This entire topic on the distinction between Christ's kingdom and the civil realm has been helpfully explained in the writings of our theologians."[5] And that is as far as the naming of premises and authorities goes. It was probably politically correct not to appeal to Luther's scholarly reputation outright when in hot debate with Rome. It is also evident that the Lutherans believed their convictions about civil authority were non-controversially ecumenical. Article 16, after all, was lodged in that section of the AC and Ap which was not significantly disputed. On this particular theme the Lutherans wrote that Rome would (should?) agree to this "without qualification."[6]

In sum, AC 16 affirms that political authority and orderly government are "created and instituted"[7] by God. This obviously follows a straightforward reading of Rom 13. Further, for Christians to occupy political office is a high good on its own merits and is all the more so as an expression of one's baptismal vocation. The administration of justice and maintaining peace, including punishment by "the sword," just war-making, the social ordering and preservation of marriage, business contracts, property ownership, vows upon taking office, and so on are all good things created by God. It also follows that people who would disagree with or even act against the God-ordained goodness of this social ordering are practically and theologically

---

5. BOC, 231.

6. BOC, 231. Perhaps one may infer that actually stating Luther's name in print would not have been rhetorically or politically helpful.

7. I argue that "instituted" carries much more weight than one sees at a first read. In ch. 5, I will suggest that the term is not a mere synonym for "created." It connotes, rather, that God instituted "institutions," even what Rom 8 refers to as "principalities and powers." This weakens claims that God personally "appoints" particular individuals to secular public office.

wrong.[8] Their actions and beliefs do not align with God's providential activity in preserving what God created as good, for, indeed, God instituted government for the preservation of the creation.

Melanchthon's elaboration in Ap 16 of the implications of civil authority as a mode of God's providence is telling. Christ's kingdom and the temporal kingdom are clearly different. Christ's kingdom is "spiritual, that is, . . . at the heart's knowledge of God, fear of God, faith in God, and the beginning of eternal righteousness and eternal life." This indirectly specifies what is not of Christ's kingdom; that is, what is of the temporal kingdom or "kingdom on the left," all those aspects of "outward" life that promote and protect both public and private life. Note the primacy of promoting and protecting, if coercively, as a response to sin. Again, the temporal kingdom is a key space for God's general providence. God provides for all of a peaceful life's necessities, including "legitimate political ordinances," oversight and regulation of food, medicine, architecture, drink, even the air.[9] To these the gospel introduces no new laws or requirements. In other words, the Lutheran reformers held to a basically conserving role of the gospel. Insofar as present laws and practices supported and strengthened the public good, they were not to be compromised by any new political imaginations masquerading in gospel terms. This is why Melanchthon called the fellow Lutheran Karlstadt "insane" when he tried to impose the Mosaic Law upon civil government;[10] or said that monks were "pernicious" for their advocacy of socialism; and that "Wycliffe was obviously out of his mind when he denied that priests were allowed to hold property." It is in the spirit of original Lutheran directness, like a Bronx cheer, for people to say today that Christians who try to impose their religious beliefs and terminology on government policy are nuts. Whether this is a "charitable" witness according to Luther's counsel against false witness is apparently debatable.

It is interesting that Melanchthon thought it necessary to include property rights and assets in his list of temporal rights. The list echoes common notions of civil rights since Hellenism. But more is meant here than prudential comfort for those who depend upon their savings and investment devices for retirement. Melanchthon's considerable length of detailing the church's monopolistic or accounting practices was not about what some

---

8. The AC text uses the word "condemned," and this with reference to the Anabaptists who held that secular government was unchristian or perhaps even anti-Christian, and monastics who held that true faith required escape from worldly matters. The Lutheran church since has apologized to Anabaptists for the suffering imposed on them under the term of "condemned" and said that the condemnations do not now apply.

9. Ap 16:2.

10. Ap 16:3.

today might call "godly resource management." His concern is to clarify that the duty to protect and manage material resources belonged to the state, not to the church. Preservation of the good of the present order for him and most all the reformers was a necessary penultimate point of God's establishing a unique authority other than the church over life's temporal dimension. The temporal world is good in itself *and* provides protected time and space for the advancement of the gospel without using any temporal force to colonize the gospel. The ultimate point then is the primacy and clarity of the gospel for the spiritual dimension of human being, God's "righthand" kingdom. The penultimate point is to cultivate and sustain a temporal space of law and order, including a fair and just economic system, wherein the gospel can freely be served. "How poorly many writers understood these matters is evident from their erroneous view that the gospel is something external, a new and monastic form of government. They failed to see that the gospel brings eternal righteousness to hearts while outwardly approving the civil realm."[11]

AC 28: Ministry Is of the Gospel, Not with Little Caesars

If one would identify just what set of behaviors and beliefs stirred the reformers' anima against the medieval church, one starts well to observe that it was the reformers' experience of priestly and papal authority having gone wild. Like the post facto rationalizations of highly placed officials who accept large gifts without needing to report them to any spiritual or civic accounting firm, church prelates happily owned property, ruled over civic affairs, and even commanded personal armies. They rationalized that such pleasures were allowable perks of their priestly office. In fact, the practice severely distorted their spiritual authority, not just by diverting their attention from the tasks to which they were called, but by compromising the trust too of their constituents. Surely there was self-damage too. These behaviors in the priesthood were not just occasional secular romps or vents of pent-up frustrations and anxieties, as when clergy might take a break to "go Babylonian." Real financial, emotional, and spiritual oppression was foisted on the would-be faithful. Priestly-cum-princely authorities thought it their duty to ensure that heaven be brought to earth by enforcing civic law, and it was to be paid for in the combination of both taxes and indulgences by pious common folk. The reformers rightly named this as oppression of those who would be both faithful and good citizens. This insistence that the

11. Ap 16:8.

priestly office include temporal authority therefore marked a major dividing line between them and the Lutheran reformers.[12]

AC 28 was no minor complaint. The greatest problem was not only a confusion of job descriptions. It was the troubling of faithful souls. The Roman Catholic response seems even to indicate that, though rejecting, they understood this point too.[13] Melanchthon acknowledges that the Catholic delegation appears to have correctly read between the lines of AC 28. He writes, "In this article we were arguing about other things" than the "privileges and immunities of ecclesiastical status." Local congregation members complained about the bishops' neglect of the most basic needs of the would-be faithful. Church authorities were not attending to the care and nurture of congregational life. They did not ensure that there was good preaching of the gospel and regular administration of the sacraments. Standards for ordination and appointment of priests to parishes were unseemly low and parishioner behavior during worship was more policed than priests' manners of catechesis. Basic pastoral care simply wasn't happening, and the authorities didn't care. Instead, they focused their energies on maintaining privilege. So sums Melanchthon in Ap 28:1–5.[14] This practical reality was bad enough. But the confessional and pastoral care theological issues involved here were (and still are) even more important to address. Inattention to them was a major disservice by the church to all who sought solace and likely was a handy excuse for those who chose to be unfaithful.

It should be no surprise, then, that Melanchthon devotes much more ink to what church authorities should *not* do than to what political leaders should do, given the separation of powers explicated in AC 16 and Ap 16. A pastor's inattention to primary duties is as much a cause of flagging faith as a pastor's moral misbehavior. This destructive confusion goes to the heart of

---

12. Ironically, this difference erupts between Lutherans and other reformers too, like the Calvinists. Neo-Calvinists and Montanistic Catholics find themselves as strange allies today with their shared positive disposition toward Christian Dominionism.

13. See Kolb and Wengert, *Book of Concord*, 289n569.

14. Ap 28:3–6: "They neglect the state of the churches, and they do not care if there is correct preaching and proper administration of the sacraments in the churches. They admit all kinds of people to the priesthood quite indiscriminately. They impose intolerable burdens on them, as if they take pleasure in the destruction of their fellow human beings. . . . But the opponents make no reply other than that 'the bishops have . . . the power to rule and to correct by force in order to guide their subjects toward the goal of eternal bliss, and that the power to rule requires the power to judge, to define, to distinguish, and to determine what is helpful or conducive to the aforementioned goal.' These are the words of the Confutation, by which the opponents inform us that bishops have the authority to create laws useful for attaining eternal life. This is the issue at the heart of the controversy."

the necessity of a Two Kingdoms doctrine that reclaims and clarifies again how the church is to work in, with, and for the world.

The "issue at the heart of the controversy," Melanchthon writes, is that the bishops insist on having the temporal authority "to create laws useful for attaining eternal life."[15] This is a fatal confusion of law and gospel. The gospel is, pure and simple, the "forgiveness of sins freely on account of Christ by faith."[16] Any "law" imposed even as an addition so to "be useful for attaining eternal life" compromises the gospel. It also suggests that an ecclesiastical lawyer has more authority over the gospel than does God. Any commanded imposition of human traditions, like worship forms, then, would bear the same implications. And so Ap 28:7–10 make clear that neither sin nor righteousness are connected with such matters as food, drink, or, for that matter, gastroenterology. If traditions can be observed without superstition so as not to give offense to others, all to the well and good. If they, like any impositions of law, detract from the gospel by obfuscation or outright contradiction, they stifle rather than upbuild a Christian's faith, and so must be denied. Obedience to leaders is commendable when their laws are not in opposition to the gospel and the common good. But when they are counter, even if "commanded by an angel," the response must be strong: "Let that one be accursed."[17] Such times are when the faithful are called to "obey God rather than mortals."

Indeed, civic leaders' "laws and the entire political structure are divine ordinances which the Christian ought to use in a holy way."[18] Many people since have interpreted this affirmation of civil obedience to be tantamount to saying that "holiness" is a nation whose politics are fully in sync with Christian principles. This is a severe misreading. The misreading comes from inattention to the reformers' distinction between the command of civil obedience and the greater law of justification by grace through faith. Melanchthon relates civil obedience and political tranquility to the need of sufficient time and space for the gospel of forgiveness to be proclaimed. The doctrine of justification here in the Ap is the "first article." That is, the good news of justification is the norming and predicating article for all else of daily life. Obedience to civil law which has not transgressed its role is normed and required by the ultimate priority of the gospel, the "spiritual law." "For frightened consciences can have no firm consolation against God's wrath

---

15. Ap 28:6.
16. Ap 28:7.
17. Ap 28:20.
18. Ap 28:23.

unless the first article is known."[19] So the church's duty is to make known the first law, the gospel of freedom in and because of Christ. The government's duty is to ensure by law the freedom of citizens to enjoy the opportunity and blessing of peaceful life together as a *civitas*, promised and delivered by the free exercise of a church obedient above all to its own spiritual and not merely its inter-social calling.

This is more than a confusion of church and state. Dangerous as that is, the confusion of church and state is a confusion of polities. The confusion of Two Kingdoms is more profoundly dangerous yet because the spirited intent and the very rule of God *as God chose to rule* through both is defied. The confusion, whether deliberate or accidental, in itself may show how human being typically goes and typically speaks by trying to arrogate everything to ourselves. The confusion of realms may be even exemplary of typical concupiscence (the desire to consume all). But what it is at base is the refusal to hear God where God spoke, *ubi Deus dixit*. It is naught else than to deny God. It is disobedience to the first commandment, a refusal to let God be God. Dietrich Bonhoeffer recapitulated this insight with full throat in his advocacy of the Two Kingdoms doctrine.[20] Here it is sufficient to underscore how even visceral were the reformers against the church's historical collapse of spiritual authority with civil authority through years of war-making and crimes of prelates against prelates betwixt and between princes against princes.

Add to this egregious history the practices of enforced celibacy, idolatry of saints, and other laws against natural conscience that enervated the faithful and denied their freedom intended to be better availed and safeguarded by wiser civic rulers. Given all this spiritually occluding miasma, Melanchthon's concluding explication of the "law" of the gospel and the law of obeying civil law could not be more serious. These two "laws" mirror the Doctrine of Two Kingdoms. The church's chronic malpractice of interfering in civil matters, as compared to the good practice of faithful princes who did not interfere with the proper work of the church, heavily weighted the Lutheran complaint.

Luther's Prior Thinking About Two Kingdoms

Now to Luther's own express considerations that helped further to shape a two-kingdoms political theology. Luther's key text that stands behind

19. Ap 28:23.
20. See, e.g., Bonhoeffer, "Thy Kingdom Come," in DBWE 12.

Melanchthon's confessional synthesis is "Temporal Authority: To What Extent It Should Be Obeyed," published in 1523. Other writings pertaining to the Peasants' Revolt and essays about Christian roles in politics and military service provide helpful examples of practical applications of the Two Kingdoms doctrine.[21] Luther also spoke and wrote directly to civic leaders about his view of the right relation between church and civil authority. His *Address to Christian Nobility* of 1520 was a proposed position description to the secular princes who were friendly to his cause. In that, he even granted that the princes had a qualified authority over certain church practices. The very next year, however, Luther refused to disavow his own publications when ordered to do so by the emperor. Why this apparent about face? What of Christ's command not to resist evil in Matt 5:38–41 and Paul's injunction of Rom 13:1 to obey the "governing authorities"?

For Luther, the difference concerned the freedom of the gospel. What might seem "churchly" but was ancillary to the prime directives of preaching the word and administering the sacraments could (conceivably) fall under certain directives from the civil authorities. But it was out of bounds for civil authorities to take any action that could hinder the reception or administration of faith's essentials, the right proclamation of the word, and the proper administration of the sacraments, i.e., the very reason and being of the church.

Luther already focused his thoughts in this way in early 1522 when the Imperial Council of Regency outlawed Luther's "renovations" (e.g., communion in both kinds, clerical marriage, insouciance as to vestments, etc.). His concern for the gospel then elided with his personal sense of mission when princes under the authority of the Edict of Worms plotted against his life. Further, those who banned dissemination of his translation of the New Testament motivated him to ask what right they had to censor the proclamation of the gospel. By mid-1522 Luther had written Spalatin that it was an elector's duty to protect his subjects from persecution and to make available to them spiritual comfort. By fall, Luther had written to the friendly knight, Baron Schwarzenberg, that he would soon publish a special treatise on the relationship between the gospel and the temporal wielding of the sword, and on this matter Luther had to rebalance his account.[22] Luther worried that von Schwarzenberg was too zealous to accommodate secular authority to the gospel. But Luther shared the greater worry that secular rulers were banning the spread of the gospel. Luther promised the

---

21. Cf. "To the Councilmen of all Cities in Germany" and "Whether One May Flee from a Deadly Plague," both in Lull, *Basic Theological Writings*, 704-35.

22. See Walther Brandt's editorial introduction to "Temporal Authority," LW 45:77-78.

Baron that a forthcoming treatise would correct this double trouble. Later that fall, Luther preached six sermons in Weimar, the third and fourth of which, though extemporaneous, became the outline for the treatise after the sermon's noble hearers begged him to publish so.

The organizing question became twofold. First, what is the source and character of legitimate governmental power? Second, what limits should government have? These summary questions provided the substance to "Temporal Authority,"[23] while its structure was threefold. The first section concerns God's instituting of civil authority so that evildoers would be restrained, granting that civil authority "in theory" need not hold over the pure Christian person (though history shows there are none). Second, Luther charts when and where temporal authority is limited; it particularly has no authority over faith and conscience. Finally, Luther offers pastoral counsel on how a prince should conduct his office. Luther finished the manuscript by Christmas of 1522, but it was not published until the spring of 1523.

We are familiar with worker colleagues who are unable to stay in their lanes. Melanchthon was clear about this in his expansions upon the divisions of authority in Ap 16 and 28. Luther was clearly consternated by the problem too. Bishops too often preferred to "rule castles, cities, lands, and people outwardly" rather than to serve as people's inwardly soul-carers (*Seelsorgere*). Secular government ministers traded the outward work of territorial governance "to exercise a spiritual rule over souls."[24] Of course, Luther was a bit hyperbolic, though not unjustly, considering the existential threat to the gospel, him, and his followers presented by the Edict of Worms and the Imperial Council of Regency. Prelates overreached into civil affairs and princes reciprocated. The backscratching had been happily mutual, though the role reversal compromised the notion that faith life be ordered in the spiritual realm and civic life in the temporal realm.

Luther begins the treatise with the usual peremptory denunciations of misbehavior all around, though rather briefly, and then takes direct aim at this massive problem of role confusion. "First, we must provide a sound basis for the civil law and sword so no one will doubt that it is in the world by God's will and ordinance."[25] Romans 13 and 1 Pet 2 are the constituting texts. He follows this by recapping the divinely affirmed use of the sword/law since the fall, through the law of Moses, concluding with what Luther interprets as Christ's confirmation of the *lex talionis* (an eye for an eye;

---

23. Here I follow Bornkamm, *Luther's Doctrine*.
24. LW 45:109.
25. LW 45:85.

retributive justice) when saying to Peter, "He that lives by the sword will die by the sword" (Matt 26:52). Including John the Baptizer as such an affirmer, Luther concludes his first point. "Hence, it is certain and clear enough that it is God's will that the temporal sword and law be used for the punishment of the wicked and the protection of the upright."[26]

With his second point Luther turns from sanctioned violence to the sanctity of peace. Yes, Christ does say in Matt 5 that the *lex talionis* no longer holds and to love one's enemies, that a follower of Jesus will not resist evil but turn the cheek and give both coat and cloak and go the extra mile. Luther cites Rom 12, too, to leave vengeance to God and, per 1 Peter, to live peaceably and not return evil for evil. Luther does not see these texts as of the same category as and so counter to the political counsels in Rom 13 and 1 Pet 2, though. They are apples to oranges. The "peaceable passages" are about the would-be Christian's internal state of faith, of love and heart, while the "political passages" are about the mixed population of Christians and non-Christians together in public life. Further, these "apple" texts are about faith vs. works, and the latter are the non-salvific actions in public civil affairs. For Luther would not go with the "sophists" who interpret all the passages equally, who "condemn to hell all those who do not love their enemies." For Luther, these passages are of different orders. "For perfection and imperfection do not exist in works, and do not establish any distinct external order among Christians. They exist in the heart, in faith and love, so that those who believe and love the most are the perfect ones, whether they be outwardly male or female, prince or peasant, monk or layman. For love and faith produce no sects or outward differences."[27]

Third, Luther uses his typical disjunctive logic of "is/is not" to make the strong distinction that follows naturally from the preceding section: "We must divide the children of Adam and all mankind into two classes, the first belonging to the kingdom of God, the second to the kingdom of the world."[28] Here begin more complications than one might welcome. There is more at play here systematically than first meets the eye. Moving straightforwardly from Christ's declaration that his kingdom is not "of" this world, but of the spiritual, Luther divides humanity into two classes: those who belong to God's kingdom and those who belong to the temporal. Luther's basis is scriptural (John 18:36–37; Matt 4:17; 6:33; 10:7). Fourth, Luther quickly elides into theological anthropology—with the loci of sin, justification, sanctification, and the Christian life standing firmly in the background—to

26. LW 45:87.
27. LW 45:88.
28. LW 45:88; also note here the allusion to Augustine's two cities.

conclude with a practical, if summary, political theology. It is fair to say that Luther's stance here is both strong and seemingly inconsistent. The implicit question he addresses is whether Christians need civil law. His answer: they do not. Those who live in, from, and for God's kingdom "need no temporal law or sword" because the righteous person "of his own accord does all and more than the law demands."[29]

Luther allows that there are "few" true believers. For non-Christians, though, God provides "a different government beyond the Christian estate and kingdom of God." It is clear that "few" does not compromise the priority transcending size of God's kingdom. The spiritual priority of God's rule elicits from God too the providential means (the "emergency order") to safeguard both the righteous and the unrighteous, along with the integrity of all creation. If there were no temporal law ordained by God, the world would be reduced to chaos. People "would devour one another, seeing that the whole world is evil and that among thousands there is scarcely a single true Christian." And so "God has ordained two governments; the spiritual, by which the Holy Spirit produces Christians and righteous people under Christ; and the temporal, which restrains the un-Christian and the wicked so that . . . they are obliged to keep still and to maintain an outward peace."[30]

Note again that Luther locates the freedom of faith in a person's subjectivity, while the point of the "objective" law is to maintain a public peace. This is no facile modern secularist's dualism of private/public. God wills that human beings would have no chaos either in the heart or in the civitas. God wants and offers peaceableness because, after all, God's first and utmost impulse is love, love for God's creation and love in particular for each person uniquely as a bearer of God's image. So God enacts two modes of God's love and orders two kingdoms with their two governments.

The Christian then lives more by the law of love than by the civil law. The Christian does so not to engage in the world's debasement of life as transactional. The Christian simply does what is good for the neighbor. This includes a Christian's suffering of injustice if the injustice stops with that Christian. A "private injustice" is of no final harm to the one whose home is secured in Christ. But if it were to extend through that Christian to the neighbor, then the Christian must resist. To live by the law of love means never submitting absolutely in all cases to any spiritual or temporal authority.[31] The law of love brooks no injustice toward the neighbor.

---

29. LW 45:89.
30. LW 45:91.
31. LW 44:92.

The law of love is to shine its light on the civil realm in all respects. Later we will see how Luther understood this to take the form of natural law. What constitutes the good is instantiated in just civil law because that is what God willed. Thus, Luther can advise that a Christian if called to such work could bear arms or even serve as an executioner; in both the Christian still would be an active proponent and guardian of the peace. We may have a differently informed conscience today and might with good reason object to Luther on this point (as I will with Luther's inability to accept the terms of the Sermon on the Mount). Luther simply accepted that violence was necessary to secure the health and safety of the neighbor and nation, even to the point of giving one's own life so to save the life of the neighbor. But Luther also insisted that the exercise of violence for one's self-protection was never justified. Luther was unmovable on this point. When it is one's mortal self at stake, the Christian must suffer even unjust persecution quietly as did Christ with trust in God's providence even against all human instinct and hope. This is what it means for a faithful Christian to be a model citizen. "Christian" citizens use all good reason with all one's given talents to orient love in one's uniquely created way toward neighborly care. That's it. This is the way. Living in accord with this two-kingdom ontology is to "satisfy God's kingdom inwardly and the kingdom of the world outwardly."[32]

The non-Christian, of course, is also obligated to obey the law and authorities. But the non-Christian's subjectivity works differently, given that it is not yet freed from its anxiety-inducing captivity to sin. Compassion and reason should and must still motivate the non-Christian too. Compassion and reason belong to the natural law that Luther recognized as working in all people. That is the Golden Rule; do not do to others what you would not want done to oneself. The difference between the Golden Rule and Jesus' command to "love one another" is a difference of perception. One sees and serves the world for oneself. The other sees and serves the world for others. At the risk of being immodest, the Christian sees things with a larger perspective, including that God is all in all and will have God's gracious way. And the Christian too understands and works with the non-Christian's perspective, which includes the Golden Rule, because the Christian sees still that God works kindly and uniquely in that legal modality because God's relation to all the world in all the world's details will not be riven. In other words, affirmation of one's civic responsibilities and living obediently under temporal authority recognizes and lives by the trinity of "love-reason-natural law." This is an elemental conviction of Luther. Everyone should recognize and live by this common denominator. Christians have the higher

---

32. LW 44:96.

duty yet to live by love with a greater sense of its severity and urgency.³³ As we will see, this triune common denominator of love-reason-natural law in the temporal realm is essential. Its weakening or absence means tragedy for any civil society.

Luther expansively cites scriptural background for this now central claim. Having shown the necessity that civil authority needs to be separated functionally and institutionally from the church, he summarizes, finally that the rule of love above all—in both the secular and religious dimensions—justifies and requires the most basic societal administrative functions. The proper organizational and administrative activities to ensure a peaceable civil life are themselves even holy.

> If the governing authority and its sword are a divine service, as was proved above, then everything that is essential for the authority's bearing of the sword must also be divine service. There must be those who arrest, prosecute, execute, and destroy the wicked, and who protect, acquit, defend and save the good. Therefore, when they perform their duties, not with the intention of seeking their own ends but only of helping the law and the governing authority function to coerce the wicked, there is no peril in that; they may use their office like anybody else would use his trade, as a means of livelihood. For, as has been said, love of neighbor is not concerned about its own; it considers not how great or humble, but how profitable and needful the works are for neighbor or community.³⁴

The Nature and Limits of Spiritual and Temporal Authority

In part 2 of "Temporal Authority," which Luther considers the main part of the treatise (though the first part is much longer), he addresses the limits of temporal authority. There is danger when authority is extended either too far or too little. The danger is greater with the former, but one must discern nevertheless just where the right dividing line is. Here again Luther's declension between public and private is weighty. In brief, temporal authority includes an individual person's body, possessions, and external affairs. How one treats the neighbor, obtains property, engages in commerce, writes policy, polices the streets, and wages war: all these are the proper purview of

---

33. Bornkamm, *Luther's Doctrine*, 15.
34. LW 45:103–4.

a just and righteous government. On these Luther will advise later. His main concern here is that government authority does not and must not extend into a person's interiority of conscience and soul. Were temporal authority to so overreach into that spiritual kingdom, it would mislead and destroy souls. Luther is clear. "Man-made law" must not be so imposed as to make people believe "this or that."[35]

Then Luther makes a most interesting observation with implications that many interpreters have glossed over. In tenor and content, one could argue correctly that Luther writes as much against those who misuse religious authority as he does about the misuse of civil authority. Explicitly in the latter case and implicitly for the former, the enforcement of laws that are not clearly of divine origin and imposed upon a person's interiority are out of bounds. Luther writes, "When a man-made law is imposed upon the soul to make it believe this or that as its human author may prescribe, there is certainly no law for it." The following sentence is even more interesting: "If there is no word of God for it, then we cannot be sure whether God wishes to have it so, for we cannot be certain that something which he does not command is pleasing to him. Indeed, we are sure that it does not please him, for he desires that our faith be based simply and entirely on his divine word alone."[36] So implicative and complicated is this simple declaration! In short, Luther declares that if there is no clear word of God for any human law, then it is not pleasing to God.

What laws might Luther have in mind to write against them so? He rehearses much Scripture to make his case.[37] The sources of his animus are revealed when he reports that in three different jurisdictions "tyrants" have ordered that all publications of his translation of the New Testament must be turned over to the government. This is not just censorship. It is the temporal realm's invasion of the spiritual. And Luther's specific advice to the faithful in answer to this unjust demand? Do not turn over one page of your New Testament; do not actively obey the prince's unholy order. But if one's home is finally invaded in search and seizure of such "contraband"? Luther answers: do not resist, but endure, even as not one finger should be lifted to

---

35. LW 45:105.

36. LW 45:105.

37. And thereby, I argue, makes this case as much against religious leaders who misuse their authority as against civil authorities. Texts Luther cites include Rom 13, 1 Pet 2, Ps 113, Acts 5, and Matt 2:16 (though he misreferences it as Luke 23:7). Regrettably, Melanchthon made just this mistake of supporting state advocacy for "true religion" over and against Anabaptists. See Witte, *Law and Protestantism*.

conform or obey.[38] In effect, Luther counsels a term he did not yet know: passive resistance.

This was the real-life case study of temporal authorities having gone rogue. They are not to stifle the gospel. But what if they were to act in a manner that supported the gospel? Is that warranted? Some people argued in the affirmative; that it was appropriate for the prince to have a role in driving out "heresy." Luther again answers "no." False doctrine is to be addressed by the bishops. And correction by temporal force or even a pope's new army would not succeed anyway. It is good pastoral care that would drive out heresy, and the best pastoral care comes with well-chosen words. Faith comes by hearing. One must "let God's word have its way"[39] and let not the temporal sword be brandished wrongly.

This is a first step toward a Protestant ecclesiology that has inspired much debate since. Anticipating that a princely defendant would ask how Christians then are to be outwardly ruled, as surely there must be authority "even among Christians," Luther answers that Christian mutuality is the key. Luther addresses specifically how Christians should manage their life together, distinct from life in the secular realm. He is not speaking about the individual Christian, nor is he speaking about the Christian in temporal society where civil law has its right role. But among Christians together—one presumes here what Scripture means as *koinonia*—there shall be no authority (!). Per Paul in Rom 12 and per 1 Pet 5:5, all Christians are subject to each other, and all that they do together is by common consent. There is no superior among Christians other than Christ and Christ alone. There is not even an innate authority among priests and bishops over Christian practical life together. Clergy authority is only about the proclamation, teaching, and sacramental administration of God's word so as to give birth to and nurture Christians. Anything else is a "service and office" from which rulings come as a matter of the faith community's will and consent.[40] That is to say, yes, Luther affirmed the role of bishops as long as they served the gospel. In the emergency situation of the new Lutheran movement in which few such bishops were handy, a new churchly system of oversight was needed for good order. But whoever was appointed to such supervision was authorized also by the community's will and consent. The similarity of this ad hoc hybridization of congregationalism and episcopacy, with scriptural warrant, to a polity of the people's will (*demos-cratia*) is striking.

38. LW 45:112.
39. LW 45:117.
40. LW 45:117.

With part 3 of the treatise Luther finally advances to practical advice. The reader might well wish that this section might have been developed into a larger book and become as widely known in Luther's time as Machiavelli's *The Prince*, such a counterpoint in tone and practical wisdom it is. Luther advises here about character, not the vast corpus of law and political science. The prince must know that corpus and know when to veer from it. To have such understanding is marvelous and rare. And since such informed elites are rare, Luther strongly encourages that most any prince, so to compensate,[41] "must cling closely to God, constantly praying that he will serve his subjects wisely, making himself above all attentive to them and their needs, not his own. This prince will, second, be neither impressed by the high and mighty nor despise the lowly. The prince will be self-confident, differentiated, and trusting of his aides, but neither too-trusting nor too self-confident. He'll be wary of the inevitable sycophants and will deal justly with evildoers, knowing when to wield greater wrath and when to wave a gloved hand, knowing when rightly to 'wink at faults.'"[42]

As for foreign policy, Luther briefly advises all civic officials to cooperate with or suffer the actions of a superior. Not unlike how Luther advises Christian to suffer personal assaults privately, Luther presumes this is an ordered relationship within the same state or federation, as, say, a district magistrate to a city official, or city official to state official, and so on. As much as possible, avoid war. Whether the antagonist is an equal, an inferior, or a foreign government, seek justice and peace first, keeping the interests of one's own citizens utmost. If caring for one's citizens—one's neighbors—requires force, then so be it. Luther doesn't formally name the code he follows here, but this is the basic structure of *ante bello* just war theory. This background structure holds for citizens, too. Presuming the people's knowledge of an official's actions, if the prince is wrong, if the war is unjust, at this point finally the people are not bound to follow the leader, for "it is no one's duty to do wrong." If the people do not know of an extant wrong, their own souls are not in peril, but abetting known evil implies otherwise.

In all this, the prince should strive to practice restraint and firmness. So goes Luther's summary of a good prince's character. Given the paucity of such good princes, Luther rails the more by declaiming most temporal and religious leaders as fools. He wasn't writing from the experience of just one bad day. The story of the Duke Charles of Burgundy, even so, epitomizes Luther's hopes in any leader. A woman pleaded with a nobleman to release his captive, her husband. The nobleman promised her he would release her

---

41. I read Luther as both wry and serious here.
42. LW 45:123–24.

husband to her if she would lie with him. She asked the husband's permission. He wanted his freedom, so he said yes. After the tryst, the nobleman killed the husband and gave the dead body to the woman. She brought her case to the duke. The duke commanded the nobleman to marry the woman, after which the duke had the nobleman beheaded and gave back to the woman her honor along with all the nobleman's property. Knowledge of the law and creative imagination devoted to the care of his subject informed the duke's judgment. Note that it was civil law and creativity, not specifically Christian doctrine, that guides the duke in this "secular" situation. While many of us today prefer a more peaceable and quite other than autocratic judgment than the default recourse to violence, one surmises that Luther would have liked to witness much more of the duke's creative wisdom amongst all his political contemporaries.

Finally, one might ask what Luther does not address in this treatise. Why would Christians as such usually not serve well as temporal rulers? Do they not "know better" than the non-Christian about how we should live both part and together? Christians are supposed to know what life with God is supposed to be like in the transcending frame of the spiritual kingdom. They purportedly know that the civil law and authority is ordained by God in its differentiation from the religious sphere. The answer to such Christian superiority is that Luther doesn't resist the idea of Christians ruling well in the temporal kingdom. It's just that there are few Christians to his liking like good Frederick. The difference is that those like Frederick know their "civil" side while most Christians didn't, as far as Luther could see. Worse, those "Christians" who believe they "know better" proved empirically that they did not. Zealous Christians who wore their faith on their sleeves and interpreted Scripture as public policy were terribly ineffective civic leaders. Given their Christian triumphalism, they lacked the humility to serve well as civil authorities because they also truly lacked a "common" sense.

Indeed, they were too "enthusiastic"—the reformers weren't uneasy with calling out lunacy—about bringing in God's reign through their own proud and proactive ignorance. The story of the Schwärmer is a famous case in point.[43] Luther wanted nothing of them as authorities in the civil realm. Their collective subjectivity was destructive. No matter their impatience, God's kingdom was and is always for God alone finally to fully manifest.

---

43. The "Enthusiasts" (*Schwärmer*), a.k.a. "Spiritualists," were adherents of the Radical Reformation who, going beyond the influence of Luther, claimed direct inspiration and revelation from the Holy Spirit. They claimed an authority of the "inner word" over and against the objective word of Scripture. Many, including Anabaptists, were involved in the Peasants' Revolt and their anarchy was punctuated by their involvement in the so-called Debacle at Münster.

Variants of what is now called "Christian Nationalism" since Constantine regularly have accompanied ultimately fatal human utopianisms. Luther recognized enough of the problem to steer clear. Therefore the distinction between two kingdoms was the more necessary to advocate. The empirical manifestation of chronic sin, which also takes form in enthusiastic stupidity throughout human history was proof enough for Luther's need to argue the distinction between kingdoms without absolutely separating them.[44]

The Three Estates

The concern for the proper declension of two kingdoms was not that the church was simply or just too political. Melanchthon acknowledges that no church could not be political. As Melanchthon writes, "Besides, we have frequently testified that we do not criticize political ordinances nor the gifts and privileges bestowed by princes."[45] The oppressive error was the prioritization of the political over the gospel. In this, the correct political ordering *apart* from the gospel was an echo of correctly prioritizing justification by faith through grace over works, or grace over law.[46]

Luther himself felt no personal constraint from acting politically. He relied on political favors when and where he could from friendly princes. Whenever Luther's bread could be buttered to ensure the freedom of the gospel, he could be as cozy or as cold with the political elite as the situation required. Luther went so far as to script a theological justification for a particular political ordering within the temporal realm. He believed it was necessary to instruct all common folk and their leaders, Christian or not, about how the temporal kingdom itself is and should be ordered as designed by God. Luther saw no internal contradiction here about doing theology within that realm that was distinct from the spiritual. Likely, he understood this as an aspect of God's providence that applied to all the

---

44. I am mindful here of that period of many permutations in interpretation of the Two Kingdoms doctrine from Luther and Melanchthon through Lutheran Orthodoxy. In that time much on the spiritual side is moved to the temporal and with that a loss of eschatological appreciation: a historical regret. My omission here is simply necessary. For some compensation, I refer the reader to Hinlicky, review of *Law and Protestantism* (Witte).

45. Ap 28:2.

46. This echo seems to be faint in Melanchthon's statement quoted above in n14, that "the issue at the heart of the controversy" is that bishops feel duty bound to "create laws useful for attaining eternal life." Though Melanchthon doesn't appear to perseverate on this actual anti-gospel theological position of the bishops, he must be obliquely noting it.

creation as an aspect of "natural law," central to public life.[47] Whatever the explanation (which we here will not pursue), Luther put forward another "position description" in clearly more secular terms that he believed should be commendable to all people in their temporal lives. I refer here to Luther's adaptation of the notion of the Three Estates.

The societal declension of "three estates" or "three institutions" (*Stände*) was not new to Luther. It was a medieval ordering that Luther adapted. Instead of a threefold medieval society of clergy-knighthood-common labor that served the church (the *corpus christianum*), Luther reinterpreted the estates. First instituted by God is the church (*Ecclesia*) as the fullness of the human race descended from Adam. Subsequently, God ordered the household/economy (*Oeconomia*) for the livelihood of people, and finally the state (*Politia*) to protect the two estates of church and economy. Luther also called these estates "masks" (*larvae*) by which God acts.[48]

The medieval backdrop was a hierarchical class-ordering that Luther's re-ordering meant to change. Like the mutual reciprocal actions of the co-equal persons of the Trinity,[49] Luther saw the three estates as mutually dependent and reciprocally serving. The church was, to be sure "more distinctive." But the household and state had a unique mutual relationship whereby the locus of the economy was in the household, with its own sort of temporal government, that the civil government was meant to "guard, protect, and defend."[50] Furthering the distinction, Luther understood the church and household/economy to be orders of creation. Temporal government is not. Though "instituted" by God, temporal government is not of the original creation orders. Temporal government is a necessity in the second generation of the postlapsarian age. After Cain killed Abel, per Luther, humanity needed political ordering. "Politics is the guard of fallen nature, economy is what remains of [original] nature, and the church is the redemption and restoration of nature."[51]

While to some this idea of Three Estates might seem to be a sidebar to our primary focus of Two Kingdoms, the Three Estates concept is actually integral to understanding and applying a two-kingdoms hermeneutic. Their distinctive and reciprocal roles underscore a dynamism that is critical for human flourishing. There is a dynamism within the triad that should

47. We will consider the role of natural law at length in ch. 3.
48. LW 1:103.
49. Cf. LW 1:103, esp. the phrase "all according to the three persons of the Trinity."
50. LW 41:177.
51. Weimar Ausgabe of Luther's Writings (WA) 42:22.2026, as translated by Westhelle in "Power and Politics," 295. I am indebted to Westhelle, "Power and Politics," for these insights.

further invigorate our understanding of and participation in the temporal realm, yet is easy to overlook and understate. I would accent Luther's strong distinction between politics and the economy. The distinction is useful when today politics links more closely to economics and less to the household than in Luther's day and vision. Luther and Lutheranism believed that a clear purpose of politics is to serve the household and the household was the source of economy. Of course, Luther did not know of Adam Smith's "invisible hand" that would loom ever larger over and even against households, finally philosophically to separate economics from its origin in the home. Nevertheless, a Two Kingdoms doctrine that is given more density by the Three Estates concept would hold that "the" economy like the sabbath should serve every household—i.e., humankind—rather than vice versa. Flourishing and equity, as in a Trinitarian life, are the purposes of economy. The temporal economy is to serve the common good (the commonweal). Temporal government, then, given its duty to protect and advance the public good, ensures the fairness of the economy. Theologians and politicians might want today to be circumspect about any character of "original creation" still extant in economy and whatever economic system best serves the benevolent purpose of economy as such is surely still to be responsibly debated. Above and beyond the newer scientific and philosophical points that regularly should be considered with respect to *oeconomia*, the principles of the Three Estates and their purposes doubly underscore the values to be preserved and practiced in the temporal sphere in any recapitulation of the Two Kingdoms doctrine.[52]

Two Kingdoms in the Christian

Were a Christian perfectly so, were one simply in one's "very nature" fully Christian, the rule of law would not be necessary. The real Christian would simply "be" Christ and need no guidance. She would quietly suffer the unrighteousness directed to her, but seek always the better ways to help the suffering neighbor and the oppressed community. But we know better. Or should. Few Christians actually act so. And Luther learned enough from real experience to know better. He heard firsthand enough baptismal promises and wedding vows to know when masses of self-identified Christians did not keep them. He knew well that workaday world that depended even daily on breaking the Decalogue. If so with Christians sincerely trying to live up

---

52. Arguably, the Scandinavian Lutheran churches have taken this economic oversight part of the theological tradition more seriously than other countries in their structuring of government. See Nelson, *Lutheranism and the Nordic Spirit*.

to the name, how much more so with the masses who cared much more for their own interests than those of neighbor and society?[53]

Per the Doctrine of Two Kingdoms, God established civil authorities as guardrails for the preservation of order and justice in society at large. This was a matter of God ordering service of neighbor to neighbor, as God's favor is like rain on the just and unjust. More important yet, for God this was and is a matter of keeping evil at bay. Every instrument must be employed, including the sword when necessary, so to preserve concord and freedom enough for every society member to pursue and enjoy what God would freely resource: daily bread, clothing, shelter, health, education, meaningful lives. Above all, per Luther, the social ordering must be protected enough for every individual to discover, hear, and be freed by the gospel. In other words, care for all people, guaranteed by a fair and just social order, and so instantiated in the temporal kingdom, is a matter of providence. God wills to preserve what God began. So the rain falls generously. Further, God intends to redeem. Therefore, the spiritual kingdom is where the church works its heart out proclaiming the word and providing sacramental nourishment all along the way. In that spiritual kingdom life in full freedom is anticipated practically until that day when neither kingdom is finally necessary, and God is tangibly and sensually all-in-all.

But let us move from the gospel's grand vision to quotidian practicality. What does this all mean for the individual Christian? For the time being, the Christian who is daily strengthened by the church when it properly stewards its spiritual authority is called to attend to one's civic responsibilities. As does the church, the individual Christian lives in and serves both kingdoms. It is equally true that both kingdoms abide in the individual Christian. This is why Luther advises Christians to rise daily and "remember" one's baptism, which is to remember whose one is. Thereby the Christian daily re-members who one is, a follower of Christ freed to serve actively and creatively in one's baptismal and professional vocation as a caregiver for one's neighbors, even defending them with the sword if need be. But, as we just rehearsed, while the Christian must "tolerate no injustice toward your neighbor," where the Christian's own self is concerned, the Christian must "suffer injustice toward yourself as a true Christian."[54]

Is this a prescription for personal anxiety, even a kind of spiritual masochism? I suspect, rather, though the thought is underdeveloped, that this is Luther's way of stating that obedience to the spiritual law of love (above and beyond the natural law of the temporal realm) includes an internalization

---

53. Nelson, *Lutheranism and the Nordic Spirit*, 89, 91–95.
54. Nelson, *Lutheranism and the Nordic Spirit*, 96.

of Luther's Theology of the Cross. Just as Christ's obedience even unto death on the cross shows the true "character" of God as selfless love, so also the Christian's suffering on behalf of others in trust of God's power manifesting through human weakness is a disciplined and holy denial of self-privilege. "Two-kingdoms" language—in fact, not just language, but a spiritual and moral *worldview*—also describes the "two sets of relationships within which the Christian lives."[55] There is one's own personal life among one's family, friends, and associates. The personal life includes one's whole Christian disposition wherein forgiveness, endurance, and sacrifice prevail. Then there is one's life in the commons, in society as a whole, where law must redress evil; where Christians strive to ensure that no one suffers injustice or victimization from others. One set does not work without the other. A life of love in service has no energy without the personal life of the cross where God gives the greater strength. As I just noted, however, this theme is underdeveloped, as Luther's keener situational interest is about the public and systemic relationship of the spiritual and the temporal. And Luther does not explicitly construct his two-kingdoms model with guidance from his Theology of the Cross hermeneutic. I will return to this problem later.

For the meantime, the systemic must inform the personal and it is to us further to draw out the implications for the inward life of the individual Christian. For these two sets of relationships, God has provided appropriate means, governments (*Regimente*), which are the free (and freeing) word of God and the coercive power of civil authority. God has ordained both, in both of which the Christian must live while the non-Christian need live only in one. So Luther: "For this reason God has ordained two governments: the spiritual, by which the Holy Spirit produces Christians and righteous people under Christ; and the temporal, which restrains the un-Christian and wicked so that—no thanks to them—they are obliged to keep still and to maintain an outward peace."[56]

---

55. Bornkamm, *Luther's Doctrine*, 8.

56. Luther, "Treatise on Good Works," LW 45:91, quoted in Bornkamm, *Luther's Doctrine*, 8. Also, and again, that Luther uses the term "governments" (*Regimente*) here is not a problem. It is his common swap for "kingdoms," thereby, I hold, helping to interpret the latter while not denying the latter's connotation of spatiality. Note Luther's furthering of the meaning of "kingdom" (*Reich*) as "domain" in his sermon of June 5, 1534: "All who are not Christians belong to the kingdom of the world and are under the law. There are few true believers, and still fewer who live a Christian life, who do not resist evil and indeed themselves do no evil. For this reason God has provided them a different government [*Regiment*] beyond the Christian estate and kingdom of God. He has subjected them to the sword" (Luther, WA 37:426, quoted in Bornkamm, *Luther's Doctrine*, 17–19).

The Christian lives eyes wide open in a world fractured by sin and grace. "Enmeshed" may be a better term than "fractured" and an image of intersecting domains more helpful than the binaries Luther employs. The Christian's spiritual world, a wondrous gift from God, is not separate from the temporal world, but fused with the temporal and vice versa. The Christian lives in that sector of the Venn diagram where the domains overlap. Only the angels and the saints triumphant live "now" in that temporally untainted part of the righthand circle. Still, it is by the love of the Creator God that both domains exist. And by God's redeeming love there will finally come a time beyond when the full unmediated presence of God to creation and creation to God means that one once mortally empty domain is all in one and one in all.

Which brings us to that end time and more, the role of eschatology in Luther's formulation of the Two Kingdoms. Luther had a lively eschatology. It is a major mistake to suppose that Luther intended any stasis with the Two Kingdoms. God's love will finally subsume all and is the *raison d'être* for both. Love abides even in the purely temporal domain, where, by God's will, love assumes natural form. Christians know they are to follow the prime directives of loving God above all else and loving neighbors as themselves. The prime directives are for Christians specific iterations of the general natural law of love. The natural law of love assumed interesting political forms in Western philosophy after Luther. But Luther was aware and fully affirming of the law of love's rule and mimetic forms over many cultures and over all history. The Golden Rule was familiar and fully affirmed as the "Higher Law" in the temporal kingdom. "For nature teaches as love does, that I should do as I would be done by."[57] Love and natural law, then, are to be exercised among all people. It is the obligation of all people, and especially civic authorities over all people, to use reason to advance the justice necessary in service to love and natural law. Indeed, love and natural law *must* be reasonably employed by responsible, clear and freely thinking administrators. They must be virtually innate for those called to public offices of societal care, like the pastor who can make quick and wise decisions without a moment's pause after a full life of challenging ministry; or like a heart surgeon whose skills and knowledge are so elided after decades of practice that she will fix a sudden arterial eruption and without worry will order an immediate change of medication. Along such lines, in the third and final section of the treatise, Luther makes clear the practical necessity that civic authorities be of the best reason and character. "First, toward God there must be true confidence and earnest prayer; second, toward his

---

57. LW 45:128.

subjects there must be love and Christian service; third, with respect to his counselors and officials he must maintain an untrammeled reason and unfettered judgment; fourth, with respect to evildoers he must manifest a restrained severity and firmness."[58]

We infer rightly that Luther would say the same of those who hold office in the spiritual realm who stay in their own lane, as temporal authorities would stay in theirs, as Melanchthon rehearsed such concerns in the *Treatise on the Power and Primacy of the Pope*.[59] Reason aligned with love are to be the hallmarks of good pastors who faithfully and creatively proclaim the word and administer the means of grace, aiding in the liberation of their hearers so that they in turn can and will effect and shape both the private and public good. The Two Kingdoms are distinct. And they are accountable to each other for the ensuring of their mutual response-abilities.

The Church's State of Exception—
Making an Adiaphoron a Rule

There is one more large question to address here that the Doctrine of Two Kingdoms hardly posed at its first inklings. I've alluded to it above, but it needs more attention. This question concerns when resistance to authority is required. Luther provided an example of his own in his treatise "The Freedom of a Christian." After the Lutherans affirmed the AC and the Ap, which were deeply informed by Luther's independent iteration of the doctrine, an occasion arose for the "second generation" of Lutherans that required another caveat as to when the church as such should resist sacred or secular authority. This occasion was the Augsburg and Leipzig Interims of 1547–48. They evoked from the Gnesio-Lutheran leadership of Matthias Flacius an article in the FC, the last official confessional document to be included in the BC. This article (FC 10) addressed so-called adiaphora, those matters usually unaddressed by Scripture that may or may not be chosen as practice by the church. They are "open questions." Insofar as they serve the gospel and befit local circumstances—such as the form of rites, ceremonies, vestments, and other practices—adiaphora are "external matters of indifference" that the local church can change when the situations seem fitting.[60]

However, when an adiaphoron becomes a rule that threatens the integrity of the gospel, it becomes a heretical legalism. It then is, as it were, a fake authority. Illegitimate authority must be resisted. Paul's debate with

---

58. LW 45:126.
59. BOC, 329–44.
60. FC 10:9 (BOC, 637).

the leaders of the apostolic church on circumcision provides an example. As Paul argued clearly, if a Jewish Christian in his freedom maintained pride in his circumcised status, that was not exactly core to the gospel. But if church leaders required that all gentiles who wished to become Christians be circumcised, that compromised the core of the gospel, that the Christian is one who is saved by faith through grace alone and not by any external human act. Circumcision could and did suppress the pure teaching of the holy gospel.[61] When what was a matter of indifference becomes required it is then a matter of Christian exigency. The Christian does not yield on this principle when opponents would so persecute the very ecclesia. A clear declaration of the faith specific to the situation is demanded.[62]

Thus the conclusion of the majority, led by Flacius against Melanchthon. Melanchthon thought it not to be a dealbreaker when the Catholic opposition proposed that an interim truce in the Smalcaldic Wars include a temporary suspension of certain Lutheran practices. For him the word "temporary" was benign. AC's definition of the church as "the assembly of saints in which the gospel is taught purely and the sacraments are administered rightly" had left it open for congregations to be dissimilar in their liturgical practices and local traditions. The interim did not appear to Melanchthon to threaten this article. But because it was the emperor who asked for compromise even on the adiaphora, suspending them and reinstating previously uniform liturgical practices, Flacius saw this as a flagrant example of illegitimate heteronomy. His team won the argument. A temporal authority had crossed boundaries to impose restrictions on the church that threatened the being and purpose of the church. The situation, like all such situations, required a strong and pointed rebuke by the church, a case (*casu*) or state (*statu*) of confession (*confessionis*). Consequently, when the church is required by an authority inside or outside the church to act or not act in a certain way that would inhibit the freedom of the gospel, the reason to resist became codified in FC and Epitome 10. And should an authority within the church mandate activity that is contrary to the gospel, the church must declare a state of confession even against its mortal self. When the gospel itself is compromised from within or without, resistance is required. It is urgent, for in such cases the space for spiritual freedom itself is in a state of exigency. But because it is a spiritual exigency, it is also the more obedient to the Prince of Peace. Resistance from the tenants of the spiritual realm always is to be nonviolent.

---

61. FC 10:10 (BOC, 637).
62. FC Epitome 10:6 (BOC, 516).

Another very pertinent example of confessionally appropriate resistance stems also from the second generation of Lutheran leadership, this time from its political leaders. In 1546, the Emperor Charles V threatened to overturn the Nuremberg Religious Peace of 1532. In so doing, he threatened the now relatively established church life of Lutherans. The government leaders of the Smalcaldic League saw that it was their responsibility as temporal authorities to resist even the "higher" authority of Charles V, as he threatened the very freedom of the gospel. So these "lesser magistrates" found themselves in a state of confession, *in statu confessionis*, which required them to disobey a supposedly higher authority. Natural law would have required them to do so, they had already concluded, to protect their citizenry. But the highest spiritual law yet, for the sake of the gospel, amped up the controversy to the state of spiritual exigency. I write at length about this case study and attend to it for different reasons in chapter four in regard to the topic of "sovereignty." To put a Churchillian gloss on this topic, when the gospel is attacked, never compromise and never surrender. This is, for our purposes, the final answer to a challenge posed to the early Lutheran movement of the meaning and application of the Doctrine of Two Kingdoms.

Questions These Texts Don't Ask

Having reflected on the primary texts, what challenges and weaknesses might we identify against or about the Doctrine of Two Kingdoms? I note (1) the evident absence of Luther's *theologia crucis* hermeneutic; (2) Luther's acceptance of violence on the civic order and, concomitantly, his interpretation of the Beatitudes as wholly impossible for the temporal Christian to follow; (3) the formally unacknowledged role of eschatology and apocalyptic in his two-kingdoms doctrinal construction; (4) his spare sense of what constitutes governmental sovereignty; and (5) the quasi-acknowledged importance of natural law in his construction. I will comment here and later again on (1), (2), and (3). I will address (4) and (5) specifically in chapters dedicated to them.

We will not find a foundational theologoumenon in the Lutheran reformers' explications of the Two Kingdoms doctrine. First generation Lutheranism was written to the situation. A more systematic reflection comes later. This recognition helps us to understand why an important component for the right interpretation of Luther's political thinking is invisible in his writing. I adopt this charitable explanation for why the Theology of the Cross doesn't show up materially in any discussion of the Two Kingdoms doctrine. Some say flat out that Luther wasn't true to the theological convictions of his early career. It is "awkward" that Luther declared the Theology of the Cross was essential to any responsible theology and theologian. He did write in the Heidelberg Disputation of 1521 that the *theologia crucis* is the key and primary lens by which any and all true theology should be done. He concluded that God's nature is revealed under its opposite in the suffering and death of Jesus Christ on the cross. What to humans is weakness is for God strength. In suffering we see not a pretending impassible god, but the solidarity of God with all vulnerable and suffering humanity, which is to say, simply, everyone who in honesty would confess that they are only human. By such solidarity, by such fidelity declared to humanity since God's promise to Abraham and Sarah, by such incarnational fidelity to God's own beloved Son unto even death on a cross, God then so identifies in the crucified Christ with all humanity that all humanity is redeemed by the power of God's overwhelming love enacted in Christ's crucifixion and resurrection.

The cross is thus the ineluctable sign of God's power with and for the powerless, even as the truly powerless illusorily see themselves as powerful and God's manner of being as foolishly weak. For Luther, this is the only way theology can be true and the only way a theologian can do theology. Luther opposes the traditioned and arrogant theology that, using the traditional Greek philosophical assumptions about deity, would speculate from "top-down" principles, from abstract principles to concrete particulars, giving to the particulars meanings that are never there. So Luther: "19. That person does not deserve to be called a theologian who looks upon the invisible things of God as though they were clearly perceptible in those things which have actually happened [Rom 1:20]. 20. He deserves to be called a theologian, however, who comprehends the visible and manifest things of God seen through suffering and the cross. 21. A theologian of glory calls evil good and good evil. A theologian of the cross calls the thing what it actually is."[63]

Having stated these hermeneutical principles, Luther expands. It is relevant to underscore, as he does, that human works, no matter how commendable, are affected by mortal sin and that God's works through human beings, no matter how evidently harsh, are not sinful. Methodologically, the theologian, therefore, must always beware of irony. The very task of theology must be done with fear of judgment and humility, for God may act in what is thought commonly to be unlike God, even in these words here now printed and read.[64] In the thick of life's vicissitudes, that is, most profoundly

---

63. Luther, "Heidelberg Disputation," in Lull, *Basic Theological Writings*, 31.
64. Luther, "Heidelberg Disputation," in Lull, *Basic Theological Writings*, 34–36.

and practically speaking, the sufferer under the ironic promise of the cross is freed to trust in the salvation of God even within the historical conditions of sin and suffering. And in that way only are we sinners freed to live, courageously and joyfully. The cross was and is the definitive revelation of God's providence from the beginning. The irony of the cross interprets even the beginning of human being. If the solidarity of God with humanity holds even in human sin, sin was not the cause of human death and death not the punishment for sin. Rather, what appeared as punishment, exile, was gift. It was providence. Not even Adam and Eve's disobedience was the cause of human death. The consequence of the fateful fruit was the knowledge of good and evil, and so, knowledge of the sting of death. Death, we must then infer, was already within God's natural created order. But God did not intend the fear of death. God does not intend for us to fearfully imagine a final separation and severance from our created communality. Beginning from the facts on the ground, rather than some speculated universal principle of something like karma, applied then to every human act, God's exiling of Adam and Eve was God's way of keeping communion even when humanity would break communion. If the exile ban from the garden was the alpha act of God's keeping communion with humanity, then God's raising the crucified Christ was the omega act that still perdures. God will not break solidarity with what God has made and loves. God does not intend for anyone's life to be reduced to longing for belonging.

Fear of death, what Paul calls out as the sting of death, is bad enough. Could there be anything more frightening? Actually, yes. More frightening would be to live forever with such awful knowledge, forever longing for belonging, forever severed from any true communion with another. This is the Eastern Christian reading of the problem. It is solved by God revealing already God's providential care for humanity and all the creation through God's having exiled humanity from the garden before Adam and Eve could taste of the tree of life. It's not the most attractive act of God. It looks and feels like punishment. But given the consequences of fateful human choice at the proto-genesis level, as it were, it is God's saving and providential act so to ensure God's eschatological intentions.

God's providence, in other words, is all-embracing. It covers all human personal and institutional designs and all the consequent implications for the creation that suffers humanity's divinely unintended inhumanity. The language and rationality of the Theology of the Cross, in other words, serves as Luther's spiritual and theological language for how God will work in this world that with other languages and rationalities does not work so well. God is not like what humans had "before Christ" construed goodness to be. God is not defined by the classic philosophical categories; not defined by "omnis" of any spatial or human-projected sort. As far as the theological is concerned, the classical definitions of deity and the canons of reason failed utterly at understanding God and the human being who desires God. And this *theologia crucis* as a primary hermeneutical mode applies, and must apply, to a "Lutheran" political theology as much as any topic more purportedly "spiritual."

Vitor Westhelle shows positively how this rediscovery of the theologically ironic in the Theology of the Cross serves us today in our faith and our politics. Westhelle writes, "Martin Heidegger was probably the first in modern times to recognize in Luther's theology, most incisively represented by the Heidelberg Disputation, an epistemological gesture that deconstructed the Western philosophical tradition known as ontotheology, which relies on the definition of God as Being constructed in analogy to beings." Westhelle then quotes Heidegger: "*Theology* is seeking a more primordial interpretation of man's Being toward God, prescribed by the meaning of faith itself and remaining within it. It is slowly beginning to understand once more Luther's insight that the 'foundation' on which its system of dogma rests has not arisen from an enquiry in which faith is primary, and that conceptually this 'foundation' not only is inadequate for the problematic of theology, but conceals and distorts it."[65]

What could this mean, then, as explicit theological backgrounding for the Doctrine of Two Kingdoms? I suggest that from the Lutheran prescribed lens of faith, we would see not only (or merely) that God established both realms. We recognize more that God did so recognize that sin—which is to act consciously and unconsciously on the knowledge of good and evil—infects the temporal kingdom *and* infects the visible church which cannot help but still limp along in the temporal kingdom, too. Persons and principalities, including the church, are *simul iustus et peccator*. But with God so recognizing, the structures in and of both kingdoms are intended for providence. Their vocation includes maintaining the opportunity for everyone everywhere to come to know and celebrate the healing and wholeness God intends for church and state together while yet distinguished, *and that* the requirements for resistance itself are providential requirements for the full "two-kingdoms system" to work. God is on the side of those who do not get to choose sides and reveals structurally how this is so through what God intends with "Two Kingdoms."

Now to a second problem. What of the apparent acceptance of violence as a component of God's justice? Related to this, I believe, is that many people have interpreted Luther's interpretation of the Beatitudes as Jesus'

---

65. Westhelle, *Scandalous God*, 30.

ironic (if not dissembling) command to do the impossible so that we would surrender and trust God only. Luther actually counsels his hearers and readers to take Jesus' words to heart when it may not be possible to enact them in this world.[66] Still, Luther's acceptance of violence in the temporal order (only) does not escape criticism. I turn to the Barthian prophet in William Stringfellow as a whetstone to consider this compound challenge. Stringfellow is not persuaded that submission to political authority is a mandate for Christians insofar as government's vocation is to keep order in society. In sum, he questions that government is a tool of God's providence[67] because the historical record shows first that violence, which Christians are never to practice or accept according to Jesus himself, is a chronic condition of all government over the millennia.

The reality of political authority rarely has corresponded to the abstract justification of political authority, which is to say that legitimate political authority is quite a different matter than lawful political authority. Political authority has almost always been based on the threat and use of violence. Though there have been instances of peaceful emplacements of new governments, one could win a big game show cash prize by naming just one example; so rare they are in our consciousness and so casually normative our recourse to violence that just war theory is thought to be a radical good. I can't condemn Luther for his taking such processes of "managing" violence so for granted that he could never imagine being a pacifist. And I have seen the most devout of pacifists ready to throw fists when body checked on a basketball court. But Luther's conclusion, that Jesus could only have meant his beatitudinal counsel for Christians to practice radical peace as an impossible law to obey so that we would despair at following that law and so depend only on God's unfathomable grace, has something of doubt within the hope in it. It also smacks of a spiritualized tactic of bait and switch.

Is not surrender to the use of violence by the Christian a denial of the regenerative power of Christ's Holy Spirit said to be given to us and to be within us? If "New Obedience" indeed is made possible and expected from the justified Christian, as Lutherans confess in AC 6, doesn't Luther's

---

66. E.g., LW 21:3–5: "Be bodily and outwardly poor or rich, as may be your lot, God does not ask about that; and he knows that everyone must be before God, that is spiritually and in his heart, poor."

67. Stringfellow, *Conscience and Obedience*, 56: "In practice, this support for the anti-anarchy brief for political obedience has often been adorned to the extent of suggesting that the order enforced by a political regime not only estops or punishes crime or other 'bad conduct,' but diminishes or minimizes sin. That seems to have been a consideration influential upon Luther where he can be found—paradoxically—requiring obedience for the sake of order even in circumstances where that means endurance of governments deemed wicked."

ready resort to violence in the civil order contradict Christ's command? And doesn't this defy Paul's own pneumatological anthropology of the Christian of which he writes in Rom 8 and prevalently elsewhere? Is there a pneumatological deficit in Lutheranism? Obviously there is long history of a large Christian witness to and practice of pacifist, nonviolent resistance that strongly challenges Luther and Lutheranism here. Peaceableness is about far more than a moment on Christmas Eve when enemies might pause war making to sing a carol's verse together. An "orthodox Lutheran" emphasis on AC 6 should ask for much more singing. Also, contemporary ecumenical dialogue progress between Western Lutheranism and Eastern Orthodoxy on our understandings of sanctification and theosis should strongly question Luther's amenability to violence as an essential component of the Two Kingdoms doctrine. My consideration of current Pauline studies in chapter 5, especially the compelling exegesis of L. Ann Jervis, looks at this problem further.

Finally, even more compelling for Stringfellow, the dominant interpretation of the commands to obey authority in Rom 13:1–7 and 1 Pet 2:17 are based on the phrase "honor the emperor," though "emperor" should properly be translated as "sovereign."[68] And the emphasis on that phrase has been a noncontextual or even anticontextual mistake for ages. Stringfellow believes these verses touch on a theological locus, the doctrine of creation read eschatologically, that neither Luther nor his early followers considered with regard to the temporal kingdom.

Paul's letter to the Romans is imbued with an eschatological sensibility (Stringfellow uses the term "cosmological") that evidently was shared fully by Paul's primary audience, that Christ and Christ alone was the Lord, the Sovereign, of the universe and that he would return soon. The latter part of Rom 13 is explicit about this, just as the conviction resonates throughout the epistle.

God's "eschatological sovereignty" is the primary frame by which one should interpret Romans. It is odd then, to read Rom 13:1–7 as if it only meant "obedience to whatever regime happens to occupy office, much less an obligation of simplistic or automatic obedience to the person of the ruler."[69] This is to have forgotten something integral to Paul's doctrine of creation and its fallen character, per Stringfellow's reading. In his and—so he believes—Paul's view, political authority "encompasses and conjoins the angelic powers and the incumbent rulers."[70] The typical non-eschatological

---

68. Stringfellow, *Conscience and Obedience*, 39–47.
69. Stringfellow, *Conscience and Obedience*, 48.
70. Stringfellow, *Conscience and Obedience*, 48.

"straightforward" reading of Rom 13:1–7, then, seems to be an acquiescence to Constantinian—and nonaccountable—authority that Stringfellow denounces in the name of the gospel. An eschatological framing of the whole of Romans, as is required, leads to a radically different interpretation. That interpretation would be this: that governing regimes are not primarily or solely "secondary" products of sinful humanity, not, as it were, consequences of human fallenness itself. They themselves are of the "principalities and powers" (Rom 8) that rule this passing age. They themselves are complicit in fallenness. They themselves delegitimize themselves when they claim themselves sovereign otherwise having known that there is only one sovereign and eschatologically so. Human pride should not be so great, though being sinful it is, as to presume that institutions and nations and governments and such are our own creations and in so doing have made ourselves great again.

In other words, sinful humanity did not transmit sin into humanity's own begatted institutions, as if Augustine's traducianism were to apply beyond individual human couplings to anything humans create. Rather, the Word of God created *all* manners and matters of life. They are, "biblically speaking, creatures with their own names, identities, integrity, capabilities, proclivities, and, as has been earlier emphasized, vocations."[71] Governments too are, per Stringfellow, among the God-created but God-supplanting and therefore fallen "principalities and powers."[72] The creation of the church, then is God's intended redress of them. If this sounds apocalyptic, Stringfellow (also serving as a prophet of later New Testament exegesis!) says "so be it!" This eschews, too, the practical liberalism, idealism, and the Niebuhrian Christian realism of those who would employ violence to stop violence. Stringfellow explores this in the case history of the early American pastor-theologian Jonathan Mayhew, whose own preaching and teaching anticipated Reinhold Niebuhr centuries later.[73] Whether American liberal or Lutheran conservative, for Stringfellow the cosmological-eschatological import of Romans is far too vast and deep for any Christian tradition's accommodations to political circumstances in any time and place, the radical difference of the gospel of Christ's rule and peaceable rule being far too profound for convenient, yet sophistic, answers couched in the Constantinian settlement.

---

71. Stringfellow, *Conscience and Obedience*, 65.

72. That God created institutions yields remarkable implications that should upend much of how we have interpreted Rom 13. In conversation with current Pauline scholars, I will address this more in ch. 5.

73. Stringfellow, *Conscience and Obedience*, 55–62.

It is, to my mind, not so much that the ideas about legitimacy or order are false, in a dogmatic sense, but that they are too abstract, too small or too narrow to accommodate the gospel, too convenient to emperors and officials, too simplistic and too misleading for the faithful. I am unable to circumvent, for example, the incongruity of Luther's tolerance of tyranny because that saves order when the order which is enforced, in fact, is disorder. At the same time, when Mayhew pronounces a tyrannical regime illegitimate and unworthy of obedience, I respond more sympathetically to Mayhew than to Luther, but I still cannot abide the resort to violence which Mayhew would advocate to overthrow the illegitimate regime because that also is incongruous.[74]

Summary

Humanity always has been a story. It is an apocalyptic story that tells truth by symbol witnessing against tyranny in terms radically counter to tyranny's usual terms. The true biblical story "comprehends tyranny and oppression as blasphemy, the denial and denunciation of the Christ the Lord."[75] To stand with those who suffer from blasphemy's terms, to stand with the oppressed and violated, to stand against the haughty and shrewd rationales of the self-serving, is to confess that Jesus Christ and no other principality or power is lord. Herein is the call to follow the Theology of the Cross, to stand on the side of those who do not get to choose sides. Does this call to repentance two generations ago from Stringfellow and his not few like-minded followers since challenge the Doctrine of Two Kingdoms? Surely it does. Like a whetstone that either breaks or sharpens a dull knife, Stringfellow challenges the standard interpretation of the Two Kingdoms doctrine. Surely also he confronts what he perceives to see as Luther's de facto dismissal of the Sermon on the Mount as impractical. It is a problem, or a perceived problem, that we must consider.

Do the problems I've just raised mean that the doctrine should be abandoned? I do not think so. I think it is possible that a reappropriation of eschatology that is more dimensional than literalism's caricature of eternity can re-enliven two-kingdoms thinking. It is possible, too, to refresh apocalyptic language that is more profoundly imaginative and stirring of truth than presumptuous univocity. A reclaimed Doctrine of Two Kingdoms calls from us renewed language that reveals God active in our "now" out of God's

74. Stringfellow, *Conscience and Obedience*, 67.
75. Stringfellow, *Conscience and Obedience*, 67–68.

eternity. And what of the peaceableness of the spiritual kingdom for us that Jesus could not have been merely analogizing about from the mountain or the plain? Eschatology and apocalyptic speech are implied throughout the corpus that encodes Two Kingdoms, while the encoding presumed every citizen's consensus on the importance of natural law and personal human sovereignty.

But are these concepts *still* appreciated, respected, and normative? Or are they artifacts left to us as philosophical museum pieces of a bygone era? If, as is also true, Luther thought this doctrine to include his whole "worldview," should we be so ready as to sing a farewell and blessing on its exit? Is there anything we can do with the doctrine not for its own survival sake, but for the better sake of gracious pluralistic life together in political orders? I offer an initial answer by turning to the concept of natural law in the next chapter.

3

Natural Law in the Temporal Realm

"Piously we produce our images of you / till they stand around you like a thousand walls. /
And when our hearts would simply open, / our fervent hands hide you."
—Rainier Maria Rilke[1]

IN CHAPTER 2, I summarized the relevant confessional and interpretive texts pertinent to the Two Kingdoms doctrine. I noted Augustine's influence on Luther's version of the doctrine along with the ecclesial and political context for Luther's explication. That context confused what Augustine distinguished: the sacred and the secular. Luther recognized the need to make them distinct again. He did so on the basis of the dual revelations of Scripture and nature/natural law. Nature and natural law had their unique provenance and terms in the secular world. But they were not wholly separate from the spiritual realm. Luther held Scripture as the primary lens for understanding nature, but he was explicit about the guiding role of natural law in all life. This relative stereoscopy was also Augustine's method.

Luther was no less committed to affirming the concept of human sovereignty insofar as the emerging concept (though not yet the terminology) was a mediation of natural law into the Reformation era's legal world. But appeal to natural law and sovereignty lessened dramatically over the centuries since. These two foundational principles for secular government's coherence with the spiritual kingdom came under devastating philosophical criticism in the eighteenth and nineteenth centuries and were all but

---

1. Rilke, "The Book of Monastic Life 1.4," in *Rilke's Book of Hours*, 49.

abandoned in the post-Christendom of the twentieth century. With secularity's loss of respect for natural law and ambiguity about human sovereignty, the supposition that God had instituted the civil order was compromised.

There are many other familiar reasons for the declined status of Two Kingdoms today. But a reconsidered Two Kingdoms doctrine cannot succeed without attending to these two integral concepts and their suitable successors for political and legal philosophy today. Thus I turn in this chapter to the role of natural law in Luther's theology and in Western philosophy since. I will focus on the concept of sovereignty in chapter 4.

The Theology of Natural Law

What is "natural" about law is implied immediately in the words of Gen 1:26. God creates humankind in God's image. *Imago Dei* has been interpreted in many ways. The capacities of reason, love, and relationality are listed as one set of markers meanings for the image of God Trinity. Commonly agreed is that human dignity reflects God's dignity. *Imago Dei* also denotes beloved originality. We are the creatures whom God created from nothing prior, in whom God delights, whom God tasks with ultimate responsibilities, the "crown of creation." Human being as God's image also connotes innate goodness. We *know* intimate sacral connection and natural obedience to God before sin triangulates the relationship. Still, according to the apostle Paul, human goodness perdures "after the fall." We know God's law "naturally" from the get-go.

In his "Lectures on Genesis" Luther writes of the prelapsarian function of God's law directing Adam not to eat of the tree of knowledge of good and evil. This law needed no compulsion or threat of punishment. Luther celebrated the prelapsarian direction as pleasant guidance for abundant life. Authority was not experienced as heteronomy, but as the good to which the loving responder cannot conceive any response but the good of obedience. After the fall, sin becomes the norm that must be normed. Now the law is experienced as threat and force, though it is still serves God's providence. Authority now is delegated for coercion and punishment of the wicked. God thus intends governmental authority as a gift of an "outward remedy" to sin. Luther favors Gen 9:6 in making this case for government. "With this hedge, these walls, God has given us protection for our life and possessions."[2]

This comment fully comports with the younger Luther's position in "Temporal Authority." With characteristic satire he likens people who would rule the world with full gospel gentility to a shepherd who lets carnivores

2. LW 2:141.

into the fold to cavort with the sheep. The sheep would not survive long. Then the beasts would turn on each other. In the postlapsarian situation power is peace,[3] and so law is required. The gospel cannot be the grammar for ruling the temporal world. Nor can the law be the primary word for the church. For the authorities to transgress their position descriptions would mean that if princes told their kingdom's people to turn their cheeks, sin would overtake everything. And if pastors ruled the church with the threat of violence, the gracious message of justification by faith on which all stands or falls would be obliterated. This also underscores how futile it is to coerce conscience. Government can command certain public behavior, but it cannot control or cure souls. Government's only authority is to maintain order and to serve justice,[4] which itself is accountable to the higher court of natural law.

In this way secularity is blessed and a blessing. In his *Notes on Ecclesiastes* of 1532, Luther directly correlates the moral law with the Two Kingdoms. Ecclesiastes 2:24 is his key verse: "There is nothing better for man that he should eat and drink, and find enjoyment in his toil. This also, I saw, is from the hand of God." What joy in the temporal quotidian! Christians can and should live their witness in all respects as faithful citizens. We do so under the authority of the natural law that calls for communal justice.[5] For politics "under the sun," reason reigns in accord with natural law. Beyond the sun reason has no authority. There the authority of the gospel lights the heavens and guides the sextant of natural law below. "The 'two kingdoms' political economy is not just there to be apprehended naturally. It must be generated by the insertion of the gospel of grace."[6]

Luther refers to natural law or its synonym more than seven hundred times.[7] Natural law equates with what the conscience knows as morally right. In his "Lectures on Genesis," Luther held that all people have a natural understanding of God as good, merciful, and truthful.[8] Even were the Decalogue not written in stone, Luther writes, "it is lodged in the conscience."[9] Luther further affirms natural law's imprint on everyone's conscience in his "Lectures on Romans"; of Rom 2:15 he says, "Naturally and indelibly the

---

3. LW 45:91.

4. For an excellent exposition of the texts and context for Luther's position here, see Whitford, "'Cura Religionis.'"

5. Hinlicky, "Luther on Ecclesiastes," 39.

6. Hinlicky, "Luther on Ecclesiastes," 41.

7. In the American edition. For more citations, see Whitford, "'Cura Religionis.'"

8. LW 6:113.

9. LW 35:164.

law of nature has been stamped upon the mind as a good testimony of good things and an evil testimony of evil things."[10] Yes, human nature is corrupted by sin, but that does not erase the natural law. For Luther's day, nature and reason are ruled by a moral order independent of Christian Scriptures and distinct from the spiritual kingdom. In his exposition of Ps 101, Luther writes, "Natural law and natural reason form the heart and source of all written law."[11] Accusing the Peasants' Revolt rebels for wrongly appealing to the gospel to achieve civil justice, thus confusing the categories of the Two Kingdoms, Luther writes that they violate "the natural law of all the world that no one may be judge in his own cause or take his own revenge." On the other hand, praise is effusive for the "heathen, Turks and Jews" who keep the natural law and highest praise goes to the "rare bird" of that Christian who keeps both the Christian and the natural law.[12] Luther was consistent in his advocacy for natural law. Natural law's very reality underscored the need for strongly distinguishing the spiritual from the temporal.[13]

A Brief History of Natural Law

Why was natural law apart from Scripture so normative for Luther's social ethics? Renewed humanist zeal was in the reforming air. Cicero's legacy in particular was hugely influential for everything other than theology and set the contextual frame for subsequent political theology. Cicero's definition of higher law was the default legal concept and praxis for medieval and Reformation era scholars. They quoted his definition from *De legibus*: "true law as right reason, harmonious with nature . . . eternal and unchangeable." Natural law was that against which all other law was measured. Later, natural law in the legal establishment would be known as higher law. Higher law

10. LW 25:19.
11. LW 4:226.
12. LW 4:226–29.

13. Some Luther exegetes believe that his commentaries on Pss 82 and 101 show a shift from Two Kingdoms to the view that the state should overtly control while being instructed by the church. However, as Whitford, "'Cura Religionis,'" 54–55, points out, these commentaries were situational; they were written in the twofold context of (1) the awful conditions of the church unveiled by the Saxon visitations, and (2) the growing anxiety at the threat of subjugation of the Lutheran magistrates in Nuremberg and surrounding regions. Furthermore, Luther's response is also directed against heresy beneath the political threats—namely, blasphemy. And Luther attacked blasphemy with considerable dependence on his understanding of natural law. Luther interpreted blasphemy to be on the first table of the law. But he also saw that blasphemy attaches to all the aspects of the second table known to all people, not just Christians. This too is the law as nature wrote it into people's hearts.

was not merely a matter of utility. It even ruled human nature. Cicero again: "We are born for justice, and right is not the mere arbitrary construction of opinion, but an institution of nature."[14]

Luther knew Cicero's work. Erasmus called Luther "the German Cicero." Cicero was on Luther's lips as he lay dying. "Nobody understands Cicero in his letters unless he has been engaged in public affairs of some consequence for twenty years."[15] Only one who himself was so civically active could say this. Melanchthon and other humanists of the Reformation were consistently public in their affirmation of Cicero and natural law, too.[16] There is "behind" and "above" civil law the natural law inscribed eternally by God for all the world to follow by conscience and reasoned teaching. Natural law constitutes the mandate for fair play between all human beings. Luther's recalls Cicero's maxim, "*summum ius, summa iniuria*," to which Luther replied "*enges Recht; weit Unrecht*" ("narrow justice means great injustice").[17] In other words, if one sticks only to a *prima facie* textual reading of civil law, one does much injustice. Genuine equity must be discerned and distributed by reading stipulative written law in light of natural law. This better way also accords with the Reformation era's understanding of well-practiced law. To practice and obey written law in light of natural law is to practice the spirit of the law. This is essential, for though the secular realm would not perceive this, for the Christian to attend to the natural law in this way is to recognize that the Holy Spirit is at work in both kingdoms. In this the temporal kingdom resonates to the spiritual kingdom.

The "spirit" of the law was oriented to the well-being of the citizenry. Cicero was the central early advocate for the Roman citizen's voice. By affirming the citizens' role of consent to proposed public law, Cicero also recognized the relative sovereignty of the Roman citizen body.[18] For this he is still celebrated as a prophet for the *demos*. Though Cicero still affirmed a meritocratic government more than the role of "the people," his argument about individual relative sovereignty, too, would influence renewed political thought about the dignity and rights of the human individual. *Imago Dei*, natural law, and sovereignty would influence theology and politics some fifteen centuries later.

The Western story of the *ius naturale* continues through Augustine, Thomas Aquinas, and its first appearance explicitly as "higher law" in the

14. Cicero, *De legibus* 1.10.28, quoted in Corwin, *"Higher Law,"* 10.
15. LW 54:476.
16. See Springer, *Cicero in Heaven*.
17. McNeil, "Natural Law," 220.
18. See Schofield, *Cicero*, 46.

work John of Salisbury (d. 1180).[19] Augustine prefers the term "divine law" to "natural law," but his meaning is the same. Of course, he identifies God as the sole source of natural law. It should interest us to see how Augustine concludes this. For Augustine, reason explores the transcendental grounds for peace so as to discern what is a just moral order.[20] If human being had obediently stood stalwart in the original beautiful garden state of justice, all would have been harmony and peace. For harmony and peace again to prevail, per Augustine, reason when it is ruled by God finds right ordering, which is also when the soul (mind) rules the body with its baser desires.

Society should do the same. A mindful society would be just. Instead, society suffers the conflicts of people living more impetuously by base and conflicting greed than by reason.[21] Because society is so inward and conflicted, government must coerce society to have a modicum of peaceable civic life.[22] Given sin, society will never achieve perfect social harmony. But Augustine is not democratically dour. Persons of grace could and did have roles of civil and military authority that Augustine commended, particularly when said authorities were Christian.[23] Nor was secular society just a hot mess. As noted before, Augustine saw the temporal city (despite Rome's egregious government) as the staging ground for the City of God.

Augustine elsewhere elaborates on his understanding of both eternal (natural) and temporal law. Eternal law perfectly orders things. It is God's way of directing things to their proper ends; that is, natural law supervises natural teleology.[24] Eternal law is immutable. Temporal law, however, can vary according to circumstance as long as it is oriented to the common good. If it is so oriented, it is just; if not just, it cannot even be a law. But if it is just, it is so for the regrettable reason that human perversity required it for at least a minimal justice to obtain in society. By such definition, no temporal law could ever be a "perfect" law. But even in its imperfection temporal law points to higher natural law. The logic leads to the conclusion centuries later that temporal law is asymptotic, always aspiring toward the higher law, but never reaching. Temporal law insofar as it keeps the temporal world

---

19. Whom Edward Corwin labels as "the first systematic writer on politics in the Middle Ages." Corwin, *"Higher Law,"* 16.

20. Augustine, *City of God* 19.21.

21. Augustine, *City of God* 19.20.

22. Augustine, *City of God* 19.15.

23. Cf. Augustine's positive letter to a recent convert to Christianity, the general and Roman senator Symmachus, whom Augustine counseled to remain in his position to do justice. Augustine alludes to Symmachus in his *Confessions*, book 5. Correspondence with Symmachus and more is presented in Ebbeler, "Religious Identity," 230–42.

24. Augustine, *On Free Will* 1.6.15.

coherent by wielding justice for the commonweal deserves applause. Luther would be yet clearer about the goodness of temporal law and the respect due to its able and faithful administrators.

A final comment on Augustine and natural law concerns how reason opens Christianity as a faith that could accommodate to any customs and practices other than those that reason denounces as immoral. Because, per Augustine, Christian faith received by grace governs a believer's actions, Christianity itself is not a divinely prescribed law meant to replace all temporal law. Christian (political) morality is defined and delivered from the spiritual domain and therefore should be compatible with any just political ordering. It should commend itself rather than impose itself on one's temporal neighbors precisely because the Christian action inspired by faith is for the well-being of the *civitas*.[25] To that degree and no more, a Christian cares for one's country without identifying her faith as belonging to or subsuming one's country. Augustine opposed Christian conversion of persons or states by coercion of law or other force. He practiced an "eerily modern political realism" shaped by his understanding of revelation and natural law, and so had great impact on Western modern law.[26]

With Aquinas the distinction between the natural law of the temporal realm and the spiritual realm was softened almost to the point of erasure. Yes, as with Augustine, natural law was a directed order from God and meant for the right ordering of all a person's thoughts and actions. Being endowed with reason, the human person knows one's purpose and is or should be immediately aware of the principles that should guide behavior. But while these general principles were known most commonly through conscience (what Aquinas called "synderesis"), they were not sufficient. Natural law had to be supplemented by reasoned human law, a subsection of which would be categorized as universally normative (like laws against murder, adultery, theft, lying) and another category as circumstantially contingent.

By asserting this, Aquinas steps beyond Augustine. His step is consequential. Aquinas contends that natural law can and should be realized in mortal life by human reason and will. A perfect, just mortal life is achievable. If so a life, so then the social order. Therefore, temporal law for Aquinas is not of the asymptotic character of Augustine's description. Aquinas believed that natural law in the human world could and should coincide with perfect justice and an ecclesial authority would have just as much responsibility, if not more, to supervise this as the temporal king or prince. An individual's

---

25. *Epistula* 138.2 in Augustine, *Letters*, 138.
26. See Brooks, *Augustine and Modern Law*.

religious and moral perfection coincides with being a perfect citizen.[27] It is not hard to see in this the justification for confusing spiritual and temporal authority that would come under attack in the Reformation and inspire the revival of Augustine's distinctions of the cities as Two Kingdoms.

In the time between Aquinas and Luther, one finds little on the continent that is consequentially different in theological or institutional appeal to natural law. Lombard's *Sentences* were common coin in Europe. Scotus, Occam, Biel, and nominalism all had their methodological formative impact on Reformation thought. But *that* natural law was a given was not debated. Reflection on natural law seeded formal legal theory, including the idea of common law in England. But back to Germany, it was, again, the confusion of the spiritual and temporal authority structures, hand-in-glove with the dangerous confusion of law and gospel, that evoked Luther's protest and stimulated his political thought.

Luther and "Higher" Natural Law

I've underscored Luther's high respect for natural law. Even so, Luther was mindful that the faculty of reason by which human beings would discern and follow the *lex naturae* is tainted and limited by sin. Luther is fully with Augustine on this point and quite not so with Aquinas. *Human* reason requires humility in its exercise, especially when solitary. Given sin's pandemic effects, it is all the more imperative that reason's temporal exercise occur in a public commons of checks and balances. Going public with the understanding too that reasoning is a communal obligation is by definition political.

Luther identified and applied natural law to political well-being. He did not lodge natural law solely under the umbrella of secularity. In his two-kingdoms paradigm Luther held to the distinction without separation between the spiritual law and the natural law. This much of "natural theology" Luther could maintain.[28] While theology filtered throughout Luther's

---

27. Fortin, "St. Thomas Aquinas," 267.

28. Recall that Luther generally denounced natural theology as such, the kind of theological reasoning that starts with observed nature and then proceeds to speculate even wildly on what it all means about God and related matters; a rather unreasonable thing to do when the definitive revelation of God comes from the cross and grave, about which human beings could have no rational imagination. Luther called this natural theology (as distinct from a theology of nature) "theology of glory." He damns it. But *after* all is defined by the "Theology of the Cross," Luther has no qualms or inability to write in the terms of a natural theology; they are accessible when tamed and directed by the cross. See all of his "Heidelberg Disputation" on these two points.

political thought, he also clearly advocated for the natural law's provenance in civil governance. The natural law was foundational for justifying the structure and sovereignty of the emerging nation-state. Natural law was and must be the primary way for a Christian authority to rule in the temporal world. In this respect, too, Luther proved closer to Augustine than to Calvin and other Reformed influencers. With Augustine, the pluralistic world would be the secular staging ground for eschatological grace. With the Reformed, no matter their explicit adoption of a two-kingdoms political-theological model, the pluralistic world would be subject theocratically to the overt legal imposition of Christian principles. Though Luther could never countenance this, subsequent Lutheranism did not avoid it either.[29]

The temporal world, we remember, is one that Luther assumed "to consist mainly of non-Christians." All the more, then, natural law in its postlapsarian modality was the only reasonable justification for civil governance. God, with grace that goes beyond religion, chose natural law for secular rule. This applies to the credentialing of governing authorities as well as to the expectations of the governed. Natural law is the mode of God's governance for the "Kingdom of the Left." It is a visionary caution, a sign of a clear mind, that though in the social reality of his day Luther only knew and expected "Christian" civic leaders, he could and did imagine the need for this caveat: that natural law, not Christian diktat, must guide civic leadership. The abstraction would turn palpable not long later. The first criterion for being a worthy governing authority is to do good by protecting one's citizenry, not to "be a Christian." The Two-Kingdoms principle strongly instructs about this. "Being Christian" is not the basis on which one deserves or is appointed to governing authority.[30] Nor is it a legitimate basis on which to campaign for any civic office. The ability and commitment to understanding and doing the good, per natural law, is.

Also, to "do the good" per natural law in the Reformation led fairly quickly to legal application with refined terminology particularly in

---

29. There is a significant period of "Lutheran Orthodoxy" after Luther that looked closer to Reformed theocracy than to the original Two Kingdoms vision. In this period natural law and biblical "principle-ism" were more closely fused. With that was the agreement that the political ruler's faith itself be that of his region, which gave back to the "state" more ruling authority over the church, too, than desired by the first Reformers. In this, Melanchthon was initially complicit, mostly because it seemed convenient under the short-term exigent circumstances. I am constrained from detailing the history of this era between early Lutheranism and the Enlightenment. That's another book. It must be enough now simply to signal the era and its further problematizing of the Two Kingdoms doctrine.

30. This Christian insight in fact is generated by the intervention of the gospel of grace. Apart from this the secular become mere secularism.

second-generation Lutheranism. What was natural law for everyone became known in law formally as higher law. That a consensus as to the character of and obligation to higher law in legal matters and questions of sovereignty had already formed in early Lutheranism is very significant. It was also put to the test already with the Smalcaldic Wars. I will comment more on higher law below. Now I turn to the philosopher after Luther who lifted and redefined natural law in a way not done before, John Locke.

Natural Law and Modernity—John Locke

John Locke (1632–1704) is famous as a political philosopher in the liberal tradition, "liberal" meaning the newer, seventeenth-century emphasis on the dignity and rights of every individual human being. Yet he is also overlooked for having defined classical liberalism with an express dependence on basic Christian principles. An accurate assessment of his impact on political philosophy underscores his intention to affirm and sustain politics that cohere with humanist and religious convictions. In this he differed from Thomas Hobbes, who, given his sour diagnosis of human nature's hostile state, could only prescribe an ethics of morally cold transactionalism. Locke wrote with a finer pen and warmer heart.

Locke describes the original state of nature as (1) giving freedom to all individuals to order their own lives independent of others' wills, with (2) equality fully enjoyed and respected by all persons. Freedom is not license, however, to harm any other person in "life, liberty, or possessions." Why? Because this is the *law of nature* established by the "one omnipotent and wise maker . . . [the] sovereign master" for every person so to love each other with "justice and charity."[31] This natural law orders, too, that persons seek to preserve themselves *and* "the rest of mankind." Peace and peaceable life are meant to be at the center of individual and corporate life together.

Locke's compact statement of political purpose is that government's duty is to see to the enjoyment and sustenance of peace, having been ordered to do so by the "sovereign master," God. When Locke first describes the state of nature and its meaning for civil government, he refers to the political condition of paradise before the event of sin. What then does natural law discerned by reason then require in the postlapsarian political condition in which we now live? What do we do with the "degenerate" person who chooses to "quit the principles of human nature and to be a noxious creature"? So far Locke echoes Luther's answer. Society has the right to punish the criminal so to prevent further such misdeeds by others. But to this

---

31. Locke, *Second Treatise*, 8–9 (emphasis mine).

Locke adds a new flowchart. This right of punishment is delegated by the people to the magistrate.[32]

As close to being as religiously explicit as he can while writing politically, without naming his biblical model, and as an implicit counter to Hobbes's account of the state of nature, Locke draws out the political implications of Genesis on paradise. "Original" natural law concerns human autonomy in the fully equalitarian community wherein persons just "do" the good in happy mutuality without reflection, because the law of love goes in all directions to love God, neighbor, and self. After Eden the as-it-were "second" iteration of natural law becomes a codex that orders all lives alienated from God, neighbor, and self. Locke understands that sin is alienation. In his temporal world the maximizing of peaceableness among the alienated in accord with natural law is the purpose of politics. In Hobbes's world, the degenerate person is the premise for politics as human resource management. In Locke's still religious view, politics and politicians are guided by the classically and biblically liberal aspiration for the City of God.

This assumption underlies Locke's exposition written in terms appropriate to the temporal realm. Jeremy Waldron argues that Locke understood his agenda to be fully Christian. One should not suppose that Locke as a philosopher is compromised by his attention to the Old Testament, especially Genesis, as he does in the *First Treatise*. In *An Essay Concerning Human Understanding*, Locke affirms that bare human reason as such underscores the equality of all persons because they bear the image of God. Further, that reason orients everyone (some better than others, but still all) in the direction of moral revelation leads Locke in his *Reasonableness of Christianity* to identify reason and revelation not as alternative ways to discern natural law, but as naturally allied and required as a team to know and do the good. Theism in the Christian frame is Locke's philosophical foundation, which he even would prescribe for all aspiring philosophers.[33] Not all philosophers agree that Locke was intentionally so Christian. Some speculate that he was being tactical, others that he was a libertarian, and others, like Leo Strauss, that Locke was disingenuous. However one regards their arguments, that they so argue in itself underscores already the softening of the Ciceronian concept of natural law.[34]

Still, also like Cicero, Locke was not equalitarian when it came to who was equipped to govern. And checks upon autonomy are necessary if a society is to be stable. Every single human being "has a Property in

---

32. Locke, *Second Treatise*, 11.
33. Waldron, *God, Locke, and Equality*.
34. My summary of Sigmund, "Jeremy Waldron," 408.

his own Person [body]."[35] This basic right does not require a sophisticated understanding of one's own life. It only requires that one understands that one *has* a life; that one is simply conscious of oneself and no one else can compromise that inherent right. But this basic right does not and cannot extrapolate to full equality of political rights. More than self-ownership is required. Locke's theory, critically curated, is not an all-or-nothing call for sheer individualistic libertarianism. That eventuates in anarchy. This is why Locke requires a second tier of those who recognize natural law by the exercise of reason, though now in a different manner than did Cicero or Luther. Those for whom reason further discerns natural law are those who constitute and populate the institutions for a self-aware liberal society. So gifted by reason, these de facto social and governmental leaders' possession of law-abiding equality is at least as much a social and civic responsibility as it is a right.

Locke understands the challenge represented here. There are many people who will not be self-governing by recourse to sound reason. There are many people "being biased by their Interest, as well as ignorant for want or study."[36] Locke recognized that many would see in this distinction a backdoor access again to a non-democratic meritocracy. This concerned him. He thought hard about appearing to grant more civil rights to those who are more rational than others. Empirical induction alone that counts the prevalence of lawbreakers might deny natural law. But induction tempered by careful reason, still for Locke, affirms natural law.[37]

Long on Kant

An interesting alternate universe to Locke's British empiricism was appearing on the Continent. Though alternate, the effects on the reception of natural law would be similar. I refer to Immanuel Kant and his epistemological revolution. Kant concluded that only pure reason (*reine Vernunft*) could achieve true knowing. Even at that, to know something is not to know the thing-in-itself, but only to know that thing as it is known by the human. Reason is critical, and reason must be criticized. The consequence is that we do "know" things by pure reason, but we know them already as predicated. Pure reason is "critically realistic." It is aware that the subject subjects the object to the subject's gaze. The distance is not far from Kant's critical realism to postmodernity's questioning of everything, except that

35. Locke, *Second Treatise*, 19.
36. Locke, *Second Treatise*, 66.
37. Hunt, "Locke on Equality," 549.

Kant never claimed or understood that the object (the noumenon) ever actually disappeared into the subject's gaze. There was and is always an essence to an experienced "something," a noumenon to a phenomenon. For Kant there is always a "there" there, even if impossible fully to know. Pure science can and does change its mind about the origins and predications of phenomena while depending upon the perdurance and even palpability of the phenomena to be described with ever thicker description.

But there is a part of life in Kant's view that is not amenable to such inquiry and progress of knowledge. That is the practical and aesthetic. They are "known" only by their effects of bringing purpose, value, and morals to life. Religion is of this kind of "practical reason." Kant's lynchpin to practical reason is the Categorical Imperative. Practical reason is the reasoning we use for daily living, especially for the negotiation of public life. Practical reason is the set and practice of formative principles by which we live, rather than a set of explicit rules to be obeyed. The Categorical Imperative is the most general principle by which to live a morally good life. One always asks if one's choice and action can "in principle" be copied by every human being without its self-contradiction. There are exemplars, Kant argues strongly, who live by such pure practical reasoning. Jesus Christ was such an exemplar. Jesus Christ indeed re-presented the best of natural religion. No real public knowledge of Jesus Christ could be attained by pure reason. But if religion is removed from pure reason to the category of personal and practical—i.e., the ethical—Kant believed he then "saved" religion; that by describing pure reason's limits to knowledge (*Wissen*) he made "room for faith (*Glaube*)."[38]

Kant's own regard to religion is mixed. He rebelled against the Lutheran Pietism and its moralism of his early life. He deplored the narrow dogmatic legalism of Lutheran Orthodoxy that conflicted with what he regarded as true religion accessible to every person. True religion, he thought, was what was natural to every human being. Practical reason takes charge in this arena of the "natural." A commonsensical religion could and should be derived from practical reason's principle of non-contradiction, as Kant in his later career would state it. It is necessary for humans to believe something the denial of which would make impossible the performance of any moral duties. Freedom and the reliability of reason itself are upper most of a person's moral duties. Since free reason concludes what is morally good, it must be possible for the good to be achieved. But then it must be possible for the good to be achieved no matter the circumstances, including death.

---

38. I of course am highly distilling Kant's program here. For a most useful introduction, see Pasternak and Fugate, "Kant's Philosophy of Religion."

So immortality is a practically reasonable, even if religious, necessity for the good to be realized.

"Pure" or scientific reason cannot accommodate such religious sensibilities, however. Kant was steeped in the implications of the post-Copernican universe, believing that the universe itself was evolving toward perfection according to the Newtonian physical laws. For Kant this perhaps even influenced his thinking about God, giving him an affect like Rousseau's, but could not be expressed in pure reason's terms. As Hume had prompted Kant, the conditions for empirical adjudications must exist for there to be real (though critical) knowledge claims. Miracles, God, religious doctrines, etc. do not inhabit the constellation of empirical phenomena whose reality can be determined. To think about the supersensible might be possible, internally coherent, and profoundly meaningful. But the supersensible cannot be known. Thus religious faith is a practical matter of even practical necessity. But whatever we might think to be the elements of the supersensible must be sequestered from critical reason, which itself is the only warranted modality of descriptive speech for the public square.

Is there law then to be revealed in nature? Is there natural law? Whatever natural law would be for Kant, it is the law of Reason. It is notable that while Locke saw it necessary (and I think rightly) to affirm natural law's independent authority by way of some relatively basic rational deductions based on the observed character of human beings being with one another (and this as a complement to his positive reception of biblical ethical principles), Kant could only do so on the basis of practical reason apart from *any* empirical evidence. This echoes his relocation of religion from the category of revelation to the realm practical reason, for which there can be no pure reason as apologia. In effect, Kant declares the received notion of natural law to be outside the purview of pure reason.

This does not mean that Kant dissembled as to the importance of religious conviction. Indeed, he was so disturbed by the consequences of the Catholic-Protestant wars,[39] that he was spurred to write *Zum Ewigen Frieden* in 1795.[40] In this influential work Kant shows his own Lutheran tendencies. Not unlike the Two Kingdoms doctrine's mandate to take the peace of the spiritual kingdom into the civil domain, Kant believed that as culture improves, religious and linguistic differences could give rise to "greater agreement over their principles, [leading] to mutual understanding

---

39. Though the wars were ended with the Peace of Westphalia, smaller religious wars continued until 1712. The huge death toll of the Thirty Years War, however, was felt for generations throughout Germany.

40. Kant, "Perpetual Peace."

and peace."⁴¹ But to make this claim, Kant also thought it necessary to make of religious belief an ethics that is palatable for everyone. This practically meant that religion should be reduced to ethics.

Kant was not consistent in this mission. On one hand, he criticized believers' dedication to worship and practice of Christian discipline instead of nurturing their own moral character. On the other, he affirmed the institutions of religion insofar as they were "instrumental" for the attainment of moral virtue and remained open to reform. But instrumental toward what? Kant's distinction between "revealed" religion and "natural" religion is important to understand here. He contrasts revealed religion to natural religion and prefers the natural over the revealed, thinking revealed religion at best to be heuristic.⁴² "Natural" religion is what reason apart from empirical or historical influence should lead one to conclude. This is tantamount to saying that knowing something as one's duty is to know it as natural law. Reason is natural. Natural is reason. Law is itself the same in both. This is a consequential stage in what turns out to be the subtle expulsion of natural law from political philosophy.

Natural religion for Kant is the religion of the rationalist. Natural law follows suit; it is the law of the rationalist. One infers then that the Categorical Imperative *is* the natural law and morality then is religion. Historical accoutrements like religious creeds and customs may be needed yet for a while. But finally, what Aquinas thought as spiritually achievable in the temporal realm is now for Kant the expectation that the temporal realm rightly ruled by reason will achieve what once was thought spiritual. Historical contingencies notwithstanding, practical religion should and must lead to a "*pure* religious faith"⁴³ that nurtures autonomous reason, which itself only and ultimately legislates the highest religion of moral law.⁴⁴ This highest religion of reason is the only religion, being truly natural, that is capable of universality.⁴⁵

It is an understatement to say that Kant's redefinition of religion and natural law is consequential. I name three positive consequences. First, we praise his strong premises for reasoning as an intersubjective public

---

41. Quoted in Tomaszewska, "Kant's Reconception of Religion," 125.

42. Kant, *Religion Within the Limits*, 142–43.

43. My emphasis. By "pure," Kant means transcendental, deduced by reason alone, devoid of all empirical predications and historical influences.

44. Kant, *Religion Within the Limits*, 145–46, 173–78.

45. Kant is positively disposed toward ecumenical and interfaith rapprochement. "There is only one (true) religion; but there can be different kinds of faith . . . [even] because of the difference in their kinds of faith, one and the same religion can be met with." Kant, *Religion Within the Limits*, 98.

necessity that will or should correct individualistic overweening self-confidence and cultic groupthink. This means that the practice of "pure" reason requires protocols and institutions to optimize the exposure and removal of the epistemic contingencies that affect us all. Democratic processes must be emplaced. Financial influence on governmental representation must be controlled. The space for a free press must be honored, and the press itself operate more as dispassionately objective journalists than as persons of maxims and contingencies that promote and demote select people's autonomy. These components of classic liberalism still prevail in an educated society, though we see evidence of their deterioration today. Second, Kant is the forbearer of contemporary epistemic arguments for legal infrastructures favoring personal autonomy in concert with a robustly healthy *civitas*. Read closely, Kant strives for a polity that respects both the rights of the individual and the community/society as such. Pure reason practiced communally allows for democratic discernment of how to achieve the good. It also can reveal the biases that constrain a person from successfully practicing the categorical imperative. Finally, rationalist restatement of natural law as the primacy of reason in the public square underscored what the Augustinian Lutheran tradition affirmed all along about the temporal realm: that it is dedicated and must be dedicated to justice for every one of its inhabitants as a matter of natural law. Kant's insistence on reason's[46] "natural" role in the *civitas* still comports with how the Two Kingdoms doctrine understood natural law's role in the temporal second kingdom. Comportment between Kant's understanding of reason and Luther's understanding of natural law allows us room for reconstruction in Two Kingdoms theory.

Still, challenging consequences of Kant's thought remain with our regard to Two Kingdoms theory. What counts as legitimate fodder for knowledge was heavily restricted by Kant. This reinforced a long period of "spiritual desensitization" that one will see in theology during and after him. It goes directly to what I identify as the loss of eschatological imagination in the spiritual realm (which I treat in chapter 5). It also meant the privatization of faith in such a way that theologians later like Paul Althaus and Reinhold Niebuhr would severely misread the Two Kingdoms doctrine as fully separating religious faith from obedience to authority in the temporal realm.[47] Rather, many today argue and colleagues to Kant argued that legitimate knowledge can come from religious experience.

Kant had his friendly influencers and dissenters regarding his reduction of "knowing" to critical reason. He would somewhat agree and mostly

---

46. Hinlicky, *Paths Not Taken*, 17–42.
47. Althaus, "Kingdom of God"; Niebuhr, *Nature and Destiny*.

disagree with Gottfried Wilhelm Leibniz, who is garnering new respect over and above Kant today on the matters here considered. Kant's long association with Johann Georg Hamann (1730–88) was regularly marked by Hamann's insistence that there is more to reason and knowing than "objective" data. Indeed, Hamann's deep philosophical acuity and argument that knowledge is given and shaped by multiple sources other than material phenomena may well have tempered Kant's rationalism (particularly Kant's aesthetics). Some summarize Hamann as a mystical fideist and have left him at that. But his warning about the Enlightenment's overconfidence in reason has proven warranted, even presaging Wittgenstein's high valuation of what the Enlightenment claimed as inexpressible and nonexistent.

Hamann argued that knowledge is informed by much more than reason alone, and pure reason was no less affected by other human responses (like emotions) than the faith which Kant thought to sequester from public reasoning. Hamann decried Kant's separation of reason from the rest of human liveliness. This has implications for Kant's virtual alignment of reason with natural law too. For Hamann, natural law is not an object to be discerned by reason, nor even an external writing upon some heavenly tablet. To construe natural law as part of the *res extensa*, of nature as separated from spirit and so nature no longer to be read as the "book" of creation, evacuates the natural law of all its "naturalness" in human being. Rather, the natural law is God's address to all creatures "gifting us with existence and life."[48] *To be open to God's address is to be human.* This is an impressive premonition of postmodern faith and knowledge to which we shall return.

Philosophy's Denaturalization of Law and the Disappearance of Higher Law

Back in Britain, other political philosophers were catching on to the same problem. Not so long after Locke, reason led Jeremy Bentham (1748–1832) to divorce reason from natural law and declare its progeny of natural rights as illegitimate. Bentham famously said that to claim rights not granted in positive law by the state is "nonsense upon stilts."[49] It is people's lack of life necessities that are reasons for wishing there were rights. But reasons for wishing rights do not make them natural. The Enlightenment's turn to the individual, in other words, led further to ethics by enumeration. What serves the greatest number for their happiness is what counts. There is no external rule by which to curate what "counts." There is only the counting

---

48. Bayer, *Contemporary in Dissent*, loc. 2645 of 3360.
49. Bentham, "Anarchical Fallacies," 53.

of the satisfied vs. the unsatisfied. Not even the words of the satisfied or unsatisfied matter. To them the Romanticists gave thick expression in music and literature. But harder headed analysts of culture like Bentham and his hard-headed industrialist supporters were interested in numbers over qualities.

"Wants are not supply, hunger is not bread," Bentham famously wrote. So he proceeded to hard-headed analysis. He was impatient with Locke's methodology and Kant's abstraction. Bentham dispassionately questioned the merits of any proposed solution to an unfair situation. What utility would this solution bring? What immediate and foreseeable maximizations of pain over pleasure could be calculated? Bentham disliked Romanticism's rhetoric du jour of "right reason" and "natural right."[50] Reason could prove just as arbitrary without a proven calculus and rights were only achieved, never natural. Up-and-coming capitalists of the Industrial Revolution liked Bentham's bent, along with his distaste for words from what they regarded as pretentiously out-of-touch salons. But their support of Bentham was ironic, for if any subgroup would come to interpret utilitarianism in the cold words of cost-benefit analysis and thereby increase the space between haves and have-nots it was them. Yet, the industrialists were the ones who would give Bentham and his program more success in promoting egalitarianism than anyone current with or prior to him in the English tradition. John Stuart Mill himself wrote that Bentham was "the father of English innovation both in doctrine and in institutions; . . . [he was] the great subversive."[51]

In all this success Bentham stood out also for removing all religious mystery from analysis of social good and ill. He ignored the terms of religion, spiritual aspiration, and sin. Bentham's appeal to the greatest good for the greatest number was fully secular. Counter that to Edmund Burke (1729–97), the English conservative philosopher and statesman deeply influenced by Montesquieu, Hume, and Locke. Burke argued for the greatest good for the greatest number, too. But in that he still aligned with his received tradition, that the greatest good was not so much in people's political equality as in their aligning with the divine ordering of the universe. Burke sang Augustine and Aquinas while Bentham murmured the material world from which he exorcised natural law. But Burke's voice, though still heard, was muffled once John Stuart Mill joined the utilitarian choir.

Mill is of course more famous for his extension of utilitarianism into the classic liberal definition and prescription of liberty and how it should

---

50. Kirk, *Conservative Mind*, 115.

51. Quoted by August, "Mill as Sage," 144; August illumines Mill's very dry sarcasm in describing Bentham.

be honored in structures of government. As for the status of natural law and natural rights, Mill was more circumspect than Bentham. He agreed with Bentham that there was nothing "natural" about them, but preferred to speak of them more as Hume did, as perceived uniform experiences and habits of thought. However, Mill was thoroughly in the vein of the new naturalism. We are wholly part of nature. Knowledge can only be had by observation and experience. We have no access to *apriori* truths and so no access to objective facts that lie beyond experience. Our minds are not imprinted with truths "from outside" nor do our minds construct the world (idealism). There are no natural laws or rights delivered to us by external deity or some other cause. We have more than sufficient cause to question the authority of those who assert such external authority to us. There are moral rights, however, and those are derived from the basic fact drawn from observation that individuals can and do think for themselves, claim autonomy, and follow one's reasonable intuition as to the trustworthiness of certain public leaders.

Mill delicately demurred from the received notion of natural law as did Bentham so loudly. Mill's is a naturalistic, not idealistic, construct in place of what had been natural law. Natural rights are Mill's signum drawn solely from the turn to the self, no outside authorization or help needed. The people (the Many) are sovereign. The state is sovereign only insofar as it represents the will of the people and makes its decisions on behalf of the people with utmost transparency. Sovereignty, like natural law, is not granted "from the top." It emerges from below, from "the people." In them natural law was first vested, no longer externally objective for all to see and follow. From them law and rights emerged as willed by their informed desires, which is to say that ultimately law and rights emerged from the people's subjectivity.

The consequences are significant. If moral, ethical, and finally legal conclusions could not be derived from an external eternal perduring reality, then they would have to be drawn inferentially from the particulars on the ground. Now not only had natural law been "moved." Further, its very "words" are questioned. So the philosophical seeds of logical positivism were lain for sprouting in the early twentieth century. The earliest language positivists believed they could encode all language into symbolic mathematical form, achieving a universal univocality transcending the builders of the Tower of Babel. They failed and Wittgenstein's famous final word of his *Tractatus*, that the truly meaningful matters of life could not be said, placed a rather emphatic exclamation mark at the end of the early analytic efforts.[52] No matter that the early Wittgenstein's word structures

---

52. Wittgenstein, *Tractatus*, §7.2.

as "reality mirrors" and the latter Wittgenstein's "language games"[53] both affirmed meaning beyond the text, analytical philosophy's legacy insofar as it impacted the interpretation of law itself was to deny meaning above and beyond the text. The significance of this cannot be overstated. There is no court available for appeal, no higher authority like natural law for "judicial review." And if no such court is present, no judge recognized as natural in the manner so recognized up to and including the Reformation era, then the structure itself of Lutheranism's Doctrine of Two Kingdoms has been dissolving under both our feet.

Where then philosophically to turn? In philosophy generally the options turned out to be pragmatism, textualism, and the relativity of postmodernity. As for legal philosophy and law, however, logical positivism was adaptively trickled down into what today is practiced as positive law. Logical positivism sought for direct correspondence between the words and/or grammatical structure to the things they ostensibly named. Words were "things." Positive law subsequently was the practice of analyzing the words that legislatures "pose" (statutory law). This practice is much influenced by logical positivism in a curious and informal partnership with pragmatism. Positive law that now only curates its own words is not concerned with what is or had been "natural." It is concerned with the narrowest referentiality possible. But, historically, positive law sustains a particular interpretation only as long as it politically can. Without universal consensus under an arbiter as was once the case with natural law, what "politically can" means is the temporization of pragmatism.

One sees clear leadership in this direction in the celebrated Oliver Wendell Holmes, from the late nineteenth century into the early twentieth. Holmes's teaching at Harvard Law School presaged the turn from interpreting law as reflective of highest principles to interpretation of law as the language of the sovereign state represent by the legislature; in other words, law is the analysis of language in case history. Learned Hand is another famed jurist who made the same point, furthering a positivistic methodology. An oft-cited exchange between Holmes and Hand proves the positivism, also called "legal realism," indicating that the law is about "is" and not about "ought." When on one occasion Hand said in parting to Holmes, "Do justice!" Holmes answered, "I do law, not justice." William P. Lapiana well summarizes the methodological shift in the teaching of law: "The exclusion of non-legal topics for legal education was part of a conscious intellectual strategy. It was dictated by the view of law as what judges actually enforce and became a valuable weapon to use against the view of law as eternal

---

53. Wittgenstein, *Philosophical Investigations*.

principles."[54] Bentham's disposition against "natural" rights was by this turn of the century now well emplaced in the highest echelons of legal education.

H. L. A. Hart, one of the most celebrated philosophers of law and practicing attorneys in the mid-twentieth century, wielded great influence in the English-speaking world of law with his teaching of legal positivism and positive law. Hart cut his teeth on Bentham's utilitarianism, but also rightly criticized Bentham's vulnerability to the politics of power and extremism. There may be no such things as a set of natural rights, Hart argued. But there must be yet some implicit premise for law. Law could not rest on an absolute moral anarchy, nor, at best, mere preservation of the status quo. Hart argued even more explicitly than Mill for a minimum content of natural law. It is the right of all people to be free from suffering. All law must be positively directed to amelioration of suffering. Hart does not justify this one natural right with any metaphysical speculation.[55] If he argues from any recognized philosophy at all, it is pragmatism. Common experience shows that it is simply unacceptable for humans to suffer. Therefore human beings have the right to freedom from suffering.[56] This one right is and should be reasonably generative for law sufficient to address all human conditions. Law then must be (positively) written and practiced situationally for the advancement of freedom from suffering.[57] "Situationally" is the operative adverb here. The freedom not to suffer is conditioned all around by socioeconomic inequity, violence, war, and many other deleterious contextual influences. Positive law's purpose is not to enforce the illusion of eternal natural law, but to serve people's freedom by addressing their life conditions. The law, in other words, must attend to and change the conditions that inhibit freedom, which is to make peace possible. Only "where peace is possible" (Locke) can a natural right have value. Other than this one premise, there are no fixed legal concepts. The idea of fixed concepts itself Hart calls "the fundamental legal error about the nature of legal concepts." There just is no such thing as fixed concepts prior to their application in concrete cases.

Hart's annunciation of "no fixed concepts" is an apt epitaph also to the evident demise of Higher Law. The unquestioned normativity of

54. Lapiana, "Thoughts and Lives," 609–10, and Gunther, *Learned Hand*. For the most exhaustive presentation of Holmes's legal philosophy, representing the formalistic move from natural law as "legal realism" toward positivism and, eventually, the contemporary regard for textualism, see Holmes, *Common Law*.

55. Hart, "Natural Rights"; Hart, *Concept of Law*.

56. I will qualify Hart's "freedom" hereafter as "freedom from unnatural suffering."

57. Hart recognizes the Marxist error here in its identification of poverty with the lack of freedom. Poverty is one "evil," per Hart; the lack of freedom another. Hart, "Natural Rights," 175.

higher law[58] was affirmed in the legal and civil arenas into the twentieth century. For the two-and-a-half American centuries so far, the legality and supremacy of the US Constitution has rested on the "belief in a law superior to the will of human governors."[59] Indeed, one may argue that until the hermeneutics of "originalism" began to command obedience in the latter twentieth-century US Supreme Court, higher law was the norming norm of all judicial philosophy. Edward Corwin identified the origin of "ultimate law" in the Hellenic mind, higher law having proceeded from Stoicism to inspire Aristotle's idea of "natural justice." Cicero amplified the concept for the Roman Senate. The concept become rule spread throughout the empire, transmuted into the Magna Carta, then British Common Law, finally into American jurisprudence. In all its phases of linguistic and legal adoption, higher law was the secular iteration of the divine law, external to human will and human passion. Aristotle's own summary still resonates: "To invest the law then with authority is, it seems, to invest God and reason only; to invest in man is to introduce a beast, as desire is something bestial, and even the best of men in authority are liable to be corrupted by passion. We may conclude then that the law is reason without passion and it is therefore preferable to any individual."[60]

Many philosophers of law[61] interpreted higher law as the ultimate benchmark against and by which all legal appeal is adjudicated. Higher law decides whether lesser laws are just. We see the concept's influence in Chief Justice Marshall's quotation of Harrington in Marbury v. Madison, that we are a "government of laws and not of men."[62] People still, to be sure, readily judge as to what is and what is not fair and right according to conscience. People still "just know" what the objectively right thing to do is. People intuit too that so doing is to do and serve justice. This certain autonomic moral compass, however deeply embedded it is in human humus, is still subliminally respected in the commons. But public intuition notwithstanding, positive law evolved into what is now called textualism and originalism,

---

58. I'll write of higher law now in the lower case, following current convention. The referent is the same.

59. Corwin, *"Higher Law,"* 5.

60. Corwin, *"Higher Law,"* 7, quoting Aristotle, *Politics* 3.15–16. One can see here, by the way, the inspiration for Kant's critiques, even his decision to write of religion only on the grounds of practical reason, as pure reason is not to be influenced by human passions. As for whether this is truly a good thing, I've already discussed Kant's deleterious effect on religious faith and his presumption to have "saved" it.

61. E.g., Alonso and Fernando, "Cicero and Natural Law"; Pettit, "Liberalism and Republicanism"; Schofield, *Cicero*.

62. Corwin, *"Higher Law,"* 8.

in which neither natural nor higher law are generally referenced nor specifically cited, as is so now in the most prescribed and used textbook on how to read law, *Reading Law: The Interpretation of Legal Texts*, by Antonin Scalia and Bryan A. Garner.[63]

The conservative legal movement of the last two generations—led most prominently by Scalia—has championed a strictly textualist approach to decisions in these statutory interpretation cases, eschewing any judicial role in determining the "purpose" of a given law or how best to give effect to a presumed broader policy represented by the law. This movement arose in reaction to the Warren Court of the 1950s and 1960s, and what it perceived to be "judicial activism" by which unelected judges imposed their own policy preferences on the community rather than "judicial restraint" that gives effect to the laws enacted by the people's representatives. Scalia was an especially articulate champion of this legal philosophy. His philosophy now dominates the writing, reading, and administration of law at all levels. As Supreme Court Justice Elena Kagan said in a now famous remark, "We are all textualists now."[64]

It still happens that presumptions of higher law or natural law may be included in the development of common law principles. Via judge-made rulings, these incrementally become a fully-developed body of law addressing a particular situation that could apply to new questions of larger significance. But given the priority of particular situations in positive law, one never sees explicit appeals to higher law. It is either deliberately neglected as a consequence of the Benthamite tradition or circumstantially ignored due to the incessant and accelerating growth of positive law. In a recent interview, Supreme Court Justice Neil Gorsuch shared that much of the majority worry behind Loper (the Chevron Deference case) is that regulatory agencies have so taken over the construction of positive law that no one can keep up.[65] This surfeit of law is due to the usurpation of the duties of Congress by regulatory agencies. Conservatives like Gorsuch see

---

63. Of course, Scalia's and Garner's text is not the only representative of legal language today. It is on the American scene the most prominent, while other approaches still abide. For a fine outline of the main approaches, cf. Obgar, "Concept of Legal Language." As for Garner, there is not much daylight between logical positivism and his methodological descriptivism, which reveals his confident adaptation of the later Wittgenstein. For a superb and humorous affirmation of Garner's skill and authority, see Wallace, "Authority and American Usage." Finally, amongst much more evidence of the elision of positivism and positive law, see Cloud, "Pragmatism, Positivism, and Principles."

64. Regarding textualist normativity now in American legal practice, see O'Scamlin, "'We Are All Textualists Now.'"

65. French, "Neil Gorsuch." Cf. also Gorsuch and Nitze, *Over Ruled*.

here an antidemocratic arrogation of policy-making to an unelected and unrepresentative few. While this antidemocratic movement must be reigned in, the Supreme Court and all courts increasingly have had to focus on interpreting statutory text, positive law, rather than discerning and restating an optimal legal rule based on prior precedent and the facts of a particular case. That had been standard practice when the notion of higher law was normative, as with the Marshall and Warren Courts.

Notwithstanding such "fine tuning" in judicial review as to be attentive only to the *sola scriptura*, textualism does not receive unanimous support. Justice Kagan's remark was made with tongue in cheek. She wryly reminded hearers and readers thereby that even when everyone practices textualism not all will agree. Supreme Court majority rulings and minority dissents both are often made on strictly textualist grounds while wholly opposite in their conclusions. This applies to constitutional interpretation, too. However, "originalism" rather than "textualism" is the primary methodological term for constitutional interpretation, as the judge is advised to discern the "original public meaning" of the words used by the Founders or subsequent amendment drafters. For example, in the famous case of District of Columbia v. Heller that decided toward an absolutist individual right to bear arms, Justice Scalia's argument on the premises of the English Bill of Rights, *Blackstone's Commentaries*, and other sources was a paragon of originalist interpretation of the text of Second Amendment. But Justice Stevens met Scalia on Scalia's own terms, answering Scalia point by point by looking to different historical evidence, concluding that the amendment protected only the right of militia members to bear arms.[66]

Something other than purported textual objectivity must be inferred from opposite conclusions made with an identical hermeneutical method. One could have no more precise an example of textualism applied to positive law, and yet we apparently still do not escape subjectivity. Heisenberg's Principle seems to have come over to law from physics and Kantian epistemology. Things are not measured as they are. They are measured according to the instruments used to measure them. Or, as the postmodern umpire says about the pitches to the batter, "They ain't nothing until I calls 'em." But the central question here regarding the Two Kingdoms doctrine is what would an umpire from the spiritual kingdom have as common ground for conversation with a colleague umpire in the temporal kingdom? If natural law and higher law no longer are normative factors in theory and practice today, what then about a theological Doctrine of Two Kingdoms that depended on them?

---

66. O'Scamlin, "'We Are All Textualists Now,'" 3.

Postmodernity and Revelation

Luther recognized law in both kingdoms, the law of love in the spiritual kingdom and the natural law in the temporal kingdom. Natural and higher law had been the means to enjoy sociality. Higher law had been the priority of justice *(ius)* as the objective right over law *(lex)*, "and so of a legislation to a goodness existing independently of the human."[67] If not independently of the human, might we identify something that is at least shared between humans and itself human, something that transcends and so heals the often-agonistic breach between the Individual and the Community? Through all the history we have briefed from Aristotle to beyond Marx, freedom with justice was the goal in reconciling individual rights with communal and nation-state interests.

Readers may recognize by now that the classically liberal era inherited from the Enlightenment on one hand rendered the Two Kingdoms more separate than distinct. The accelerated cultural evolution toward secularism since cannot be detailed here. Charles Taylor covered that with a depth and breadth that makes him the standard authority on the matter.[68] How I have framed the question for the Two Kingdoms doctrine about the absence of natural law echoes postliberal theological laments about the absence of normative moral value. Postliberal political theologians ask if there is any place for the sacred in secularity, given its absence of God.[69] David Congdon helpfully parses postliberal antipathies as tending either to a class of separatists against liberal culture on one hand and, on the other hand, new Christian colonialists of the culture and, even, the state.[70]

Postliberals of postmodernity eschew the tried liberal praxis of correlating theological assertions with purported counterparts in secular culture. In other words, they deny any effectiveness to apologetics and so advocate its abandonment. For Kantians that's a win. For postmoderns, the turn from the self to the biblical narrative is trust in a bigger win. The strategy has had no little success, unto the point that, unexpectedly for postliberals, biblical literalists in the tradition of Carl F. H. Henry celebrate and name postmodernity as their warrant. We who accept many critiques against modernity, however, fear that in this response the Enlightenment baby is thrown out with the bathwater. We can't accept the now de facto undergraduate creed that everyone has their own truth, even subtly affirmed in the fights over

---

67. Milbank, "Natural Law," 430.
68. Taylor, *Secular Age*.
69. Gordon, "Place of the Sacred."
70. Congdon, *Who Is a True Christian?*, chs. 4 and 5.

who gets appointed to a supreme court disposed toward textualism. Insofar as I here have been asking for just such a correlation, I've kept to the liberal project. If the Two Kingdoms doctrine is to be of any value, it must on its secular philosophical side have roots that are more sustained and sustaining of moral social behavior than the pragmatics of fickle opinion.

So we look for a postmodernly "foundationless foundation," an acknowledgeable given that commends itself by its immediacy, something that *is* known and knowable that Kant would not have accepted as epistemically legitimate. One postmodern theologian in this quest is John Milbank. Milbank is among those Congdon lists as more inclined to cultural supremacy instead of liberal hospitality to differentiated mutuality. Supposing that Milbank is so inclined, he serves as a sharpener for my questions and answers. In any case, Milbank seeks a retrieval too of Augustine, as well as Aquinas, for our age. He sees them not as the overstated advocates of God's grace on one moral political side and human potential on the other. In them Milbank sees the prospect of mediating the current dyad of individualism and communitarianism, of individual human rights with community rights. He finds a hopeful clue in Aristotle's linking of the human necessity of friendship—a theretofore "foundation" for healthy human being not previously listed on the eternal subset of natural law—with justice and freedom.[71]

John Milbank argues that for the "real" Aquinas the proto-natural law of grace was destroyed with the fall, transmuted after sin as a providential instrument of external restraint and punishment, then restored into its originally intended function of grace in Christ's incarnation; the *Logos* become new *Nomos* itself.[72] Almost to oversimplify Aquinas, if the prelapsarian natural law was discerned intuitively in relationship with God and nature, the refusal of divine government known as the fall is the fall into individualism. To redress this, the new law of Christ re-presents God's new order of communion. For Aquinas, revealed law is distinct but not separated from the intentions still of natural law, supporting Luther's own double recognition of law. Both revealed law (in the spiritual order) and natural law (in the temporal order) intend justice to be realized in the recursive good of friendship and community. Pursuit of the good actualizes community and community impels the good. The good is *intuited* by the community as objective. This is an example of the foundationless foundation that we seek. The communal good, impelled by the individual's need for association/community, is not merely heteronomously stipulated. It stands apart from community while is yet discerned from within community and

---

71. Aristotle, *Nicomachean Ethics*, books 8–9, cited by Milbank, "Natural Law," 420.
72. Milbank, "Natural Law," 419.

builds community. It comes into public perception by the give and take of spoken reasoning within the community. Insofar as the community is also always diverse in its perspectives and ways of knowing, the discernment process of the good necessarily includes religious intuition and tradition as community epistemic claims. This natural, practical discernment of the good when transmuted into law echoes Kant's insistence on reason as public and consequently defining of government's role, while it also corrects by the addition of the affect of friendship to Kant's narrower canon of reason.[73]

The discernment asked for here is that sort that had been expected of democratic governments. To discern together, to be associated, to exercise sociality: these activities imply already a communal covenant. It is that to which Locke gave words. But the point here is that the covenant already preternaturally exists in the very "spontaneous" effort of discerning the common good, if even step by step, "crossing each problematic bridge" when a group of people come to it. Later we will identify this more particularly even as the existence and exercise of language itself. For now, we emphasize the commitment to the *common* good, if even step by step. The "covenant to the common" is foundational. But the group effort finally is only artificial when lust for power trumps the commitment to the common, as is so when electoral outcomes and public emotions are manipulated by external interests uninterested in genuine public good, as when democracies like the United States are marked as "flawed."[74]

At this point, the loss of natural law to positivism and, finally, textualism, threatens also the concept of human sovereignty, to be considered more in the next chapter. History shows unstoppable repetition of individuals acting against individuals. Boundaries must be imposed. Authorities must be established to enforce the contracts. Authorities achieve statehood, "itself defined by artificially achieved stasis, rather than by any claim to participation in divine equity."[75] Liberty is now defined and enforced by the state, which today is quite likely to be groups arrogating to themselves increased power and doing so by employing vast media to "persuade" a public as to what freedom in their moment of history means. That is when Jews, gypsies, transsexuals, and illegal aliens are scapegoated as robbers of the freedoms of "real citizens." Milbank, with many, sees that any claim to an "absolute" natural right of freedom is necessarily and paradoxically constrained by principalities and powers if freedom is to exist at all. Schmitt is proven

---

73. Milbank, "Natural Law," 421.

74. *The Economist* ("Why America") for the eighth consecutive year indexed the United States as a "flawed democracy."

75. Milbank, "Natural Law," 427.

right. Whoever or whatever represents the state—an executive, a legislature, a supreme court, a corporate oligarchy—is the only arbiter of rules and their exception. The state—not the individual together with the *natural* whole of the community built from friendship—is exceptional because the state alone defines and decides law. In its own eyes, then, the *state* is natural, and the state then is the natural law. This is the state of the state that many contemporary interpreters believe we have reached and to which postmoderns of all parsings are opposed.

Today as a citizen I still am able to exercise some rights. But they are not natural. They are posited insofar as they are textualized. Yet, as we have shown, because textualism ultimately is subjective, even when subjected to judicial review, sans genuine commitment to the common good, there is no sociality, and so there is no true justice. And the converse is as true, *because or when* there is no justice, I am stripped of my truly natural (!) right to sociality. My claim to the right of religious freedom may warrant my refusal to pay my portion of taxes diverted from public to private religious schools. My freedom to do that aligns with the MAGA militia member who opposes the federal government's reach. We may be allied Lockeans; but having no justice, we are not friends.

Milbank reminds that reason must lead the individual and society together to the justice of freedom to be common and sensical. This would honor the natural right to be free of unnatural suffering. Recognizing this may draw us with Luther back closer to Aquinas, wherein the natural law of reason, being the chief task of temporal government, correlates with God's law in the spiritual order. Still, the freedom for which natural law inspires us in the temporal realm is a necessary rightful goal. But it is relative freedom. That is, it is freedom that relates to others' freedom. And, therefore, it is freedom that faces the neighbor and the *polis*. In fact, freedom alone is not freedom at all. It is not yet full. Freedom is to lives one's life without unnatural suffering, with the conscious duty freely to ensure the freedom of the other. Freedom is duty bound. It is responsible to the other. The fully free individual is response-enabled, thus response-able, and so responsible to all other individuals. To be that is to build justice in friendship and to deepen friendship with justice. To coin a phrase, the human being is wholly, rightfully sovereign, subject to no other; the human being is wholly relative, subject to others' rightful sovereignty.[76]

---

76. An important topic for which I have no space to follow satisfactorily here is obedience. Obedience is distinctly related to freedom. Obedience also has its own nuances the most distinctive being the distinction between voluntary obedience and involuntary obedience, as it were, the "obedience of obedience." The former is always volitional, and so freedom attaches to every moment of decision. The latter is volitional only once,

How has it come that autonomy must abide necessary heteronomy? He stated the problem differently, but this is the aporia that worries Milbank. Christians, of course, would answer with the word "sin" and refer to our postlapsarian human condition. But that is the answer for the spiritual kingdom, while here we converse in the terms of the temporal kingdom defined by philosophy, law, and the human and natural sciences. An answer to the grave problem facing this "most natural law of freedom" and its aporia is that perhaps natural law, whether construed as eternally fixed or contextually implied, is not where to find congruity and congress between the Two Kingdoms in the first place. The congruity is not so abstract. The congruity involves the spiritual fullness of divinely sourced love on one side and friendship's drive for justice on the other. Both concern affects of love. The language of the spiritual kingdom is love ever striving how to love more. The language of the temporal kingdom concerns friendship, what I have called sociality, and so love's protection, components of which include human sovereignty, freedom, and peace.

These would be the measure of Hart's criterion of freedom from suffering. Love has its form with its distinctive language in the revealed law of the spiritual realm and its differing form with its concomitant different language in the temporal realm. Hart points to love's many temporal incarnations. Compassion, a component of that foundationless foundation called friendship/association, is a "natural" and dynamic motivation that calls for different words from and for different occasions without having even temporally been ordered into practice. New "natural" law, in other words, is "what happens" when compassionate human being meets suffering. Compassion—more generally, friendship—is dynamic. But it still needs a guiding language within a societal structure, as with positive law written by reason, so to remediate the suffering and so also to protect and amplify friendship. This is when friendship, freedom, and justice cohere. The rule of friendship, and so justice, when defining ever larger societies may thus require language that seems more prescriptive than liberating. But when reasoned for the common good with the least possible cause of suffering to

---

when one first says "yes" to the temporal period or whole life thereafter of nothing but obedience to the specific purposes and situational decisions of a life in community, like life in a monastic community or military service, under a stipulated leader or chain of command, the exception being when one's conscience and fundamental human rights are at stake. It is a good question as to which of the two the individual clauses of Luther's definition of Christian life in "The Freedom of a Christian" fit, that the Christian person is perfectly free and subject to none *and* perfectly servant, subject to all. The philosophical implications of freedom and obligation are superbly explored in Kaurin, *On Obedience*.

individuals, the most effective "language" of government will complement the immediacy of sacral relationships in the spiritual realm.

Language Is the "Most" Natural Law

Our present state in the cloud of textualism and originalism offers another silver lining. It is that we can be grateful that words matter and are most basic for judicial adjudication. This is not a trivial observation. Indeed, that words count as more than a convenience—*particularly when they are understood to bespeak the common good*—suggests something of ontological importance, the *event* of language. The natural law, implicit in its joyful benevolence in the spiritual kingdom and explicit in its dynamic conditionedness in the temporal kingdom is revealed in the event of language. Its location is twofold, spiritual and temporal. Its origin is one. *Deus dixit*.

Luther understood that God gave language to humankind so we could speak to and name creation in addition to giving voice to our sociality. Humankind is charged to relate and distinguish with language. Rather than exempt religion from his thought about natural law, Locke underscored religion as constitutive of natural law right alongside reason's discernment of the law. Kant's colleague, Johann Gerhard Hamann, insisted on a correlate of divine revelation as a necessary "reasonable" complement to Kant's rationalism. Hamann considered even that Kant's dissociation of reason (and so true knowledge) from personal and historical experience was a kind of Gnosticism.[77] Always prevenient to thought is language. Hamann recognized what Kant in practice did not: that language is either the necessary clothing of reason or, even, reason's forbearer. "Without language we would have no reason," wrote Hamann. Likewise without language, no religion.[78] Per Hamann, language bears revelation and reason, and so both are sources for true knowledge. Giorgio Agamben, like Luther and Hamann, and in no ill accord with Locke, places language in the category of revelation. Agamben does not clearly state the relationship of language to reason (perhaps wisely choosing to avoid analytic philosophy's contortions). But he reasons to the conclusion that the fact of language implies an ontology of revelation.

Language is the mode of revelation. Language reveals what is and what can be. Language therefore is useful. It is action. It connects people to a world, people to people, and persons to themselves. Language also negates relations. This can be a blessing or a curse. Language initiates a person's separation from one's self and from others even as one would commune

---

77. Bayer, *Contemporary in Dissent*, loc. 2581 of 3360.
78. Quoted in Bayer, *Contemporary in Dissent*, loc. 2030 of 3360.

with others. To the extent that language is so used and how it is so used, language falls under the category of reason and is political. "There is politics because man is the living being who, in language, separates and opposes himself to his own bare life and, at the same time, maintains himself in relation to that bare life in an inclusive exclusion."[79] This statement is a dense reiteration of the aporia of individual freedom we discerned above.

But *the fact that* language exists is a revelation. In his reflection on "the idea of language," Agamben writes, "If the content of a revelation were something, however absurd, that human reason and language could still say and know with their own strength . . . this would not be revelation. What revelation allows us to know must, therefore, be something not only that we could not know without revelation but also that conditions the very possibility of knowledge in general."[80] Revelation doesn't transfer facts from one sphere to the next. It does not entail linguistic propositions about a being, not even about God. Revelation reveals rather that language exists, that we can see and speak the world through language but do not see language, like we see reality through the most transparent window, but do not know the window exists until we come hard against it.[81]

Here Agamben is now the explicit theologian. He ties the now revealed *mysterion* (mystery) of God of Col 1:26 to its appositive base-less *ton logon tou theou* (the word of God). What is revealed? Not a fact. Not a worldly or otherworldly event. What is revealed is simply "the word of God"; more yet and finally, that God gives the word by which we live while God remains yet invisible. "The invisibility of the revealer in what is revealed is the word of God; it is revelation."[82]

Mystery remains beyond revelation; "Being" beyond "a" being. Revelation does not disclose and exhaust mystery. God is not fully exposed, consumed, or dead. All human language has at its root this offering of "infinite transcendence." This potentiality is only for language. But also being of infinite transcendence, language begets reason, and so revelation is the ground for reason! Says Agamben, quoting the neo-Kantian philosopher Hermann Cohen, "The meaning of revelation is not that God reveals himself *in* something but *to* something." Revelation is "the pure event of language before or beyond all particular meaning."[83] And since the revela-

---

79. Agamben, *Homo Sacer* (HS), 8.
80. Agamben, *Potentialities* (P), 39.
81. P, 40.
82. P, 40–41.
83. P, 40–41.

tion of language as such is open, thought has the possibility of going beyond meaningful propositions.[84]

Agamben closes this reflection with a political observation. Language mediates things (thoughts, persons, values) but is itself immediate. The attempt to force language to "go beyond" itself in the immediacy of revelation cannot happen. Revelation cannot be instrumentalized. There are no seven steps toward successful apocalypse. Still, there is potential because the immediacy of language as such is always open. Language always opens itself to beyond itself. Language, like poetry, is capable of self-transcendence: *finitum capax infiniti*. Language as such is immediate. To *use* language is not to engage in immediacy, though use at its best aspires to immediacy. The immediacy of language is an event to which human beings can be open, but from which human beings are separated once spoken. The immediacy of language itself is, therefore, presuppositionless and only being open to the *idea of language* provides the prospect for community. "What unites human beings among themselves is not a nature, a voice, or a common imprisonment in signifying language; it is the vision of language itself and, therefore the experience of language's limits, its *end*."[85] Its end, indeed, is a communion and a sacrament; a "*communicatio* between the speech of God and the speech of men" and a *sacramentum*/oath[86] by which God dedicates God to a specific purpose. Agamben intends its meaning as in medieval law in which a sacrament is an official oath or promise.[87] What is *sacer*/sacred is dedicated to a purpose.

There are two major implications in Agamben's analysis, only the second about which he is explicit. First, as I've already said, originative language—*Logos*—is God's eschatological revelatory gift that enables the human use of language. "Eschatological" is not Agamben's term here. It is mine. I use it to underscore that God's gift is not the consequence of a teleology embedded in the secondary human use of language. God comes *to* and *into* the event while also offering the event,[88] becoming incarnate but also thereby reserving transcendence and mystery. Agamben's phrase "the Sacrament of Language" concerns the performative word that gives an experience of mutual immediacy between the giver of the word, God, and the receiver of language, human being. It is the primal "experience of language in which

---

84. P, 42.
85. P, 47.
86. Agamben, *Sacrament of Language* (SoL), 339.
87. SoL, 349.
88. Jean-Luc Marion writes similarly, before Agamben, in *God Without Being*.

it is impossible to separate name and being."[89] The Sacrament of Language is original and originative communion.

Agamben also poses language's use as "the Sacrament of Power." It is important to remember that by "sacrament" Agamben intends its non-ecclesial meaning as "oath" or "covenant." With "Sacrament of Power" he refers to a secondary but necessary function of language. Here the implied oath is on the part of the human language user, though, regrettably, of the gravity here the human is usually unaware. At best, children are taught and remember as adults to use language charitably and accurately. But even when advocating the best in the use of language, that a person simply by the act of speaking takes an oath like a sacrament, however true this is, is practically ambitious. There is common work to do on this matter. But nevertheless the sacramental "power" character of language is a fact that Agamben emphasizes. The terms are authoritative even so. Simply by using the gift we in effect promise to respect the gift by the manner of our use.[90]

What God spoke as act with the originative language of the *Logos* was good. What human beings then are to do by implied oath with language (*logoi*) is to dedicate ourselves to the *Logos*. This is existential risk. The human being is *"the living being whose language places his life in question."*[91] Speaking truly as constituted by and to the *Logos* is to speak to the spiritual and temporal purpose of *logos*, the integrity of the individual in community and vice versa. To speak the lie is to dissociate, fracture, alienate, all of which is to murder, and all of it implicit in the original sin. Of course, like the petulant child who puts self above the house rules by crying out, "I didn't choose to be born!," we aren't given the practical choice to speak or not to speak. But the corporate self-reflection of the species has brought us to the conclusion found and forgotten repeatedly, now found again by Agamben, that the givenness of language itself necessarily implies its function as revelatory and its ground as God.[92]

---

89. SoL, 340.

90. One could make the case that the animal and plant worlds are more responsible in their use of language insofar as their communication serves only the good of their specific communities. Language has not evolved (eaten of the apple) in those places that would deceive others in their own communities. The lie is the first sin after the original sin of disobedience.

91. SoL, 353.

92. SoL, 340.

Summary

We've covered much ground to ascertain the situation with natural law. Cicero affirmed that natural eternal law gave rights to "the people." Augustine affirmed that natural rights were God-given. God's divine law enspirited the heavenly city while natural law birthed and oversaw civil law in the earthly city. Aquinas fixed natural law even more as eternal and added that every person had the capacity to be so morally good as to be a perfect match with natural law, and this was at the same time to be spiritually pure. Luther restored Augustine's differentiation of divine law and natural law, keeping both still "high," that is, transcendent and eternally fixed. Divine law was revealed as grace in the spiritual realm and natural law revealed in the conscience. Kant liked the fixity, but allowed that the moral good could only be discerned by reason, not revelation. Locke agreed, but called the inductive/deductive process natural, starting from the reasoning individual, but this also cohered with scriptural testimony. In effect, both Kant and Locke re-located natural law in the human mind. Bentham thought that there was no such thing at all as natural laws and that the decision for what was good lay with the people, period. Mill ironically agreed. Logical positivism's coincidence with positive law and pragmatism extended the ramifications of Bentham's utility into the current hermeneutics of textualism and originalism. We concluded with Hart's "freedom from unnatural suffering" as at least a minimalist condition in the philosophy and practice of law that, when discerned communally with dedication to the common good, could still point to something more trustworthy than the subjectivity of textualism to safeguard that good.

As for the search for a suitable renaming of what serves as natural law, in concert with what positive implications can be inferred from textualism, we segued to the ontological implications of language itself, with debt to Giorgio Agamben. He titled originative language as a sacrament, even implying language as the proto-sacrament. Originative language is the gift of words in immediacy of relationship. We had identified sociality as a preternatural driver in the new search for a natural law. Agamben (with my offer of Hamman and others in support) writes of the "Sacrament of Language" as the revelation both of God and relationship with God and each other. As for the use of language for purposes other than the immediacy of relationship, which use is vowed for the common good but obviously so-oft broken, Agamben suggests the "Sacrament of Power." Both of these he intends for his own still developing political philosophy, though I borrow them for rethinking Luther's political theology of Two Kingdoms.

For a human being to have received this original sacrament and then to promise to live with it and by it, is to live as one who whenever naming will bless or curse. In language we unite or separate. Living from and by the immediacy of the gift is to live in the "Sacrament of Language." To *use* language then for the good of community and aspiration toward immediacy to God or for ill purpose in either way is to perform a Sacrament of Power. The Sacrament of Power communicates and discommunicates political life. The Sacrament of Power is a trust, not a privilege. It is a trust funded by the Sacrament of Language, and the language of the Sacrament of Power is meant to be consonant with and accountable while not necessarily referring explicitly to the greater sacrament.

Agamben's notion of "Sacrament of Power" is not acutely developed. He may intend irony, given his assignment of it to politics. Given its de facto exportation into the realm of political theology, I take it as suitable for the temporal kingdom because it likens the governmental function via "sacrament" to churchly function while yet differentiating. It reminds of the promise that must not be made casually when a regime assumes political leadership. Political authorities in (the best of) theory take an oath to use language for communality more than for division. The oath is implied in the very speaking of language. Agamben's insight is profoundly philosophical and theological. Agamben has shared his thought with civic and religious leaders.[93] But no one can claim that the implications have trickled down into common speech and conviction. That language is revelation of God's intent for sociality requires much faithful further teaching. That the purpose of language in faithful teaching and in political leadership is to enact communion obviously requires further thought before constituting even a political campaign platform. But if it is true that secularity has functionally abandoned natural and higher law, then Agamben's definition of linguistic duties could suffice at least to cohere with the duty to minimize suffering. Agamben, meet Hart.

In the temporal kingdom, then, the purpose of Sacrament of Power language is that it be spoken and heard in the aspirational tones of communion and the healing of unnecessary suffering. This is the most natural ambition for raw temporal life. Our work in the temporal kingdom with that ambition will grow nearer to but never reach its final aim of freedom *and* beloved community vowed in the Sacrament of Language spoken in the spiritual realm. The vocation of temporal authorities is to speak so to protect their people and to preserve space and time for spiritual freedom. In my iteration here, God's intended vocation for the state of preserving human

---

93. Agamben, *Church and the Kingdom*; also, Agamben, *Coming Community*.

dignity (a.k.a. the *imago Dei*) then differs little from the original Augustinian and Lutheran statement of purpose. Proposed revision of the doctrine centers on recognizing that redressing suffering may be the new "natural law"—given the "original" natural law's evacuation—in the temporal realm for which the use of temporal power is divinely purposed. Into that, space and time has come and can come the moment when the Sacrament of Language happens. Agamben calls this the moment of messianic time, an intersection of human historicity and divine transcendence wherein if even but for an apocalyptic moment the human *knows* immediacy with God. To "messianic time" and Pauline metaphysics that commend Agamben's vision as real I will turn in chapter 5 after next exploring in chapter 4 the concept of sovereignty.

4

Sovereignty and the State

> Terms such as *sovereignty, right, nation, people, democracy,* and *general will* by now refer to a reality that no longer has anything to do with what these concepts used to designate—and those who continue to use these concepts uncritically literally do not know what they are talking about.[1]

IN DISCUSSING THE FATE of natural law in the previous chapter, I touched on the nexus of freedom, fraternity, and justice. One cannot ignore the relationship of all four of those abstract subjects. Indeed, one must also add the fifth element of human equality. The terms of the eighteenth-century French rally cry that have influenced all democratic impulses since—of *liberté, égalité, fraternité*—are mutually implicative; no one element can be enjoyed without the other. So, if we agree with Milbank's postmodern[2] recourse to Aristotle and Aquinas to retrieve friendship as integral to a just society as "something" of a "natural law," friendship/*fraternité* needs further attention.

Recall that friendship denotes "association." We are more attuned yet to the riches of the French slogan to understand friendship as "free association." "Friendship" of course in its popular take since nineteenth-century romanticism refers to affectionate closer human relationships. But its use here is political and affectively neutral. I can be a member of a "community of diversity" in which I don't have to "like" everyone in the community, but for the sake of the healthy continuance of the community I can and

---

1. Agamben, *Means Without End*, 109.
2. Whether or not Milbank is "postliberal" (and I'm not sure) does not affect this argument.

do regard every community member with respect. Respect includes our abiding by the covenants that formally constitute said community, in which we also agree that our personal freedom is relative to each other's wishes and needs. *Liberté*/freedom and *égalité*/mutual equality are essential in the covenant if the constitution of the *fraternité*/community is honored, which is, practically speaking, to live by it. Freedom, equality, community (or sociality) are never had on their own. They can only "happen" as identifiable parts when all happen together.

And so anyone, like Milbank, who assays the philosophical history of freedom discovers that the classic liberal notion of the free individual can only become self-canceling when absolutized. "Absolute freedom" includes an aporia. It cannot be. But to react (rather than to respond) as if its opposite is an absolute "community" reveals that as an aporia, too. Between neither of the poles of libertarianism and communitarianism can equality be realized and respected. It is either both and all or none, and each part in the "all" is relative; freedom, equality, and friendship are related to each other as identifiable distinct notions in a complex unity.

This complex unity may seem obvious, but, if so, it has been a hard-won realization. Our political memes are necessarily simpler if they are to provoke and rally a significantly sized following. In that process of psychological management of a population, one word must stand as a cipher for innumerable sentiments and aspirations. "Freedom!" when vastly shouted in 1776 meant freedom from burdensome taxation for some and freedom to hoe one's potato fields for others. "Freedom" meant respect for one's personhood no matter being a peasant in Reformation Germany and also meant freedom to worship and believe without a priest or pope saying how and what. "Freedom" has also become the justification today to impose one's moral universe on others or to privilege one constitutional covenant over another. Freedom's aporia has exploded into clarity in postmodernity. Its shrapnel are widely felt.

This discussion was conducted under a different primary term during the Reformation period. The term is still used and only recently has come under philosophical fire. The term is "sovereignty." To be sovereign is to have the freedom to do as one will. Free people—sovereign persons—learned that their personal sovereignty, believed to be both a Christian truth and a human right, could only be secured "relatively" by leasing it to another or others, whose offices finally might be recognized as institutions. In Western culture, this awareness did not happen manifestly until the Enlightenment. Before then we see that the concept of sovereignty evolved politically from the concept of Divine Right (excepting the limited Hellenistic experiments in democracy), ordering both the church and the emerging nation-state, into the eighteenth- and nineteenth-century movements that were more attentive to the *res publica*. In those centuries "sovereignty" was the key word philosophically and theologically for mediating its valence between human beings, the state, and God, no simple conversation. In all this, human equality and community are deeply implicated, too. In the thoughtful temporal kingdom "sovereignty" could never be a simple topic over drinks and cigars. This meant in the spiritual domain that saying that God appoints persons to political posts according to Rom 13 is unacceptably simple for the temporal philosophers. So, echoing again my abiding question regarding the viability of two-kingdoms thinking, what about "sovereignty"? It too was an essential consensus premise in the temporal domain to which the Two Kingdoms doctrine was correlated. Change in the understanding of sovereignty since the Reformation requires change in thinking about the Two Kingdoms doctrine also. Assaying how "sovereignty" fared in those centuries also might help explain why the doctrine was damaged since, especially in the early twentieth century. So to sovereignty we turn. In so doing, I will show why the understanding of sovereignty and statehood today do not cohere with the Reformation era's understanding

Sovereignty in a State of Flux

Sovereignty in political language today refers to a governing power's right to rule over a designated territory against the possible claims of other internal and external powers. A person's victory on the battlefield and ability to keep the loyalty of his military and financial supporters characterized the "right" to sovereignty of individuals throughout early history. In Greece and Rome this arrangement still held, though it was mediated by a Senate of prominent citizens who to some degree represented the *res publica*, the voice of the people. After Constantine converted to Christianity, the emperor's claim to a divine right was supported by the pope. The claim to a divine right to rule, linked also to primogeniture, characterized the investiture speech of kings and queens of the Western world from Constantine into the Reformation era. A ruler's ability to marshal a military, of course, helped sustain the usual claim to sovereignty. War-making, deal-making, and favor-dispensing garnered as much support as, if not more than, an episcopal blessing. Usually deals are remembered longer, too.

The formal bases for claims to sovereignty changed dramatically after the end of the Thirty Years War with the Peace of Westphalia in 1648.[3] Until

3. This is the conventional summary of the rise of the concept of sovereignty per Meckled-Garcia, "Sovereignty."

then, the formal authorizing sources for sovereignty were religious; the pope authorized the emperor and bishops blessed their "lesser" rulers. After Westphalia, the ruler of a territory set the religious brand. The prince's faith would be the faith of his region. This arrangement still had with it a certain scent of a claim to divine right. But for practical purposes, a secular basis for claiming sovereignty was now established; the prince, not the prelate, declared the faith, the spiritual authorities of which "in turn" affirmed his right to rule. After all, the prince was a de facto independent entity, recognized per the now operative Two Kingdoms doctrine as secular, yet with the duty to protect the freedom and rights of the spiritual realm in addition to assuring the relative freedom and welfare of his territory's citizens. Sovereignty was a secular given with some responsibility for the safety of the spiritual.

The origin of the idea of sovereignty is debated still. Luther had no such word in his head when he wrote to and for the temporal authorities. It is also unclear whether he had a somewhat parsed idea of it. As for any "Lutheran" speculation about the origin and legitimacy of temporal authorities, then, i.e., the purported sovereignty as such of princes and magistrates, Luther had no opinion. It is reasonable to agree that he simply accepted them, knowing no other temporal model of civil administration, and that they were included generally as "God-established" per Rom 13. Luther also reminded them of their God-given responsibility to care for the public welfare by the keeping of lawful order and relative economic freedom, seeing to institutions like schools and hospitals, any service that could maximize the public good. But unless temporal authorities were egregiously monstrous (Luther's own terminology), their decisions were to be unquestioned. If Luther had any idea akin to "sovereignty," it was of the sort that a plain and literal reading of Rom 13 would evince; to wit, God instituted government; all we know is this sort; it is what it is, and therefore must be obeyed.

It is easier to understand how practically useful Luther's iteration and application of a two-kingdoms political theology could be when all the players and political processes were familiar. The complex idea of sovereign rulers with sovereign nation-states did not yet affect the political conversation in the initial kindling of reforming fires. Basic authority structures were in place and framed the understanding of church and government relations. But that began to change even as the ink was hardly dry on Luther's treatises. Local alliances around faith and civil authority stances were made and grew. Languages and accents helped harden lines of identity. The conversational standoff at the Diet of Worms was theological, to be sure. The gospel was at stake! But factors of empire and local interests conflicted there too. Latin may have been the legal language, but German, French, and

Italian made their appositions felt. Finally, after the awful bloodshed of de facto nation against de facto nation, the 1648 Peace of Westphalia initiated what historians and scholars of international relations for centuries since have called the Westphalian Era, during which emerged the nation-state over against imperialism. It is as if Westphalia marked when the concept of sovereignty was born and the modern theory of the state took hold of public consciousness.

I name the concept of sovereignty as a problem for the Doctrine of Two Kingdoms for at least two reasons. First, numerous scholars today deny that Westphalia birthed the notion of sovereignty and that those who claim it did are guilty of anachronism. International Relations scholar Andreas Osiander[4] makes such a charge, asserting that the Westphalian origin is a myth invented by nineteenth-century historiographers and was irresponsibly Eurocentric, notwithstanding the fact that Jean Bodin[5] used the term "sovereignty" as early as 1576. Thus the challenge. If the concept of sovereignty was absent in the Reformation mind, one is hard pressed to explain why Luther accorded authority to temporal princes as God-instituted. That God is invoked clearly signals the dispensation of authority from one who is the highest authority, the sovereign. But this implies something that a committed secularist disavows or, at best, ignores, that the origination of the idea of sovereignty was at base religious.

Other arguments in favor of the idea of sovereignty as extant before or with Westphalia before the rise of the word's use are more compelling. Andrew Latham agrees that the formal term of "sovereignty" was the apotheosis of a long medieval tradition that speculated about the source and character of authority.[6] He summarizes how a *lex regia*—a kind of common law—was in use alongside the longer and stronger tradition of a theocratic strand. In support of the former, Julia Costa Lopez traces how various thirteenth-century legal debates about property rights were conducted and settled by authorities of varied statures and contexts. *Suprema potestas* and *merum*

---

4. Yes, Andreas Osiander is a contemporary, twenty-first-century writer with the same name as the Osiander of original Lutheranism. There may be irony here in that the original Osiander may well have known enough from firsthand experience to dispute the contemporary's claim that Westphalia's generation of "sovereignty" is a myth. See Osiander, "Sovereignty"; Osiander, *Before the State*.

5. Jean Bodin (1530–96), *Six livres de la république*, translated in Bodin, *On Sovereignty*. Bodin, while a constitutionalist, argued that absolute sovereignty was the defining principle of the state and that monarchy was the best way to assure the well-ordered state. It was his fear of civil war, like Hobbes's, that led him to lodge absolute power in the royalty, even though he also asserted that the natural family unit was the mainstay of social order.

6. Latham, "IR's Medieval Sovereignty Debate," 496.

imperium could be weighted differently; the local and "inferior" authority could have greater sway than a higher and distant *potestas*.[7] Politics could be local. Or not. "Authority" was multivalent, and jurisdictions could be more practically powerful than an empire with a different language base.

Religion mattered, too. Even the conceptual strand of sovereignty that accented the will of the people had still at its base the conviction that people bear the image of God, and by such a premise, their voice must be respected. The modern concept of sovereignty, then, was the result of a trajectory fueled by two sources: the direct revelation of God's will per Scripture and the indirect imprimatur of divine dignity on the human soul. From "heaven" and "earth," with God heard through text and discerned in the justification of temporal polity, sovereignty was conferred on magisteria from greater to lesser. One does not read of sovereignty so explicitly in the thought of Luther, but one cannot help but see it between the lines.

Put differently, the heretofore common concept of sovereignty does not represent a break with the emerging reformation tradition instantiated at Westphalia. Westphalia formalized the trend already long begun. This fact is lost to many today who insist that a progressive secularity alone should inform our political imagination. Latham notes that this is tantamount to an "odious essentializing" of a false dichotomy between progressive secularity and "backward" religion. Further, while we are obviously more secular in our politics today, the secularization is only superficial. Scratch deeper and one finds that theology drives the sense of sovereignty.[8] So, with reference back to my asserted first challenge regarding the very term of "sovereignty" and the Two Kingdoms, the theological basis on which Reformation era leaders depended for asserting a certain sovereignty to government authorities still obtains. Their incipient understanding of political sovereignty coheres with ours insofar as theology still informs our terms of statecraft. But this "insofar," this *quatenus*, today is another obvious challenge that will be extended when Carl Schmitt virtually invents political theology in 1922.

Back to Westphalia, however, again, though the term is not explicit, the concept must have been at work in its predecessor Peace of Augsburg in 1555. Many of us were taught that sovereignty and its relation to religious choice became concrete then with the slogan *cuius regio, eius religio* ("Whoever rules, so his religion"). Curiously, the slogan actually never shows up in the Peace of Augsburg document. The Augsburg phrase was "the right of reformation" (*ius reformandi*) that Protestant princes used in their lands. The idea of *cuius regio* antedated 1555. The idea was used at the Diet of

---

7. Costa Lopez, "*Merum Imperium*," 501–2.
8. Latham, "IR's Medieval Sovereignty Debate," 498.

Speyer in 1526, allowing Lutheran rulers to act as emergency bishops (*Notbischofe*). The first secular territorial reform actually happened in Prussia under Albrecht of Brandenburg, who, in 1525, transformed the lands of the Teutonic Order into a secular duchy, thereby breaking with Rome. This was not a full-fledged sovereign reform, but it shows that notions of what came to be called sovereignty were afloat well before Jean Bodin wrote about them and provided the first explicit naming and definition of sovereignty in 1576. The formal *cuius* expression first appeared in the late 1570s in the work of two Protestant lawyers, Joachim and Matthias Stephani. In sum, "pre-Bodinian" leaders spoke of the idea of sovereignty before using the term and the eventual fragmentation of Europe required finally both the idea and the term. All this is to say that if the concept of sovereignty was struggling to be born during the Reformation, the incarnation of the term itself fixed a political arrangement of authorities and nation-states that was always in dynamic debate. "Sovereignty," like natural law, would have a challenged life in which the practical political challenges may have had more agency than theological convictions.[9]

A Case History

So how might we know of what would accord with Luther's and the reformers' understanding of a secular ruler's sovereignty and associated duties? A case study that centers on the emerging consensus about sovereignty illumines how compelling the consensus already was early on if even the term was not yet so standardized. The case history regards the looming Smalcaldic War. Two ethical questions framed the debate and decisions that led to the start of this brief period of conflict (1546–47) between the Lutheran Smalcaldic League and the forces of Emperor Charles V. These questions, related to the classic principles of just war theory, were (1) whether governments should defend their citizens from unjust power exercised by other authorities, and (2) whether the oppressed governments could initiate a preventive war against the oppressor. The leaders of the Smalcaldic League, particularly Elector John Frederick I of Saxony and Landgrave Philip I of Hesse, saw that Charles V was making alliances with Pope Paul III and even certain Lutheran princes in preparation for battle against the Smalcaldic League that would overturn the Nuremberg Religious Peace of 1532.

Charles was preparing to turn back the clock to withdraw the religious rights and achieved autonomy of the now devout Lutheran regions. Luther, who had died the previous February, would have strongly counseled as he

9. Holm, "Conclusion," 515.

did rigorously before that only a monster could be resisted by his subjects. Luther had not concluded that Charles was such a monster. But, as of July 1546, these "lesser magistrates" thought differently. They believed that their religious freedom was at stake. Thus they saw it as their duty to invoke a case of confession—*in statu confessionis*—per the Formula of Concord (FC), Article 10.[10] Using two-kingdoms language, along with the obligation of church authorities to protest when the obligations within the spiritual kingdom are attacked, authorities of the temporal kingdom are duty bound to protect religious rights. The recognition of a "state of confession" in the spiritual domain called for the exercise of just war by the temporal domain.

Adding fat to the fire, the temporal authorities appealed to higher law—a legal synonym for natural law—to make their "secular" case. In other words, they used terms from the political sphere that were amiable correlates to terms of the religious sphere. These were, in fact, their correlative terms that came to be known in legal parlance as the "magisterial principle," that it was by "*natürliche und gesetze Rechte*" ("natural and legal rights") that in this situation "the bond between the inferior and superior is dissolved *jure naturae*." Further, the defender has the right to anticipate an attack in this situation, "for the Gospel does not forbid, rather it confirms, the office of government and law."[11]

The pretext for the initiation of this First Smalcaldic War was weighted on the side of higher law.[12] It also exemplifies how and when a two-kingdoms formula was employed early in its life. But we do recognize complications, not the least of which is that the Lutherans misread Charles's warring capacities, having believed that they could mobilize faster than he. They also could not agree on how and when to block Charles's movement of forces from Austria. The result: the League lost, some Lutheran princes submitted, John Frederick and Philip Landgrave were banned, cities were fined and occupied, though Bremen and Magdeburg still resisted and eventually successfully outlasted exhausted imperial forces.

This led to Charles's dictation of the Augsburg Interim, which only upped the ante for the Lutherans truly dedicated to the identity of the church and their religious freedom. Melanchthon's irenic disposition led him to accommodate to certain of the emperor's demands for change in

---

10. Recall this conversation in ch. 2 with respect to adiaphora and required resistance to any proposed requirement that would compromise the essence of the church, particularly as expressed in AC 4 and 7. Also note again the criteria for declaring a state of confession (*in statu confessionis*) as discussed in ch. 2.

11. Cited in McNeil, "Natural Law," 227. See also Larson, "Theology Confronts Wrongdoing."

12. See the discussion of Higher Law in ch. 3.

Lutheran practices, but other Lutheran leaders, led by Flacius, took a harder interpretive line as to what could be given up and what must be kept at all costs per Augsburg Confession 4 and 7 (which finally would be encoded in FC 10 in 1557). The Second Smalcaldic War, initiated in 1552, was based then again on the same reasons as the First, only this time the oppression of the "greater" magistrate was even clearer. Perhaps even Luther would have agreed. This time the Lutherans won. The official acknowledgement of Protestants was made in the Peace of Augsburg of 1555. Charles V then abdicated. It was with the Peace of Augsburg that the idea of sovereignty emerged with the compromise language of "whose rule, his religion" (*cuius regio, eius religio*). It looked like the Lutherans really had finally won. This, of course, was not fully instantiated until 1648, and then the unintended consequence was in fact the instantiation of the concept of nation-state sovereignty. If the Lutherans had won, it looked more like a nation-state secular-political settlement generated by religious affections, as well as the succumbing of empire to incipient nationalism.

The general point here is that the two-kingdoms principle was invoked and exercised in both Smalcaldic Wars. The finer point is that the concept of Higher Law was warrant enough to claim sovereignty about rights within a given territory. *Natürliche und gesetze Rechte*, particularly the right of religious freedom, inspired Smalcaldic leaders to rise above their mistakes in the first war to win the second. Higher Law was an explicit and normative criterion for what to do legally and morally, even when appealed to by opposing Catholic and Protestant interests. We should also acknowledge that "Higher Law" likely was used as a pretext for poor decisions with tragic consequences. It became a motivating slogan for the devastating Thirty Years War (1618–48) in which principle yielded to the lust for personal power. Like the motivations for the Smalcaldic Wars, that war began with claims for religious freedom. But it finally centered on who would rule, making the official state religion contingent on the person of power. Any theological and political dedication to the doctrines of Two Kingdoms and Higher Law must have suffered concomitantly with the familiar surrender of religious and rational principles to human bias and greed for power.

There are two more major consequences suggested in the case history. The Philippists' irenic disposition could well have led them to accept a sacrificial peace. Surely their own grounding in natural law, too, as part of their renewed excitement for Renaissance humanism, would ensure a path toward concord with reasonable people. But Flacius and his Gnesio-Lutheran party could not support this anticipation of Chamberlainism. They believed that if there were ever a time that required clarity and resistance, this was it. Charles's authoritarianism and Melanchthon's temporizing were unacceptable. This moment illuminated for the Gnesio-Lutherans what is at stake when natural law, as they saw it, intersects with the apocalyptic event of the gospel.[13] One cannot overstate this point. *Apocalypsis* is clarification. It is a revelation of an either/or situation that must be decided immediately, with no time for baroque reflection. Apocalypsis is the exigent moment when all is at stake and one must decide to resist or surrender. In this historic case, the Gnesio-Lutheran choice was the politically correct one so to secure Lutheran religious rights. And so Lutheranism is still with us. The Two Kingdoms doctrine's success in this case suggests to us that we could discern better when and how religion's voice should be sharper when politics otherwise would oppose the apocalyptic event of the gospel. Whether or not a temporal or spiritual question requires an apocalyptic redress is an essential criterion for any reframing of the Two Kingdoms doctrine, for at such moments it is precisely and finally the question of sovereignty that is in crisis. Further, the reframing will require the reclamation of apocalyptic as the distinctive language of the spiritual realm that must be differentiated from the flat dimensionality of Christian Dispensationalism's and Dominionism's misuse. *Ubi Deus dixit*.

The second consequence is more ecumenical than intramural. In addition to the genesis of the concept of sovereignty, the "magisteria vs. the state" outcome of this case history exemplified also the Augustinian principle that perfection in spiritual and civil things is impossible to achieve by mere human will and force. For the temporal realm, the Augustinian line toward pure sanctity is asymptotic; the trajectory of sanctification will get ever nearer, but never finally touch the finish line this side of the mortal coil. The best of Christians are still *simul iustus et peccator*, however better weighted on the former side than the latter we are. The Thomistic trajectory thinks itself as targeted for convergence. Often when considering sin, theological commentators today express a loathing of Augustine, as if his views, and Luther's also, on sin so awfully abuse the current psyche of humanity. But it is the optimist Augustine, and so also Luther, who with his limiting doctrine of sin (*non posse non peccare*) concluded that only God's grace mediated from the spiritual kingdom takes us totally beyond sin into God's pure beauty. This is a theological point of divergence from holiness movements and even new explorations in the Pauline view of sanctification, for which we can and should nevertheless exercise intellectual hospitality and personal respect.[14] But as for civil government, the Augustinian caveat here means

---

13. I address the character and renewed necessity of apocalyptic language in chs. 5 and 6.

14. As we will see in ch. 5 with considerations of Martyn and Jervis.

that government must and can do only its best to ameliorate sin's inevitable effects in the temporal realm without stepping into the spiritual realm's salvific role. The Gnesio-Lutherans' Smalcaldic decision exemplified that principle well. But it counters the Thomistic conviction that the enspirited attainment of pure righteousness is possible on the mortal side of eternity. This meant in Thomistic Christian practice that government should work with and support the religious establishment so to teach, shape, and ensure righteousness throughout the civic order. The natural law that governs the temporal world thus should accord with and intimately collaborate with spiritual rule. In that case the confluence of prince and priest would not be a surprise and its influence now ironically is felt and followed in nationalistic forms of both Catholicism and Protestantism.

Philosopher Giants on Sovereignty

All above suggests that the causes and consequences of not only the Smalcaldic Wars but also the later Peace of Westphalia are complex indeed. Natural and Higher Law were more than consequential as warrants for the emergent concept of sovereignty. This would set the terms for centuries as to how nation-states would negotiate their common interests and differences. All the leaders of the Reformation movement provided the religious impulse and theological groundwork for the concept of sovereignty. It was to the political philosophers like Hobbes, Locke, Mill, Rousseau, and Kant to reflect more keenly on the idea as they not only defined and justified the resultant nation-state, but sought diligently to define the difficult relationship then between the supposedly sovereign citizen and the supposedly sovereign state. This was the urgent philosophical task especially with the fracture of empire and the rise of the new nation-states with Westphalia, each of which now had their idiosyncratic "identity politics" at the collective level.

As the de facto summarizer of the unstated notion of sovereignty held by the reformers, Jean Bodin, the first to use the term and called the "father" of the modern concept,[15] actually rather muddied the term from the start. Jacques Maritain argues that Bodin's choice of "sovereignty" is a misleading translation and elision of two words, *principatus* and *suprema potestas*. For Aristotle the terms simply meant "highest authority," not "sovereign."[16] Bodin himself did not see the king as having supramundane sovereignty. He had in mind a *human* sovereignty that "submitted to the law of God and nature." The sovereign's duties then were to attend to the human moral

15. Maritain, "Concept of Sovereignty," 343.
16. Maritain, "Concept of Sovereignty," 344, quoting Aristotle and Aquinas.

laws and tribunals that themselves were derived from natural law. Bodin differentiated sovereignty in several ways. For example, sovereignty that was granted by the people may be lifelong for a named "*Majestie et Soveraigntie*" if the people have willed it. But a clear sense of contingency is embedded in the concept given the status of the people's will.[17] It can also be recalled if such a caveat was included at the outset of a sovereign's administration. And if the exact term of "sovereign" is not used at an installation of a governor, or magistrate and so on, that person is only that, an officer and "keeper of another man's power."[18] So the earliest explicated notion of sovereignty has with it a contractual quality. A human authority was a sovereign only if named so by the will of the people. And at that there could be a codicil that allowed the people later to act on their changed mind. And then there could be officials who were more easily recalled by the people's will, such officials having no stated status as "sovereign." It appears that in the early Reformation era, something rather like democracy was incipient in at least the nations of Protestant princes. And this not so much along the lines of what the religious tradition had bequeathed as what the new humanism was inspiring!

If democracy was nascent with the Reformation, in a certain respect it was quieted quickly in the thought of Thomas Hobbes (1588–1679), right on Bodin's heels. In his classic text *Leviathan*, Hobbes argued that every citizen of the new nation-state was sovereign insofar as every citizen was implicated in every decision of the titular sovereign, the king or legislature or dictator or whomever. Hobbes also subtly contradicted himself. He also wrote that the sovereignty of the prince/officer/magistrate/state was the consequence of each individual's willing transfer—a gift!—of personal sovereignty to the unaccountable sovereign and that personal obedience of the individual to the state authority was the replacement. Willingly to give one's sovereignty incurred the further cost of obedience, a once-in-a-lifetime deal. But the state/authority is in place especially to safeguard the people with peace, as protection from one another and protection from foreign enemies. This was Hobbes's political happy exchange, the first iteration of social contract theory. It is clear already, however, that if the people have given up sovereignty to an unaccountable sovereign, how they could continue themselves to enjoy sovereignty without a formal cyclical democratic system of "giving-up and taking back." The only meaningful way for the people in such an autocratic or plutocratic arrangement is to acknowledge

---

17. Bodin, *De la République*, book 1, ch. 8, p. 122, quoted in Maritain, "Concept of Sovereignty," 345.

18. Bodin, *De la République*, 127, quoted in Maritain, "Concept of Sovereignty," 345.

the religious normativity of the *imago Dei* to abide side-by-side with the political without any crossover.

John Locke (1632–1704) understood this problem. He did not share Hobbes's ease about the *vox populi* being taken from the people, repackaged, and then reified in the monarch/state at the expense of practical individual freedom. And given Locke's clearer Christian convictions (as we discussed in the previous chapter), he held to the dignity of the image of God in all persons, which includes personal sovereignty/freedom. Thus Locke further detailed a structure and justification of the state that included a hierarchy of contracts from the bottom up. The people rule through intermediary representatives, to whom the people have delegated their own authority. Sovereignty is nuanced in Locke's thought. The only absolute sovereign is God/Law of Nature. Then there is relative sovereignty, which is further divided into "potential" and "actual." Both of these are vested in the community, the heir to God's gift of God's image and God's protection after Eden. The community establish law for the common (i.e. common law). And the community structures and appoints the government, which is charged to carry out the law. It is this latter function that constitutes the actual sovereignty of the monarch/state. The sovereign is so, again, *insofar* as the sovereign acts for the good (weal) of the common; the sovereign is duty bound to see to the common wealth. Locke's genius, in sum, is a synthesis of theological, social, and political perspective based on a personalist concept of polity, like the hierarchy of authorities in a military structure, but appointed for yet more generalist duties of societal care. In sum, Locke worked harder to negotiate the conflict of freedoms of citizen and state. He improved on Hobbes, to be sure. But it is evident already that the aporias of natural law and freedom we recognized in the previous chapter have their impact on the notion of sovereignty too. That becomes yet clearer with Rousseau.

Jean-Jacques Rousseau's (1712–78) *Social Contract* is of a different character than Hobbes's "gift" theory and Locke's separation of powers. But Rousseau still was closer to the former than the latter. He argued that it is the tendency of a public's "general will" to promote liberty and equality, as both arise from a spirit of fraternity. Already one discerns a more optimistic spirit in Rousseau than in Hobbes. But because it is society that corrupts the original good in human being, the general will must prevail in such a manner as to govern itself as a whole sovereign citizen body. "I say, then, that sovereignty, being nothing but the exercise of the general will, can never be alienated, and that the sovereign power, which is only a collective being, can be represented by itself alone." Also, "the social pact gives the body politic an absolute power over all its members; and it is the same power which, when directed by the general will, bears, as I said, the name of sovereignty."[19] In other words, Rousseau asserted a monadic entity issued by the people that ruled over the people in the form of a monarch. I agree with Maritain that the idea is both nonsensical and actually inserts into a veneer of democracy an impetus toward totalitarianism, eventuating in "the Legislator" whom *The Social Contract* honors as a superman. Rousseau saw himself as giving the state imprimatur to Hobbes's religious impulse, writing, "the philosopher Hobbes is the only one who has clearly seen the evil and its remedy, and who has dared to suggest to unite in one single authority the two heads of the eagle, or *to reduce everything to political unity, without which never state or government will be rightly constituted.*"[20] Maritain's summary: "Rousseau's State was but the Hobbesian Leviathan, crowned with the General Will instead of the crown of those whom the Jacobin vocabulary called 'les rois et les tyrans.'"[21] It is no overstatement to summarize of Hobbes and Rousseau that they both were the modern anti-Augustinians whose aim was to abolish the Two Kingdoms doctrine. Political unity was their fondest goal.

It is important to note that Rousseau's charisma was at least as important as his Hobbesian substance and that his muse crossed the ocean with Jefferson, returning from revolutionary France to catalyze the colonies' declaration of freedom. The exemplary detail of Locke then could be said to have much shaped that new country's constitution. But if a totalitarian impulse snuck its way under inspiring populist rhetoric to embed with a well-parsed Lockian social contract, how long would it be until the hidden sovereign claims the absolute immunity that the founders had thought they preempted? What condition and shape of a preferred modest sovereignty could they have were they to have any sovereignty at all?

It isn't the case, of course, that Kant picked up on that particular question and wrote yet another treatise on it. But his impact endures too, especially with regard again to sovereignty and its relation to public life, morality, constitutional law. Kant seeks a path that mediates Hobbes and Rousseau, while he is aware, too, of Locke's positive influence. Kant routinely uses "sovereignty" with regard to the hierarchy of norms in reasoning. But he also makes clear that the highest sense of "sovereignty" is the autonomy of the human individual. About this Kant even passionately describes Christ as the exemplar for persons to fulfill their own autonomy, while Kant also

---

19. Rousseau, *Social Contract*, book 2, ch. 1, p. 119; book 2, ch. 4, p. 125, both quoted in Maritain, "Concept of Sovereignty," 352.

20. Rousseau, *Social Contract*, book 4, ch. 8, quoted in Maritain, "Concept of Sovereignty," 353.

21. Rousseau, *Social Contract*, book 4, ch. 8, quoted in Maritain, "Concept of Sovereignty," 354.

alludes to different states of dominion. He also here defines divine agency as the power of example for individuals to fulfill their own human agency:

> That is, by example (in and through the moral idea) he [Christ] opens the portals of freedom to all who, like him, choose to become dead to everything that holds them fettered to life on earth to the detriment of morality; and he gathers together, among them, "a people for his possession, zealous of good works" and under his sovereignty, while he abandons to their fate all those who prefer moral servitude. So the moral outcome of the combat, as regards the hero of this story (up to the time of his death), is really not the conquering of the evil principle—for its kingdom still endures, and certainly a new epoch must arrive before it is overthrown—but merely the breaking of its power to hold, against their will, those who have so long been its subjects, because another dominion (for man must be subject to some rule or other), a moral dominion, is now offered them as an asylum where they can find protection for their morality if they wish to forsake the former sovereignty.[22]

Kant mixes his signals as to the meaning and hierarchy of "sovereignty" in this above quote. Christ is explicitly sovereign. But we must believe so with respect to Christ as the definitive model for humans to follow, not as if Christ's agency alone redeems people and makes them by his work newly righteous. The works-righteousness of the previously pietistic Lutheran, and so its strong penchant for moralism, are still strong in Kant.[23]

How does this parlay, if it does, the concept of personal sovereignty in government? Common philosophical opinion is that Kant understands the legitimation of the nation-state's sovereignty similarly to Hobbes, Locke, and Rousseau, attending more expressly to the latter couple. Autonomy/sovereignty is freely given by the people to the state. The problem with Hobbes and Rousseau, however, is that it is exceptionally difficult for the people to wrest any autonomy back from Leviathan or that the transfer is too vulnerable to recall by a people quintessentially defined by *liberté* and *égalité*. In his essay "What Is Enlightenment?" Kant gives great weight to individual autonomy, seeming to align more with Rousseau. But in his later *Critique of Judgment*, Kant strikes a closer balance between personal and state sovereignty. Therein he describes the relationship of the citizen and state in a more democratic sense as a dynamic relationship of mutual debate

---

22. Kant, *Religion within the Limits*, 77–78.

23. Interestingly, this moralistic model of sovereignty morphs into Nietzsche's *Übermensch* and now fuels explorations of transhumanism.

and accountability.[24] "The people," though, is not just a cipher for an abstract entity of anonymous individuals. "The people" are the gathered individuals, each giving considered consensual voice in apposition and sometimes opposition to the also sovereign state.

In effect, Kant's polity is of a dual sovereignty in which the sovereignty of the people is lodged and enacted by their right publicly to challenge the nation-state. So we see that for Kant the state has a rational origin as the necessary institution that establishes the conditions for persons to realize their own full autonomy vis-à-vis other persons in political community without regard for their unequal possessions and/or threats of power.[25] The state, then, by practical necessity must establish consent conditions so to exercise its vocation of defending and coordinating the natural right of individual freedom. For government to meet this obligation to higher law under Kant's transcendental conditions of ensuring personal autonomy amid differentiated personal interests, legislators' devotion to the "general will" must override devotion to the identity politics of particular constituencies. Not all particular interests can be satisfied. But good faith in securing and maximizing as best as possible the general will of freedom can be satisfied. It is not just the utilitarian interest of the "most" to be met, but to serve the "least" (in its quantitative and qualitative meanings) also with decision-making and conclusions still in service above all else to the concept of "general will." This requires that legislators engage *public* reasoning unencumbered by would-be dominating partisan interests. Communication prior to, during, and post decision-making would be paramount, and not as bad faith, dissembling, and maskings of intent.

Stating again, a transcendental condition for the rightful authority of the legitimate state, in other words, is epistemic transparency. So Kant: "All actions affecting the rights of other human beings are wrong if their maxim is not compatible with their being made public."[26] It is not that such lawmaking simply is hidden from public debate, though that is wrong enough. For Kant, that the very possibility is denied for individuals to object that they could not follow the law without self-contradiction makes such lawmaking

---

24. Vatter, "People Shall Be Judge."

25. This is my synthesis of Kant's overview of a person's transition from the state of nature to the state of a nation-state. "It is true that the state of nature need not, just because it is natural, be a state of *injustice* (*iniustus*), of dealing with one another only in terms of the degree of force each has. But it would still be a state *devoid of justice* (*status iustitia vacuus*), in which rights are *in dispute* (*ius controversum*), there would be no judge competent to render a verdict having rightful force. Hence each may impel the other by force to leave this state and enter into a rightful condition." Kant, "Doctrine of Right," 124.

26. Kant, *Practical Philosophy*, 125–26.

illegitimate. As Kant writes in his famous "What Is Enlightenment?," a long-standard text for classical liberalism, "One age cannot enter into an alliance or oath to put the next age in a position where it would be impossible for it to extend and correct its knowledge ... or to make any progress whatsoever in Enlightenment. This would be a crime against human nature, whose original destiny lies precisely in such progress."[27]

Arguably the final founder of the classic liberal tradition with regard to personal and political sovereignty is John Stuart Mill (1806–73). The impact his *On Liberty* had on political consciousness is foundational and yet still not fully measured, though of course I here can only salute his significance. His core principles with regard to personal sovereignty are two. (1) Over one's own body and mind the individual is sovereign. (2) The only part of an individual's conduct for which he is accountable to society is that which concerns others. As for (2), the do-no-harm principle is normative within the parameters of the utilitarian ethic of maximizing happiness and minimizing suffering. Governmental authority steps in to ensure as maximally as possible the do-no-harm maxim. Because little conduct in public life is fully self-regulating, government must protect liberties. Harm prevention may not be sufficient to protect liberty, but it is necessary. Punishment thus may be a necessary second function.[28] Finally, it is not full liberty as such that Mill promotes. That would be self-canceling, as with the aporia that Milbank bemoans. Mill advocates for a limited liberty (and so sovereignty) of conscience, expression, aesthetic tastes, lifestyle, association.[29]

Mill's guiding light, we must emphasize, is that the individual would know and live with maximal enjoyment. This is not an endorsement of mere hedonism. Maximal joy is served by the attainment of inner and social peace; by fullness of bodily and psychic health, personally and communally; by the attainment of a mature aesthetic personally and societally with the arts, literature, technology, science, and other avenues, all of which would promote the virtue of responsible autonomy. Thus government also has the responsibility to provide institutions for its people to grow into the greatest understanding of themselves and their society so to exercise and enjoy their sovereignty.

How does government then garner its authority? Mill recognizes that the strongest connection between the normative utilitarian principle and a government that would operate on that principle would be a direct democracy. But he also recognizes that a direct democracy can only function

---

27. Kant, "What Is Enlightenment?," 57.
28. Mill, *On Liberty*. These summary observations are drawn from chs. 2, 3, and 4.
29. Mill, *On Liberty*, ch. 2.

well in a finely localized situation. A representative democracy, therefore, is the most desirable. A representative democracy must have epistemic transparency (like Kant's requirement) and expectation that representatives are fiduciaries of a public trust, not identity groups, sectarian interests, financial benefactors, and such. Further, representative government will be elected by the people (truly) on a proportional basis; parliamentary, as it were, not on a winner-take-all majoritarianism. This is one of the requirements on which Mill insists that individual rights would still be recognized. There can be no tyranny of the majority. He goes into impressive detail about the structure of federal government so to ensure this point, though the passage of time will always require more nuance.[30]

Mill rarely used the term "sovereignty." After his definition of the individual sovereignty over mind and body, he builds his political thought on a criteriology of what serves the utilitarian principle. Freedom and autonomy become the preferred terms and a government's authority is accorded by the people to their state only on the expectation that the government will serve the people's informed desires in an idealistic climate of epistemic transparency. The people's autonomy is such, then, that government authority can always be recalled. If the government is not sovereign (and Mill does not apply the term to government), its authority is always temporary and its leadership always of the servant type in aid of Mill's overall political ambition that every individual participate in the noble agenda of personal and social human progress. Note further that the utilitarian principle is sufficient as the inspiration and goad for society to arrange itself toward progress. As with Bentham,[31] the trajectory is one of reason alone; discerning from the real empirical data of lived, suffering, and joyful life is sufficient to build a government from and by and for the people. Natural law need not be invoked for this. God need not be invoked for this. The Golden Rule can be cited as a long-held proven slogan to kick-start reason's pursuits. Politics is but social analysis and theology would be irrelevant.[32] This thoroughgoing

---

30. Mill, *On Liberty*, all eighteen chapters of "Considerations on Representative Government."

31. See ch. 3.

32. Raeder provides an even more negative judgment than do I. She merits a full quoting. "Mill muddied the waters of classical-liberal philosophy and practice by his conviction that the end of government is the all-encompassing 'improvement of mankind' and not the preservation of individual liberty-under-law, as well as by his self-conscious embrace and advocacy of the 'social' moral ideal. Moreover, Mill's ambition to replace the theologically oriented society of the Western tradition with one grounded in and oriented exclusively toward Humanity necessarily entailed a departure from classical liberalism. For individual liberty-under-law, as historically understood in the West, is crucially and inseparably wed to the belief in a law higher than the

secularity informs a compelling ethics and political scheme. And still it has never worked, likely because Mill's critical view of human behavior could never be transcended by his insistent idealism. Mill represented much of the best of liberalism. But its acme was seen in the failure of liberalism and liberal theology to stanch the revanchism of fascism, which not even the revised language of God in Kant's system could hold back. So "sovereignty" both was gutted of respect for its religious moorings and then as a lesser term was seized for the idolatrous amplification of a particular land and bloodline of human being. It would require apocalyptic language to expose this massive conceit of modernity's sovereign self, which self was then claimed by the state with the words "I will protect you."

When Sovereignty Takes Exception

What stands out for my purposes here is the implication left to us by Latham, representing scores of writers in political philosophy, political science, and international relations, that the concept of sovereignty is inherently theological. Recent history shows this to be both true and ironically demonic. When Hitler used the idea of a theonomous basis for sovereignty as the hinge to turn the German church toward himself, he subverted the very core of Luther's understanding of Two Kingdoms. The philosophical inspiration for him to do so came from his nominal "chief" political philosopher, Carl Schmitt. A further demonic irony is that Carl Schmitt would not have done so so easily apart from his own reading of Kant. If the idea of God is a rational necessity for Kant but secularization with politicization has become the name of the game, then the transposition of religion into the limits of politics alone is exactly what Schmitt believed he achieved.

Carl Schmitt famously declared that "all significant concepts of the modern theory of the state are secularized theological concepts."[33] Schmitt is right. He does not mean simply that the religious language was transferred to the secular. He is more radical. He means that "God" as the original and only legitimate sovereign delegated God's sovereignty to the political

---

enactments of mankind, as well as to the sanctity of the person that derives from his or her source in God. In short, Mill's attempt to replace God with Humanity not only eviscerates the higher-law tradition crucial to the preservation of individual liberty and limited government but their spiritual foundation as well. For it is the transcendent spiritual purpose of each human being that, historically and existentially, engendered and sustains resistance to the pretensions of merely political power. When 'Humanity' is elevated to the ultimate source and end of value, the political rulers become, in effect if not in name, the new gods." Raeder, "Mill's Religion of Humanity," 4.

33. Schmitt, *Political Theology*, 36.

sphere. The more secularly inclined would object to this claim immediately and understandably so. But they/we should take pause.

What happens when individual human sovereignty, which every philosopher we've noted and more agree is a human attribute and therefore according to natural law or reason deserving of human rights (even if not "natural," per utilitarians like Bentham), is conceived only in temporal terms? The ideal, of course, is that personal ego would always take second place to the legitimate rights of the neighbor. This requires, as we've discussed, agreed-upon systems that enable healthy expression of individual and communal interests, trust in the systemic conventions developed so to protect and mediate interests, and obedience to the governing entities and their laws required to sustain and maximize the good for all, which also ensures that the minority whose interests are not met will still be heard and attended too, again, with all possible hospitality. Obviously, the character of such a government would be of the "servant leadership" kind; yes, an ideal. The ideal might be met on the rare occasion that a governing authority's character meshes well with the institutionalized system that put him or her in office. One might see such a model in the celebrated local relationship between Luther and Frederick the Wise. Maybe such a satisfying model was achieved in Calvin's still local Geneva experiment with a linguistically and religiously homogenous demography. One possibly could make the case that such mutuality of honored sovereignty was practiced in the Smalcaldic cities wherein magistrates and citizens were of common mind religiously and politically. In each very local context, the sovereignty of "the people" and the authority of the sovereign prince could be honored. It worked in the manner that Locke's personalist accounting could describe.

But this finally proved impossible in Berlin, London, and Paris. In those dominant new symbols of Western temporality, the emergent concept of the nation-state had both the geographical distance and human heterogeneity that rendered impossible the hope that "politics is personal" relationally and conceptually. Thus the necessary creativity of a Hobbes, a Rousseau, a Kant, a Mill, more, all of whose ideas informed the constitution of a new democratic experiment. Yet, however noble and ambitious the dream, however even successful for almost 250 years in the American test case, there has been and is always the danger of two destructive possibilities when the fundamental factor of individual human sovereignty is morphed into nation-state government.

The first possibility is that "the people" becomes the abstracted and depersonalized term that rhetorically legitimizes the institutionalized system of an autocracy or oligarchy, whether in a person or large system (today complainingly labeled as the "deep state"). Nobody cites Kant's correctives in capitol halls, though many are perfectly glib in pronouncing naive theology there. The "will of the people" may be measured at the polls. But sovereignty transposed only into statistics dishonors and even despises the sovereignty of countless heterogenous (the "other"!) individuals and identity caucuses. The practical reality is that the sovereignty of the individual simply disappears when transferred to the state with its obfuscating language mechanisms notwithstanding political philosophy's proven cautions and prescriptions. It will be an enigma to a particular ethnic group when one of "its own" aligns with a political party and agenda that historically had oppressed and denied justice to that very group. But if individuals really are sovereign, any individual has every right to the choice and deserves hospitable respect for doing so, at least until she denies the rights of any others.

The second possibility is that "the people" really do exercise a collective will, though it may be the groupthink of the crowd when inspired by the call of a charismatic leader, as when a Robespierre exploits the genius of a Rousseau. "The people" on their own demonstrate that neither anarchy nor communitarianism will succeed without long-lasting institutionalized norms that help manage a society's internal plurality and competing individual values. Without the mediating and necessarily complex "middle" institutions, as Maritain recognized, all we are left with is dispositions toward different totalitarianisms at both ends of anarchy or any-archy, whatever their conservative or liberal forms. "The Sovereignty of the totalitarian State is the master of good and evil as well as of life and death. [What is] *just* [is that] which serves the interest of the Sovereign, that is, of the People, that is, of the State, that is, of the Party."[34] In other words, when sovereignty is only political—which is precisely what Bentham argued with his denaturing of rights and what Rousseau so successfully marketed as *liberté, égalité, fraternité*—the individual and then the people lose it.

If the understanding of sovereignty is only political, strikingly parallel to law's being only positive, it also means something yet more dire. What we might call an innocent exportation of a foundational theory of human dignity from the individual to the state is itself a second exportation, having already moved from the religious to the secular. In effect, to move from the religious through the individual religious and secular person to the secular state alone is more than a simple and appropriate desacralization of the state. For the state to understand itself as sovereign is finally to replace God entirely by having denied the image of God—the sovereignty—in the individual person and whatever authentically self-willed collective voice "the people" may actually raise. To deny and attack the sovereignty of

34. Maritain, "Concept of Sovereignty," 354.

anyone—black, brown, gay, trans, non-Christian, whatever—is to deny and attack the sovereignty of everyone.

These are the initial steps of a state theologizing itself into its own solitary sovereignty. Whenever the state—whether as an individual executive, a complex oligarchy, or institutional mouthpiece of corporate capitalism—claims itself as truly sovereign, it claims its unaccountability to the people and God. It claims absolute immunity. It no longer coheres with any sense of the *res publica* (republic) or *demos-cratia* (democracy). In so being self-uprooted from accountability to history and to its people, in so being singularly political, the state dismisses and takes the place of God. Oh, it may still appeal to God, claim God's imprimatur on money and classroom walls, and ask for God's blessing after legislating presidential primacy. But here is the *telos*. When the state dismisses the natural law of neighbor care, it denies the image of God in its people while yet claiming God's appointed sovereignty. When the state dismisses human dignity, the state for the sake of its own enlargement orders the death of God even as it praises Him.[35] In contradistinction, the Doctrine of Two Kingdoms depends upon the premise that only God is absolutely sovereign and that the individual human being possesses the gift of relative sovereignty. Further, when the doctrine is taken with Luther's two seminal treatises on Christian liberty and Christian anthropology, one should get very clear that Christian freedom is *always* directed by the real needs of the neighbor personally and systemically, and that no person, not "even" the Christian, enjoys an exception from the influence of sin in body and mind.[36]

Carl Schmitt emphasized two principles for the legitimation of the Nation State and the reclaimed honor of the human individual. Most summaries of Schmitt neglect the human part of his agenda. But nation and the individual must align for Schmitt, and both under the concept of sovereignty, Schmitt's most important principle that he announces straight out in his 1922 publication of *Political Theology*. "Sovereign is he who decides on the exception."[37]

Sovereignty pertained to "the outermost sphere," where unprecedented questions arose because of the unique circumstances that generated them. So Schmitt's definition is much broader than at first read. It pertains to the unusual question that must be answered, to the unusual situation from which the question came, and to the creativity of the one who answers with a real and free decision. In fact, the decider who proves himself sovereign

---

35. And for the State, God is always "Him."
36. I have in mind Luther's "Freedom of a Christian" and "Babylonian Captivity."
37. Schmitt, *Political Theology*, 5.

issues an unprecedented answer even because he has recognized, named, and thereby created the unprecedented situation. Schmitt's definition is as exceptional as can be. It is not about a "one-off." True sovereignty must be as absolute as possible, without contingency, an "unnormed norm." The sovereign is by definition free of contingency. He is an unmoved mover, in his very being absolutely immune and unaccountable to counter forces. And he creates the systems to sustain sovereignty.

Schmitt intends his totalizing conception of sovereignty, immanentized in politics, to be ontotheological. Thus Schmitt's famed second principle is like unto the first: all politics are theologically driven. He firmly asserts this as his lead in to chapter 3. "All significant concepts of the modern theory of the state are secularized theological concepts."[38] This is Schmitt's second most famous and important principle. In other words, the form of modern politics (as of 1922) was not simply a developmental or evolutionary consequence of the history of religious reasoning about the nature and character of government authority. The disappearance of natural law that we have tracked, for example, was not merely a grand editor's striking of a trope. It was an intentional "denaturing" of a norm above all norms, making the writing and enforcement of law specific only to a given situation. Schmitt affirmed the character of law as attending necessarily and positivistically to particular situations. But he also insisted that theology was immanent and impelling in politics, even if the theological terminology was changed.

For example, over the centuries the all-powerful and impassible God becomes the all-powerful and legally immune monarch. The concept of the miracle in theology becomes the exception in jurisprudence.[39] Schmitt in effect argues that analogy is "more" than analogy. With warrant from Catholic Counter-Reformation philosophers, Leibniz, and especially Hobbes, Schmitt argues that the analogue is not just "like" its source, the source *drives* the analogue even as the source has receded from lively memory and been canceled as a spiritual reality claims. So "God" and "God symbols," though now materially gone, *actually* fund human social management. Even though no longer "real," the source motivates revised analogies and their justifications. Imagine what *this* means now for "originalism after God."

Schmitt, the conservative Catholic who gave up the substance of the faith, thus tracks and confirms the loss of transcendence in politics since the sixteenth century. Back then, God and the Bible were foundational for Western culture. Metaphysics and rationalism with their "discovery" of natural law characterized the seventeenth century. With the eighteenth,

38. Schmitt, *Political Theology*, 36.
39. Schmitt, *Political Theology*, 36.

the humanistic turn emphasized human dignity and moral virtue arrive. Economics came to dominate philosophy and industry in the nineteenth century in the competing voices of Marxism and capitalism. Per Schmitt, twentieth-century technology began to erase individual human dignity. Now in our century the Great Algorithm threatens to accelerate the erasure.

Schmitt's recognition of this history up to his day did not evoke from him an existentialist lament. In effect, he called rather for the restoration of the proud and strong human self-image—the image of God—to the hollowed-out political body. Resonating to Hobbes and Nietzsche and against liberalism's penchant for "discussion" instead of action, Schmitt promoted power. Real power, like the real decision made in and for a State of Exception, creates something from nothing. For example, if no president ever before had to demand immunity, a new figure who claims to be exceptional might name a theretofore unrecognized question about his nation-state and then proclaim the solution that re-roots the nation's identity. The sovereign is indeed radical. Wide-ranging action would be necessary, and so finally legislation and juridical fiat recognizes the exception, in effect declares a State of Exception, and thereby bestows on him absolute immunity, while yet the sovereign is connected to the legal system which he might need to suspend in part or whole.[40]

Schmitt yearned for smart leaders who would delay the ravaging political end of days, end-time resisters like Hobbes and Hegel, who would tame Christianity's tendency to encourage political rebellion. So he (contra his preference for church/state separation) linked religion to the state. Schmitt interpreted Paul's term of *katechon* in 2 Thess 2:6–7 as "one who holds" the coming apocalypse in check. Schmitt feared that last days were in store for

---

40. Before publishing *Political Theology*, Schmitt endorsed what he calls "commissarial dictatorship," that sovereign leader who would act in solidarity with the institutions and values that preserved and protected all citizens, because, otherwise, human nature is given to little other than mutual challenge and conflict. But not long after Article 48 with its commissarial tone was issued in 1922, order was not restored. Thus Schmitt saw the need for a sovereign who would create a new condition with a new constitution. Struggle would be required to establish and preserve a truly stable new order. See Schmitt, *Diktatur*. Indeed, Schmitt later would interpret the Trinity as the eternal struggle against each other of the divine persons. It is the Trinity's internal "struggle" that exudes creative energy for the life of the world in which human beings conflict as friends and enemies, ever creating new order out of chaos. And so his political anthropology was of the warring yet affable Strong Man type. It is impossible to resist noting that Schmitt's attempt to analogize the Trinity here rather contradicts the Augustinian notion that "the external works of the Trinity are undivided" (*opera Trinitatis ad extra indivisa sunt*). I never suggest that the non-theologian Schmitt's theological claims are sound, just as I note that Schmitt also wished that theologians would quit meddling in matters of the nation-state. He wasn't the church-state separatist he thought himself to be.

his country. He now added eschatology to the list of theological themes to be immanentized in politics. He argued that a strong man, a *katechon* himself, was needed for the people against the perceived existential threat to the nation. The substance of the Christian faith would not serve this purpose for Schmitt. Though shaped by conservative Catholicism, Schmitt himself abandoned spiritual faith for political form. Indeed, he confessed that he was an *alientor* over and against theology. A sovereign who himself need not be religious could serve as the *katechon*. A *katechon* could save a redefined Christian Germany from destruction and restore it with classical elegance. Schmitt invests the sovereign as the *katechon* with a nigh totalitarian power. To have the authority to declare a state of exception, after all, is not simply to make an occasional surprising and even anomalous choice, say, like suspending the right of *habeas corpus* so to win back a *United* States during a civil war. To always have the power to declare a state of exception is to put the *civitas* always within the anxious knowledge that everything could be different tomorrow, that all is contingent, on the decision and speech of the sovereign.

In so writing, Schmitt inaugurated political theology and framed it as eschatological. The question of the nature of eschatology itself was also renewed. It was no longer a strictly religious and theretofore usually esoteric doctrinal theological category. It was now theological, philosophical, and political. It would need to be addressed again broadly, deeply, and vigorously. This posed another challenge to the Two Kingdoms doctrine. Luther's vividly immanent eschatology was still lodged in the worldview of time as linear. That sensibility with respect to religion was given up by interminable impatience long before Schmitt and helped lay the grounds for eschatology's transmutation into politics. Politicized eschatology could inspire "realistic" politics. It would spur the Christian Realism of a Niebuhr and the generation of liberation theologies. But Schmitt's de facto final theo-political solution also raises the question of whether the spirit he thought he had restored to the hollowed-out political body had not actually furthered the hollowing.

I do not need to describe further the tragic consequences of Schmitt's support of fascism. Nor do I need to cover in any detail how the church was so compromised by Hitler's opportunistic use of Schmitt's political thought and reputation. Ironically, Schmitt objected to theological arguments that supported political hierarchism because he thought they were fascistic. His concern was to secure the order and stability of the state because without them society would fall back into the violent state of nature. His Hobbesian "realism" thus led him to support a strong man who fit the need of a sovereign.[41] Schmitt's juridical theory was coincidentally ripe for Hitler's picking, as was the people's need for personal "meaning," given that technological age's regard of them as ciphers. In sum, his concern to prevent the nation's fall again to chaos informed his "realistic conservatism," striving in his writing to inspire the return of strength, courage, valor, and purpose to a clearly identified people obedient to their sovereign because he loved and cared for them. His was a valuation that connected still with a society's previous respect of God and nature, whose and which laws would secure that society for a thousand years. His concern, the real economic and social problems which prompted it, his legal philosophy as answer, and the tragedy of a self-serving demagogue's hijacking of them are not unfamiliar a century since.

Agamben on Sovereignty and the State's Machinery of Language

The course just tracked shows that modernity could not sustain the differentiated unity of freedom-equality-fraternity. Liberal political philosophy could only think of sovereignty as a subject's control of self and world. As I argued, this ignoring of the necessary relativity of sovereignty to personal human dignity and community makes of sovereignty an aporia. As freedom absolutized finally self-contradicts, so does sovereignty when politicized. Not all persons can be sovereign if fraternity also is to be sustained, and so forth. Further, when each of the related notions are separated unto themselves, they imply their separation from all else. Friends without the covenants of freedom and community connote enemies. Freedom without equality and community connotes tyranny, as does also community without freedom and equality.

Further yet, each unto its own implies its own fracture. Arguably this is the least recognized damage done by modernity. The centering and ascension of the human thinking self above all else in modernity's unrestrained celebration of the individual made of the thinking self an observer of one's self even to the point of opposing oneself. Self against self! Or, more benignly interpreted, the thinking self ruled over one's extended self. "*My* body, *my* self as a self extended from *me*." In either case, the distinction of self from an extended or second self led to the philosophical justification of the state as the receiver of a person's sovereignty as a loan, ostensibly a loan to be called when the individual bank is unhappy. Let me be clear. That the Enlightenment's turn to the self meant and included the secular

41. Elert and Althaus used the same rationale in their support of Nazism.

formalization of individual human rights, be they natural or contracted, is among the most important celebrated moments in human history, be the state a person or a system. But the recognition of autonomy, epitomized by Cartesian dualism's *cogito*, entailed the unforeseen consequences of separating or ceding selves. This problematized the meaning of state sovereignty and the point of politics.

Giorgio Agamben addresses this challenge by rethinking the human being's situation as political. He argues that Western politics should not be defined by its typical friend/enemy pairing, but by the dyads of bare life/political existence, *zoē/bios*, exclusion/inclusion. "There is politics because man is the living being who, in language, separates and opposes himself to his own bare life and, at the same time, maintains himself in relation to that bare life in an inclusive exclusion."[42] An "inclusive exclusion" is a nuanced correction of the Cartesian problem I just outlined. Sovereignty here for Agamben is not the freedom of the thinking being from its extended being (which perhaps goes on loan to or is taken by the state in claiming its own sovereignty). Sovereignty here in the terms of "inclusive exclusion" is the self's stewardship of self, a subtle but consequential move. It is a stewardship of one's "bare life" with one's own wonderful voice (*zoē*) within the conditions of politics and communal language (*bios*). Popular terminology often speaks of one's own life and voice as "being authentic," but even authenticity is a judgment too often left to a public. A genuine life and voice can only be claimed and stated so by one's self. Agamben calls this—me, you the reader—the *Homo Sacer*, the self who being always self-possessing is never sacrificed, though the state is regularly so presumptuous as to kill selves figuratively and physically. *Homo Sacer*, the Sacred Human, is the self who might be killed but never involuntarily sacrifices.

Our humanity is now double-sided. My body is *mine*. Yet it also extends through all my relationships. My relationships include those I choose personally and all to whom I am involuntarily related if for no other reason than language. We communicate. Speakers and hearers, writers and readers grow connections at light speed. Language simultaneously frees and binds. The liberation is into truly mutual understanding, authentic self to authentic self. Language's aim is, ultimately, communion. Language is the medium and mediation of my extended self, my "body." I am doubled as a bare/authentic life with my own sweet voice. This double is doubled again as a body extended into other bodies by the givenness of language, being a person under *logos*. Already doubly-doubled as authentic *zoē*, I am emplaced necessarily by language also as a political self, *bios*, ineluctably being

---

42. Agamben, *Homo Sacer* (HS), 8.

impacted by all other relationships as well as the relationship of relationships called the state. I cannot not exempt myself fully from this *fraternité*, not even if I were to stake a life deep in the woods, unless somehow I were born without a public identity, delivered into life by myself as my deliverer, to exist without language. I cannot not be *known*, if even only minimally, if even God were dead. Others chosen by me and simply just situated and implicated in my life by taxes, votes, and the avoidance or waging of war, the state itself: all have a stake in me as my extended body. All the public side are my *bios* self, my political being, which does have an integrity to it and having an integrity, belongs to my stewardship of myself. Which is the point. When the usual economy says I steward those things to which I relate and am related, the truth is that I am stewarding myself. And so my personal responsibility to myself is compounded immeasurably. And the care of my "self-investment" is thus of ultimate urgency. I steward myself. Even when and despite when the state presumes to steward me, while yet I do need the state insofar as it serves the purposes for which it is made—freedom, equality, community, and so justice.

Agamben discerns an ontology for my—our—doubled-identity. It is an ontology implied by the fact of language. And not just language, but that language is lively, that its purpose is to connect and distinguish extended selves in our ever-new instantiations and differentiations. In other words, though Agamben does not say it quite *this* way, Heraclitus is right and the more things change, the more language must bespeak potential rather than the past and the less helpful will be the received understanding and practice of sovereignty. For Agamben, sovereignty is related to ontology. The long-accepted ontology since Aristotle is that actuality is of greater value than potentiality. But if sovereignty really does cover everything as Schmitt desired, and not just matters of positive law, then sovereignty would result in an actuality that negates all potentiality. In such a modern reception of sovereignty, the result is inevitably tyranny. Agamben sees instead that the only way to free up the possibility again of the truly authentic life, *zoē*, is to demote the state's political "sovereignty" at least back to its initial iteration of servanthood (my term). But still we must recognize that, even when sovereign power is given willingly by the people to an executive function, this still threatens every political ordering including democracy. An historical-philosophical relationship of democracy and totalitarianism must be acknowledged as the threat against which to guard if a new politics is to be found that heals the fracture "between *zoē* and *bios*, between voice and language."[43]

---

43. HS, 10–11.

A moment is required to flesh out what such an acknowledgement entails. Agamben tracked the division of personal real/biological life (*zoē*) and a politicized/way of life (*bios*) back to the Greeks who excluded *zoē* from the political space, confining it to the home (*oikos*). In other words, Hellenistic philosophy settled on a keen distinction between the rights and private "authentic" life (*zoē*) of human persons and the rights and public life (*bios*) of persons as constitutive of the state and over which *bios* the state claimed some responsibility. Political life, life with language/*logos*, for the Greek was all about the public. This was the limited purview of the state. Today the state sees both *bios* and *zoē* in its purview. Now the state no matter its form is innately totalitarian in exactly the way that Hannah Arendt had defined totalitarianism when it is explicit. It happens in today's ideological manifestation of statecraft and definitions of rights that, increasingly, birth is the argued condition for full citizenship. Agamben turns to the reality and the metaphor of the camp as that place where the state takes further control to remove people from their own *logos* and so then to rule more facilely with the "politics of the living dead."[44] Camps—to which I would add prisons and jails—have become the biopolitical form for "curating" who is the true citizen. They are the state's concentrations of those who might receive asylum, who might be legitimate refugees, who could be legally scapegoated for society's violence, and who should be stripped of all identity. The camp, that place once in the limen of legally defined society, now is at the center of the nation-state domestic and foreign policy discussions. The figure and the reality of the camp is no longer even a "hidden paradigm of the political space of modernity" and "the hidden matrix of the politics in which we are still living."[45]

Agamben recognizes this. In effect, he calls the situation of the state and its claim of sovereignty for what it is. Its claim to sovereignty is the state's claim of purview over all expression of thought. To exercise this sovereignty, the state, in league with technological capitalism, pretends to be the voice of the people for the security of the people. To do this, Agamben observes that the state builds and employs a machinery of language. The state can use the machine to promote community, which is honest immediacy to each other and to transcendence. This is what I summarized in chapter 3 as that positive use of the Sacrament of Power that strengthens human orientation to the *Logos* and positively complements the Sacrament of Language, the font of unrestricted reason, honest speech, and deep community with diversity. Or the state can choose only that aspect of the Sacrament of Power that

---

44. Norris, "Giorgio Agamben."
45. HS, 123 and 175.

ignores its duty toward the greater Sacrament of Language and thus separates its people from *Logos*. History and the deformation of philosophical structures that support good government, like natural law and the notion of sovereignty, show the preponderance of nation-states choosing the "lesser sacrament" that in its "promise" to its people binds them in a negative way. It is the machinery of language that separates and subdues. It is the bad faith use of Agamben's named Sacrament of Power.

Žižek describes this function of the state as yet more deleterious. As exemplified in the COVID-19 global pandemic, the state is perceived by the people in the most basic way as an authority structure functioning as a neutral space to manage the competing interests and conflicting notions of freedom of its people. This neutrality is an illusion. But it is a "real illusion" codified in the judgments of administrators, legislators, and courts and instantiated in "a series of material social and ideological apparatuses from education to health."[46] The executive will declare exception in the name of "freedom" and the "will of the people" by mandating that face masks cannot be mandated. The court will opine with final authority that the executive insofar as he is formally the executive is immune to the law he must enforce. And then a legislature can write new law that severely restricts the public's ability by vote or otherwise to change the picture, while a majority of the public applauds that such will be in their interest because they "believe" in the "neutrality" of the state, and the state will perdure insofar as the people's collective subjectivity is so controlled. An impressive machinery of language instructs, in-forms, deepens, and expands the whole ruse far beyond the Potemkin Village strategy that initially conceived it.

Still, Agamben, with many more like Žižek, Nussbaum, and Caputo,[47] holds to a certain hope. Nations almost always practice a "politics of the past," depending on the metaphysics of causal agency, i.e., what we know from history. Much of this penchant is based on an ontology of causal agency supporting a false primacy of nostalgia. Agamben's proposed revision to serve his hope is of an ontology of potentiality over actuality. Likely without knowing of their theological impact, he resonates to theologians like Pannenberg and Moltmann who argued for the causal agency of the eschatological future over our temporal present. Like Jüngel, as well, Agamben considers the implications if potentiality were to have priority over actuality. What could sovereignty mean if it were wrested from the absolute normative status of the political, if sovereignty were no longer the question of who or what within the political order had the final answer, if what is

---

46. Žižek, *Freedom*, 95.
47. Nussbaum, *Political Emotions*; Caputo, *Weakness of God*.

actual is not the dominant form and substance of the potential? What *does* sovereignty mean when it is associated with the priority of language, which service is always toward potential, the potential of community *and* the authentic bare life of the *Homo Sacer*?

Thus the rationale for Agamben's statement at the outset of this chapter. The state is legitimate only insofar as the state allows and avails avenues for its people both to engage potential (to become more than their conditioned selves) *and* to achieve and enjoy the immediacy of language as a community. If other than this, if the state transmutes sovereignty into its self-aggrandizement, it only presages its final dissolution. Agamben instead founds his new politics on an ontology of potentiality. Only in this way can we conceive of a "political theory freed from the aporias of sovereignty."[48]

Gathering Strands

In the previous chapter I argued that the vacuation of the significance of natural law in the temporal realm meant the vacuation of "God" from the secular realm too. Though the lazy response could be and has been that we should "put God back in the classroom," God's apparent suspension from school is not the material issue. Hosting a back-to-school event for God would not change the intention of the Two Kingdoms doctrine anyway. The doctrine meant and still means to pair in a positive dialectically constructive way the realm of spiritual truth with the temporal realm of pluralistic secularity. In the realm of secular pluralism, wherein language is the only means to sustain and deepen societal coherence, practical "universal" convictions like the Golden Rule, natural law, and individual human sovereignty over one's own body and mind could and would still guide public life. That Kant and his epistemological heirs "saved" religion by placing it in a closet of subjectivity beneath the stairs of public traffic is not the root problem.

Nor is Kant even as the hegemon over modern Lutheran theology the only scapegoat for having so confined faith. That line-up is thick and long since Hume. What is "real" can never be fully defined because wherever I go there *I* am. The claim is that I always impose my history and my subjectivity on the external world. Critical realism, per the Kantian criteriology, is the only epistemology I can have. It has served well. But it also meant that language finally not only turns to the self, but turns on itself. As Agamben argues for a metaphysics of potentiality before actuality, so also he prioritizes *Logos*—originative language—over knowledge. This is a radical counter to the Enlightenment's eventual consequence of anti-metaphysics.

48. HS, 44.

If no metaphysics beyond the strictly phenomenal and critically rational are possible or allowed, language itself can be only entropic. At some time, having philosophized itself into its own closed system, language, and so knowledge, denies funding from a suprarational world. If the possibility of philosophical metaphysics is rejected, if even there is a "there" there beyond the self of which no one can reasonably speak, then language itself is merely self-referential. What then is that but the fall of language into only politics? What other than the cynical embrace of temporality to the resigned exclusion of all else? What is this other than the fall to totalitarianism?

If Agamben's correction to Kant's longstanding court is taken in fullness we agree that there are sources of and for real language, and so legitimate knowledge, that have been disallowed as evidence. Bentham's proscription of "natural" and "revealed" makes sense in a total positivist language system for a totally temporalized worldview. Consequences have been dire. Lying has always belonged to the tactics of politics. Hannah Arendt reminded us of what temporal authorities have always quietly known, that lying *as such* is not even denounced by religions. Textualism leads us necessarily to the conclusion that religion disallows "only" false witness. One can drive any size of government through that loophole. Most government has been so driven. The consequence? "Neither the truth of revealed religion, which the political thinkers of the seventeenth century still treated as a major nuisance, nor the truth of the philosopher, disclosed to man in solitude, interferes any longer with the affairs of the world."[49]

Language then is but the tongue of politics that lies to preserve what it can only have temporarily in temporality. If lies are at least as much the stuff of language as truth, then to what can even legal textualism and originalism refer and how much further will it devolve?

Western culture's source and size of knowledge has been shrunk and hardened. To be sure, since philosophical positivism's quieting, existentialism became normalized as a welcome corrective. Jungian therapy has mainstreamed, and the authority of the shaman in aboriginal cultures receives keener interest from anthropologists. But for insurrectional cosplaying, however, none of this yet influences political party platforms. Western culture's prefrontal cortex has hardened to regard only critical reason as the only conduit for real knowledge, as if there are no other kinds of knowledge and no other ways to "know." But we know of other sources, and so other ways of knowing. Which is to say that language is deeper and broader than we conceive and practice. Hamann succeeded in making this point against Kant, but yet has not been adequately heard. Hamann's compelling case

---

49. Arendt, *On Lying and Politics*, 15.

against Kant was that Kant dissociated reason from history and sensible affective life. Different modes of knowing, including the mystical, need not be dismissed as fideism.

Poetry, music, and visual art surely speak from an intimate knowledge into another person's intimacy. The arts even have their own specific science to explain their structure. But they can never be reduced to simple arrangements of energy in motion among themselves. Nor can their communication beyond themselves be adequately explained only as waves of sound and light. Reductionist language cannot account for the immediacy of a larger supernal knowing that happens when a certain perfect choral resolution of notes achieves overtone and raises both the hair on one's neck and one's theretofore undiscovered emotions to sublime attention. Reductionist language cannot address aesthetics and it must even yield to prayerful silence when the event of meaning is so large that it cannot be contained in words. Oxytocin is inadequate for complete explanation of spiritual experience. Critical reason rightly denounces epistemological reductionism about matters in its own purview. But critical reason also has denied a greater scheme of things. If critical reason instead affirmed a greater scheme, an actual ontology, it would be forced to concede its own reductionism.

Christian theology has suffered the same fate as critical reason. It is by now a long-rehearsed confession, but nevertheless bears repeating. If for no other reason than to sustain its job description as faith seeking understanding (*fides quaerens intellectum*), it was necessary for theology to affirm and adopt Enlightenment principles. But it did not need to reject the epistemology of communal intersubjectivity, its catholicism, when it recognized the dignity and importance of the individual. Conversely, theology need not have sacrificed the spiritual integrity of the private person so to be accepted as critically reasonable. Lutheranism's greatest systematic theological error is its having affirmed Kant's removal of revealed religion from his newly installed canon of pure reason.[50] Hinlicky tracks a direct line from Kant's isolation of the individual from the communal (from catholicity) to Ritschl's accent on the church as a concatenation already of atomized individuals. The line extends through Harnack and Troeltsch's de facto reduction of theology to ethics, all in the name of liberalism, all in the cause of denying the possibility of metaphysics, all to commit the unforced error of suspending eschatology so to stay reasonable, finally to have little with which to resist the manufactured faux-apocalyptic language of Hitler.

Liberal theology's mirroring of Kant's reduction of Christ to a paragon of ethical humanity is stunning. Christ is the totemic exemplar, a practical

---

50. Hinlicky, *Paths Not Taken*.

example, a (!) paragon of ethical humanity. Christ is "inspiring" as the model of moral life and what trappings still adorn him are but to keep his profile high and encourage individuals (!) to "be like Christ." Clearly, the sovereignty of Christ is compromised by this line of thought. Pope Leo's astute recognition that der Führer's claim of messiahship must be countered by affirming Christ as the only Sovereign (and so the insertion of Christ the King Sunday into the liturgical calendar) was on point. But it was too late. Catholicism's long-standing enmeshment of church and state would prevail. The Barmen Declaration was of course correct, too. But Protestantism's domestication of Christ under Kant's moral hegemony already had practically isolated Christ's sovereignty from the commons, already had separated the Two Kingdoms such that the mutual accountability of church and state was morphed into the subservience of the former to the latter. That was not a difficult goal for the Reich to meet when the church itself no longer knew itself as the visible embodied presence of Christ, *Christus praesens*. When the church instead treats Christ as our historical example and inspiration, at best waiting for us at the end of human time's arrow, when the church is mindless about its own *being* as Christ's present body, it negates its ability to *act* from its being. It trades its *communicatio idiomatum* for deism. It is then prostrate before temporal powers. It is not how Paul meant the faithful to obey the temporal authorities.

Christian liberalism did not recognize its self-canceling language until Bonhoeffer demonstrated the courage of faith in Christ's sovereignty present *to* our temporal lives and Barth shouted his famous "No!" to liberalism's illusions of kingdom building by temporal standards, including illusions of political sovereignty. In any language, and implied in Agamben's Sacrament of Language, sovereignty can only belong to God. If sovereignty is to distinguish any human being it must distinguish every human being, and that only as the consequence of a Sacrament of Language graciously given from beyond every human being. This conviction must be held in both kingdoms or else in neither. In this new era of post-Westphalian illiberalism, voices like Agamben's recognize that sovereignty has lost its substance. The loss, however, is not only because of philosophical dissensus. The loss is not even due primarily to positivism's overreach, though that is a major mistake. The loss of sovereignty's meaning is due to the avoidance of ontotheology, the turn away from *Logos*. *Logos* was the active agent for being for Hellenism and for Christians. This is Agamben's answer to Heidegger. When language/reason is separated from *Logos*—or as I would rephrase Agamben, when the temporal use of the Sacrament of Power separates from its parent tongue of the Sacrament of Language—political language can no longer point to a purpose beyond its own words. The language of the temporal, of the political, reduces then further from the governing authorities who speak from the Sacrament of Power for the cause of relative peace to those who constrain and lie by that Sacrament of Power toward their own negation.

Tied to *Logos*, language reveals. Separated from *Logos* and constrained by temporal myopia, language dissembles, lies, controls, all so that the self-serving power of a few is fed by the many. The whole epistemic and metaphysical debate has been dictated by what Heidegger calls the ontotheological structure of our Western language. The structure is inescapable. Schmitt recognized this. So he rendered the final concretion of the conversation as only political in which the religious terms were imported so only to remind us of their absence. After Heidegger, there is only the political greater than which could be no other while its own language was built on the memory of the ontotheological. Agamben agreed with the problem, but argues that the political has its origin and inspiration still or again (!) in a language region that is indeed other and greater and "there" just beyond the edge of temporality. Judith Butler criticizes Agamben for carrying forward Heidegger's totalizing frame.[51] She thinks his focus on sovereignty is too narrow and too controlling of political analysis while also in the thrall of the agenda set by Carl Schmitt and Hannah Arendt. But she didn't (or doesn't) recognize that Agamben did move forward finally by decrying the received concept of sovereignty and its machined malignity. And then, as we shall see in the next chapter he moved on beyond sovereignty to where Butler still would not go.[52]

In this history of ideas that I have followed, I have indirectly acknowledged that the language of the Western religious worldview (i.e., monotheism) has controlled political philosophy. At the risk of overstating, political philosophy's options while remaining in that language game include endorsing religion and then finding a way humanistically with theology to respond. That would be a modestly postmodern strategy. The alliance then can react against the notion of the domineering God, or accede to religious hegemony, or venture on the postsecular path of a "return to religion" wherein the apparently smallest potential can transform what is actual to beyond critical rational imagination, a zone where the butterfly changes Tokyo's weather, where the recognition of God's weakness makes all the difference, and where language can and does reveal to senses beyond the critically reasoned a realm of truth to which we had been opaque. Happily, theology has within its own language select terms which can release it from its post-Kantian captivity. That zone for theology is known as eschatological.

---

51. Butler and Spivak, *Who Sings the Nation State?*, 36.
52. See the fine analysis by Dickinson, *Agamben and Theology*, 53–59.

The language that reveals it is apocalyptic. The structure that enables it is catholic, *katholos*, according to the whole wherein we human subjects are meant to be intersubjective.

I propose that eschatological imagination and apocalyptic language suitably confirm and fulfill intersubjectivity in a postliberal understanding of life in the spiritual kingdom. We must rethink eschatology and apocalyptic and their pertinence to the Two Kingdoms doctrine. Agamben does not speak precisely to either. But he does suggest a new way of understanding life in the spiritual kingdom that coheres with eschatology and apocalyptic that will have payoff for our temporal lives too. Agamben questions the human image that we humans ourselves have constructed with the "machinery of language." How does Agamben envision liberation from the machine? He answers that there is potential that trumps actuality. Potential presents itself in the contingencies and softest voices of life. Here tempests and whirlwinds of yield to the quiet intersubjectivity of creatures with their creator. *Logos* suddenly enters our time and space from its distinctive time and space. A new time, at least for a time and then a time again, enters human *chronos* by its own gracious initiative, not by human force, and offers by its speaking the Sacrament of Language the potential for *homo* to be *sacer* without the threat of injustice. This different time, a time testified by Paul of Tarsus himself, is not like *chronos*. By its surprising presence it is even more promising than *kairos*. It is a time when messiah speaks from his time into human time with words that can only come from messiah's time. Agamben calls this "messianic time." It is a qualitatively different time—a different time "zone," as it were, of which Paul himself speaks and, as Agamben discerns, Messiah brings but for a moment, repeatedly, always available for our seizing, always with the potential for us to realize new life.

To engage this potentiality theologically is to entertain the prospect of renewed eschatology, with which cosmology now coheres. The spiritual domain's language for renewed eschatology is apocalyptic, the medium in which Paul wrote. Opaque to the modern mind also was something Paul touched on in his apocalyptic way, what Agamben calls "Messianic Time." To meet Messianic Time is to welcome for its moment a goodness in bare life that can change politics for the temporal better until Messianic Time irrupts again, and then again and again into the fullness of the eschaton, when eternity suffuses temporality. To this potentiality we now turn.

5

Paul's Eschatological Politics

"For as the heavens are higher than the earth, so are my ways higher than your ways and my thoughts than your thoughts."
—Isaiah 55:9

WE KNOW THE SCRIPTURE texts that are most relevant for the Doctrine of Two Kingdoms. I've alluded to them. Now we turn directly to them, having gained some understanding of how Augustine and Luther read them amid the politics of their days and given their respective eschatological imaginations. Romans 13:1–7 is central to any conversation on the Two Kingdoms doctrine, especially v. 1: "Let every person be subject to the governing authorities; for there is no authority except from God, and those authorities that exist have been instituted by God." This text arguably has regulated Christian civic life more than any other text since Paul wrote it, though it is commonly supported by references to Matt 22:17–21 and John 18:36: "Give therefore to the emperor the things that are the emperor's, and to God the things that are God's." "My kingdom is not of this world."

It is an understatement to suggest that people on the street when quoting these texts link the texts' seeming plain sense with original intent. But popular interpretation also, as it were, plants a national flag next to the cross as the symbol set of two different worlds come into one common mind. But the placement causes dissonance, too. Conflict breaks out between those who insist on the dyad and those who defy it. A surface reading of the book of Revelation then competes for equal billing with the surface reading of Rom 13. Deeper readings of both reveal, as they should, deeper dissonance. John's Apocalypse condemns empire while Paul's civic-mindedness would seem to abet it. Yet the popular reading of Revelation does not see its condemnation of empire while the same popularists approve it smoothly with dependence on Rom 13:1–7 as well as 1 Pet 2:13–17.

Romans 13:1 is the preferred proof text for unquestioned nationalism, oft quoted from pulpits and prayer breakfast rostrums. The prooftexters read this passage as if Paul extrapolates as we all routinely do from the temporal arrow's flat trajectory; as if he means: "Christ is coming soon. Stay awake for his coming. Wait for it. And while you are waiting, just respect the governing authorities. They will be done soon enough." This is but greeting card advice to "hang on. You'll be okay." This is temporal eschatology in only the one dimension of length; history as one arrow flying that has not yet met its target, its literal last thing, its eschaton. Romans 13 does resonate with Paul's eschatological imagination, but his is an eschatology with dimensions far beyond a line ending with a period or perhaps a semicolon. Paul charges his readers to remain awake to what they have already seen: a life together even in the civil realm that is embraced by the presence of messiah and his kingdom. Those who are awake to this *manifest* enfolding already of history into God's life and rule are called to action. We are not called to act as an act of our own will and strength while waiting for messiah to come. We are called to act because we already are acted upon. It is this that in-spires and en-courages us to respect secular authorities out of respect for the kingdom that already has come and a divine will already done. Creaturely temporality may again prevail, as we are accustomed. But it is not the last word. Messianic time can and will enter again and again until it need enter no longer. Having been taken hold before, having been awakened, we stay awake for the next coming of messianic time; awake for, as I would put it, the next more evident coming of God's kingdom in Christ into the kingdom of this world. Until it need come no longer. Until Augustine's vision of the City of God has so suffused the Earthly City that all humanity's eyesight beholds it 20/20.

Eschatology frames Paul's political counsel. And eschatology for Paul means much more than speculation about "end" times. Eschatology is "now." For those with the ears to hear, that makes the epistle good political news. It also means a world of difference for how we understand and live the Doctrine of Two Kingdoms.

Romans 13 and Contemporary Interpretation

How can good news be shared in empires of exception and when empire sets the communicative rules? To put a finer point on the matter, how is the church's message to be said and heard if the message of a church that is separate from state should sound alien to today's politicized ears? The secular and religious public expects invocation of God with country. It also expects regular stated blessing of country by God. The usual audiences are unable to welcome counsel based on an eschatological exegesis of Rom 13. There is much that we must help relearn about "God and country."

Over the past forty years scholars have gained much new insight about Romans and Paul's overall work with the "rediscovery" of eschatology and apocalyptic. What Stringfellow[1] intuited is now made clear decades after him by scholars of the Pauline letters. They have rightly reframed our reading, reminding that it is not Rom 13:1 that determines the meaning of the chapter. It is the eschatological penumbra of the chapter that shapes the reason for and the meaning of Rom 13:1. This shift, incidentally, further supports Luther's own caveats about this section of Romans. Pauline scholars and continental philosophers also have surprised readers by placing Paul again at the center of literary and political theory. Adding surprise upon surprise, it turns out that the very nature of time hinted at by Paul, too, has become a favorite philosophical topic even apart from its long-discussed place in the philosophy of science. "Time" is now a significant topical thread throughout Pauline commentary. Time—temporality—is thus also a priority for our reconsideration of the Two Kingdoms doctrine.

Consider tone and context. Paul wrote this section of Romans in the second-person plural. He presumed his readers' collective identity as the *koinonia* in Rome, even as his audience was but an aggregation of house churches, each with its own ethos. He wrote to them with a keen and yet unmet aspiration to visit them personally. He saw himself in deeper relationship with them than regular folk because of their mutual bond in Christ (Rom 1:4-6). He knew them already as of the beloved community, the body of Christ. With an urgency that could only be generated by such profound spiritual intimacy, by the time Paul began writing his thirteenth chapter he had exhorted his readers to live in harmony with each other, to practice humility, to turn away from revenge, to care for the enemy as one would care for a friend, and to do good even when it would seem natural to repay evil with evil. Such exhortation is hardly trivial when troops coaxed by Nero are standing by and ready to do ill.

Recall that Nero was another self-proclaimed god who had no time for the gentle political atheism of Christians. Instead of regarding him and the state above all else, Christians lived by love and conscience rather than the code of emperor and empire. That code respected and worshiped the

---

1. See ch. 2.

emperor above all else. Christians instead respected everyone as a bearer of God's image, as objects of God's love, and so subjects with divine-ordained rights. For Christians to love and respect all others notwithstanding others' scruples and idiosyncrasies (Rom 14:1–23) was no simple lifestyle. The challenge was amplified and the danger to Christians greater as Nero's shadow of the state in his narcissistic image loomed large over them.

Paul understood this. Yet his exhortations to Roman Christians were not original to him. His counsel reflected Jewish teaching (e.g., Wis 6:1–3) and his urgings cohered collegially with apostolic teaching (1 Pet 2:13–17; 3:13). Paul, Peter, and others were on the same page of the same script. Yet Paul also underscored Jesus' own words that the authorities who must be obeyed in this world have no jurisdiction in Christ's kingdom, as it is "not of this world" (John 18:36). Pauline paraenesis itself was an ad hoc and apt application of Christ's second great commandment. Scholars acclaim this as a paradigmatic instance of the transreligious natural law that we know as the Golden Rule, "Love your neighbor as yourself." "Love does no wrong to a neighbor; therefore, love is the fulfilling of the law" (Rom 13:9–10).[2] We don't know that Paul was so delicately parsing natural law in comparison with God's revealed law of love. We can infer that Paul, who knew the Stoic as well as the political philosophy of the day, knew the natural law as enfolded already in God's higher law.

Evidently Paul was comfortable in his conviction when writing Romans that Nero's administration presented no real danger to Christians. Perhaps this made it easier to regard Nero as a neighbor. Had Paul known what Nero would do later, would Paul have been so demure? It should not matter, particularly if it is the institution of government which the person represents that is to be respected as established by God. Even protest when necessary implies respect for the office. The book of Revelation four decades later would symbolize Nero as the oppressive apocalyptic monster, representing the evil of empire against Christian faith. Nero was an amoral narcissistic tyrant, no question. He was his own "state of exception," and he reveled in it. His willful chaos during Paul's writing may have stayed within the lines of Roman executive privilege. Not until near his death did Paul perceive that Nero was an egregious authoritarian who used Christians as false flags for his own evil deeds.[3] In sum, when Paul wrote Romans he did

---

2. Bornkamm, *Luther's Doctrine*, recognizes Christ's love commandment as a localized iteration of "natural law," too.

3. The story that Nero blamed Christians for burning Rome was written later by non-contemporaries and cited in a letter of Pliny the Younger around 110 CE. Then, without fact checking, Tertullian repeated the story, which went viral after its retelling again by Tacitus and Suetonius. See Harrill, "St. Paul," 285–89.

not think that obeying the authorities would pose temporal problems for his sister and brother Christians.[4] And, again, it was the office more than the person for which he counseled respect and obedience.

Paul understood government's purpose as promoting good and punishing wrongdoing. And so he acknowledges the need for civil law, the necessity to support government with taxes, and the need for trustworthiness of the economy beyond formal government. "Pay to all what is due them—taxes to whom taxes are due, revenue to whom revenue is due, honor to whom honor is due" (Rom. 13:7). Paul even seems to speak more plainly about this than was Jesus with his own wry answer to a question about taxes. Jesus' answer had two parts; first was the question of whose picture was on the coin. Then Jesus said to give Caesar what belongs to Caesar (Matt 22:21).[5] Jesus' answer here left much room for further questioning. Paul's admonition did not.

Simple declarative sentences invite more opposition than do rhetorical statements. Readers of Paul have questioned him ever since he advised unquestioned obedience and respect. Did Paul really mean to be so final and so summary in this preciously concise exhortation, only then to turn to much more about personal behavior in the verses following Rom 13:7? Was Paul really so stoic about Roman administration? Was Paul politically credulous and "just didn't know" how evil can hide behind politicians' smiles? Or did Paul know that Nero was a real-life test case for the radical call to Christians to love the neighbor as oneself?

Nero was a fiend. History shows it. As we know, one-and-a-half millennia later Luther and his followers included an escape clause for when government broke bad. They said that social protest was appropriate when temporal authorities abused their position and their constituents. Personal protest was not affirmed. When individuals were unjustly treated, they had to take it, instead fully trusting in God for deliverance in God's time. Violent protest by the abused community as a rule, however, was not affirmable,

---

4. There could be a question here as to whether other contemporaries of Paul did see danger in the political order and so argued for a cautionary discernment that Paul perhaps here lacked. That would be another way to read 1 Pet 5:8, the language of which is otherwise strikingly consonant in its tone and content with Paul's grammar: "Discipline yourselves, keep alert. Like a roaring lion your adversary the devil prowls around, looking for someone to devour."

5. John Howard Yoder in his *The Politics of Jesus* was of the earlier liberation theologians in the Anabaptist mode in the twentieth century to write of this deliberate ambiguity on Jesus' part, offering the perspective then that this text addressed idolatry. Commentators since often read this as Jesus and the Synoptic writers (diplomatically) speaking against empire, but the standard interpretation more aligned with Paul seems still to hold.

though adjustments were eventually made for the redress of egregious wrong. But Paul does not concede anything on this point because the person of the emperor was not Paul's point. The *institution* of governing authorities is the point. It is the *institution* of government to which Paul urges obedience. Every person is subject to the governing authorities because God instituted the governing authorities, i.e., governance. Note that Paul did not exhort Christians to take over the government or even to inhabit government where and when they could, as if a Caesar would make such appointments. "How" government even comes to be is not a question for Paul. It just is. It is "instituted" (*tetagmenai*) by God.

The popular understanding of individual appointment to governance has strong Old Testament roots, of course. But for that very reason Paul's choice of *tetagmenai* commands further attention. It correlates with 1 Pet 2:13, where Christians are encouraged to "accept the authority of every human institution" (*hupotageite*). The root word for each concerns a "mechanism," or "ongoing process," an established way of doing something, which here is for the public good. It is an enduring process, and so it is an "institution." We therefore infer that God "institutionalized" government, that God established processes by which societies cold survive and thrive. God instituted institutions as the temporal means to preserve and promote common good. In 1 Peter, government clearly is an institution meant for human beings. It is on the basis of divine institution for the cause of the public good that government is good, worthy of trust, and should be supported. We do not have other New Testament cues about the origin, character, and necessity of human government. But in these instances of a shared and uniquely chosen lexicon of *tetagmenai*, we have a compelling cue. The Roman and Petrine epistles agree in their use of the same root word. Individual appointees are not in the mix. Luther could be happy and exceeding grateful to God for Frederick of Saxony and quite nonplussed about Charles V. We don't know if Luther thanked God for appointing either. We know amply of Luther's exhortations to obey governmental authority as instituted by God. We know too how and when the exception proves the rule. The exception to be resisted and corrected is when selfish rulers intentionally harm the people in their domain.

The distinction between individuals and institutions may not make much difference to us when it becomes manifest that wrong people administer right institutions. We put "faces" to institutions. Having grown weary after so long a while of wrong faces we easily yield to the temptation to remove both the face and the institution. But God is about promoting the common good and established government as God's mode of divine providence. It is consequential that *God* instituted government and commanded human beings to steward the ecology of it all. God did not appoint (which would be a wrong translation of *tetagmenai*) Nero. We cannot say that God is so politically micromanaging. Notwithstanding Old Testament wording that so often is used to supersede New Testament insight, the New Testament speaks differently about God and government. Nowhere does the New Testament indicate that God directly appoints individual persons to individual positions of political authority. Stringfellow reads this even further to say that God created and creates the "powers and principalities" including governing institutions. Like humankind created by God, the powers and principalities too may go wrong, for which they should and will have their own accountability.[6] God's providence is not deployed as a politics of puppeteering.

Yet Paul was not passive in the face of authority, and he was not a political naïf. He played the political game when he needed to, as when he informed captors that he was a Roman citizen and so must be freed on his own recognizance. It is not even the institution of governance that is the ultimate point. When one accounts for the yet broader context in this climactic chapter of Romans, Paul says that respect for the institution of government is urgent because it conserves the necessary machinery to serve the common good. And yet there is an even more important reason!

Paul also observes that God has given a gift for "the time being" so that politics might be redeemed and fulfilled. Government is the gift. Government is for "the time being." In the time being, government sustains and perhaps even extends the human space and time needed for to stave off final judgment and prepare for redemption. Government is a *katechon*, implying that government's vocation includes its role as the defender against disaster, to serve providentially as a preserver of the status quo against all threats of destruction, especially if the destruction threatens the freedom of the gospel. And so government ironically is the delayer of the coming kingdom precisely so that the coming kingdom may arrive to a people who (finally!) have been readied for the arrival. It is a Paul, whose vision is sparklingly eschatological, who counsels Christian patience and endurance of the present government principalities and powers so that we would be ready rightly to welcome the coming kingdom, irruptions of which are already known.

It's About Time

Whence Paul's eschatological eyesight? One adds error upon error to suppose that Paul counsels simple institutional obedience because he

---

6. This is a unique insight by Stringfellow that I discussed in ch. 3.

was neither eschatological nor apocalyptic. Quite the opposite, Paul is a sophisticated eschatologist as well as a winsome apocalyptic linguist while also technically adept in his writing. In concert with the Gospel writers, Paul's vision is of a larger dimensionality of time that *already* enfolds human temporality. Paul's eschatological appreciation is not unique to him. What he knows suffuses the language of the Gospels. The Gospels announce a reality other than the temporal. Jesus throughout the Gospels speaks with an apocalyptic discourse that witnesses to spiritual reality already present that contradicts and challenges the banal unreality humans believe and have constructed as ultimate. I note first Mark's "mini-apocalypse" and its coherence with Mark's recounting of Jesus' passion and death. Then I note briefly other Gospel "apocalyptic" accounts with Paul; all this as a fulsome New Testament apocalyptic univocity as to Paul's eschatological imagination.

In the "mini-apocalypse" of Mark 13, the disciples ask about the end of everything. Jesus answers not with a prediction, but how to live now. Like Paul's call to "wake up," Jesus says to be alert. Be alert. The master will come when Jesus is handed over to the authorities. Be alert to when the sky darkens at the crucifixion, for then Jesus will be seen "on the clouds" (Mark 14:62). These are non-literalistic Semitic tropes for seeing Jesus in what is unseeable to the world.[7] Look to the subtle in the daily routine. Hear the wind's differing pitches in the different sizes of fluttering leaves. Look also to those times like the present when injustice happens, as when the Son of Man is handed over to the temporal authorities. In such familiar times too the Son of Man will appear in solidarity with the faithful! Jesus' answer to his benighted disciples is that he comes not in temporality's terms of power as with larger sword, but as the eschatological lord who already has the last word of grace that transforms the world.[8]

This brings us to the question of just what apocalyptic language is. Apocalyptic language, as in Mark's "little apocalypse," is not a prediction only of something yet to happen. Apocalyptic language is not relegated to temporality's flat arrow, nor of this temporality's terms of cause and effect, action and reaction, loss and compensation, bad deed and "karma." Jesus' kingdom is "not of this world." Those who unsheathe swords to defend

---

7. Alison, *Raising Abel*, 145. Alison argues that most, if not all, the New Testament witness is to the risen Christ's solidarity with the victim. Alison speaks to something like a "continually re-realizing eschatology" under the terms of the Theology of the Cross (though he does not assert this Lutheran methodological connection). But I disagree with his conclusion that the word "apocalyptic" itself should be sequestered from proper Christian speech. I'd rather reclaim its meaning and aim toward it with as much poetic imagination as can be mustered.

8. See Caputo, *Weakness of God*; Caputo, *Cross and Cosmos*.

him are. Jesus adjures the fantasy of self-justification enacted in retributive violence under secularity's terms.⁹ Though popularizers of such titles as *The Late Great Planet Earth* and the *Left Behind* series call their language so, theirs is not apocalyptic according to the biblical norm. *None* of such human projection is God's plan. None of it is truly apocalyptic.

Regrettably, like many important terms, popular culture has appropriated "apocalyptic" as the placeholder for magna-dramatic end of world destruction. Rather, apocalyptic language is about supernal truth telling, about disclosing the really-real against the machinery of language and its unjust consequences. Apocalyptic language is the evocative inspiration of God's Holy Spirit into human speech, promising and already realizing the promised reconciliation of all creation with God. Apocalyptic language belongs to the new language of the gospel of grace apart from any prospect of human work spoken or physically acted. Amos Wilder elegantly puts it this way: "It was the novelty of grace and the fundamental renewal of existence which brought forth a new fruit of the lips, new tongues, and new rhetorical patterns." Further, the gospel "was also creative in all that it has to do with image, symbol and myth. Here, too, the substance of the faith brought forth a new liberation of speech evident in its prodigality of imaginative vehicles."¹⁰

Apocalyptic speech is the en-couraging word of Christ about how to live amidst the thick destruction of the human and inhuman powers and principalities that simply will happen, despite which faithful people will live anyway (if not literally) because the risen crucified Christ is with them. This is the gospel. This is how and why Jesus exhorts his disciples to be awake and alert to the presence of the victim so that we may go out to meet her. This is why Jesus speaks apocalyptically, "to train the disciples with respect to what must be their deepest eschatological attitude: the absolutely flexible state of alert in order to perceive the coming of the Son of man, the one who is seated at the right hand of God, in the most hidden and subtle forms in which, in fact, he comes."¹¹

This eschatological attitude with the rhetoric of apocalypticism is a real knowing unlike the lesser rationality to which modernity would keep us in thrall. The gospel's apocalyptic rationality is new wine that cannot be carried in Kantian skins. So Amos Wilder: "Our congenital modern demand that such language be rationalized must be resisted, as well as our readiness

---

9. Caputo, *Cross and Cosmos*.
10. Wilder, *Early Christian Rhetoric*, 118.
11. Alison, *Raising Abel*, 149.

to put all such forms of knowing out of court."[12] To be sure, we must still use all the critical tools at our disposal to clarify Scripture's "original intent" and so responsibly to correlate such intent for the current day. But transposition from "then" to "now" never frees entirely from the heteronomy of "then," and so cannot by definition be fully apocalyptic. Apocalyptic language/imagery instead when yoked with eschatology "breaks into" the closed worlds of human speech to capture us anew. Wilder again makes the point:

> We thus vindicate the intrinsic importance of the early Christian rhetoric in its aspects of imagery. The new myth-making powers of the Christian movement meant more than an overthrow of rival myths and more than a liberation from letter and from law. It meant the portrayal of the real nature of things and of the course of existence so far as human speech could encompass such mysteries. Comparing lesser things with greater, we appropriate the myth and symbol of the New Testament by opening ourselves to its wisdom in the same order of response with which we encounter art or read poetry. Though this order of knowing is closer to that of ancient spell or visionary realization, or the world-making of the child, yet it is, for this very reason, a total and immediate kind of knowing and one that involves us totally.[13]

Returning to the Gospels' apocalyptic alignment with Paul, we see them make the same point repeatedly. Jesus himself uses familiar language in a new and evocative way so to lead his followers from the rule of death to unimaginably new life. In Matthew, Jesus' parables use familiar daily life tropes to undercut and overturn routine human understanding, revealing a gracious God whose will of love will establish a theretofore wholly unimaginable kingdom and include the most commonly unexpected people. This in turn leads people to realize that they who judge are judged and in need of as much mercy as those whom the elites had marginalized and condemned. The winsome revelatory language of Matthew, in other words, is a proper apocalypse of God's democratic society of forgiven sinners. The theme is similar in Luke, albeit with Luke's stronger political illumination of those who will be graced by the coming of the Son of Man (e.g., Luke 17 and 21), when the "risen victim will be the principle which illuminates all of human history and reality."[14]

---

12. Wilder, *Early Christian Rhetoric*, 127.
13. Wilder, *Early Christian Rhetoric*, 127.
14. Alison, *Raising Abel*, 150.

In John, finally, the Son who came not to judge becomes the resurrected victim and criterion by which the murderous mechanisms of society are judged. And so the Johannine apocalypse is about the judgment that inverts the social norms, heralding a coming hour when indeed the dead shall live. The good news is not only about all who have fallen "asleep." It is for those whose lives have been dulled to death by the inexorable social systems that starve one set of citizens so to feed the depravity of another set; of commanding those who sit at the head table to stand off so that those who had no tables at all may finally be rightly honored. And yet all will eat, for apocalypse means God's banquet for all when all inhuman biases finally are removed. All this, too, is apocalyptic language for those who discern the presence of God's time here and now. Apocalyptic language is for the en-couraging of eschatologically sighted disciples to remain faithful, and so also, finally, joyful.

So, what is apocalyptic language? It is language that tells the truth. It reveals the time of divine grace, the substance of eschatology, that already is at hand. Apocalyptic language also bespeaks a new and different kind of time not at all similar to the time we know from day to day. We are familiar conceptually with time as *chronos*. We are familiar with another kind of time theologically as *kairos*, what Paul introduced as the gift of an opportune time. Physicists and cosmologists also speak of multiple dimensions of time that Paul, of course, could not anticipate. But Paul does allude to another kind of time, a "remaining time" that is different from *chronos* and *kairos* and would not be negated by contemporary cosmology.[15]

In fact, Paul had a particular sense of time in mind to which he exhorted his readers and hearers to stay awake. In 1 Cor 7:29, Paul refers to "time remaining." This time is not merely what seems to be left of an unconcluded linearity, as if we thought we finished a race and then are told there is yet more to run. "Remaining time" has its own integrity, its own pregnancy. This "remaining time," a certain time apart from many other unique temporalities, is, to understate it, special. This is the time to which we must awaken (Rom 13:11). This is the "remaining time" full of its own promise for the fulfillment finally of divine dreams. More than about obedience to government, more than about righteous behavior and morality, Paul writes so that his unmet readers would jump to action under the spiritually existential urgency of this utterly unique and gifted moment. He writes revolutionarily with a new recognition of the characters of time, advocating now with the zeal of the theologically converted about the present priority

---

15. I will discuss later in this chapter.

of a particular kind of time above all else. He writes so that *this* time—this time remaining—would transform and norm all quotidian Christian life.

This time is not a reprise of a time like other times. This time is metaphysically different. This qualitatively different time, which means the end for now of human common time, calls for the response of a new praxis of daily honoring and loving. "Besides this, you know what time it is, how it is now the moment for you to wake from sleep. For salvation is nearer to us now than when we became believers. . . . Put on the Lord Jesus Christ, and make no provision for the flesh, to gratify its desires" (Rom 13:11–14). This time, the time long pleaded, this time has already come. And this "now time," this new time, which is the end of banal time, has reframed everything public and personal. This is a new and particular "now time" within the time that we thought was the only time, that only time of remembering and waiting and repeating. Now *this* time has broken into our time and now waits for us who have been waiting to grasp it. This new time waits for us who have been dully waiting to make something of this new time, to appreciate its eschatological ultimacy and hear even in our hearts its apocalyptic address. Imaginations have been wearied by their captivity to modernity's reduction of Christian faith to a docetic life "as if" (*als ob*) the distant model of Jesus were consequential. Rather, Paul heralds real, exceptional consequence. The only real state of exception is Christ who was crucified, raised, and as true sovereign exercises the law of love as revealed in his church, the Beloved Community, and the exceptional Christ with his kingdom is graspable in the gift of the "now time," the remaining time that is qualitatively wholly other.[16]

In Rom 13:11, Paul writes, "Besides this." The phrase is not simply a convenient transition. Nor does it signal an afterthought. "Besides this" is an amplification. It is an up-ramp to a more important point. Like when "by the way" in a personal conversation is understood to mark why the conversation was even had, "besides this" leads the reader to the central reason why Christians should obey temporal authorities. It is because "we know what time it is." We *know* that *this* time is the time to "wake up," to be proactive in light of the coming dawn that has already come, this new time being so unique. This time requires energetic honoring of self and others, not dissolution and ennui. This time now known means us to don the party clothes of righteousness for the new day, leaving behind the shreds of cynicism and hopelessness of too long a night. This time calls for wearing him

---

16. Hinlicky's synthesis of several philosophers, and particularly Agamben, is on point. See Adkins and Hinlicky, *Rethinking Philosophy*, 200–209.

who already wears us (v. 15), for welcoming and telling of the owner who has returned to those he had left to care for all he loves (Mark 13:33-37).

Roughly two-thirds of the brief Rom 13 concerns Christian public life. The final third, vv. 11-14, is about the urgency of "the moment." Do not mistake the chapter's compactness for an interlude within the majestic whole of the letter. Here is a light from within the epistle by which to understand the import of the whole. On this point Paul is far from passive. The irruption of messianic time into Paul's personal *chronos*—many have call his Damascus Road encounter a mystical experience—changed Paul's imagination from taught and habituated to eschatological. His new vision compelled him to become the faith activist who exhorts the church to live messianic life because messianic time revealed itself.[17] This means for Paul that living the messianic life is a life for the temporal world, not against it, and not to overwhelm it. Thus Christians should honor and respect themselves by honoring and respecting others. Pay taxes. Be fair. Respect. Do so in the new messianic key. In this way Paul advocates for the well-being of the heterogeneous (multicultural) *civitas* as much as he cares for the unity of the ecclesial *koinonia*, though his immediate audience of the would-be faithful in Rome needs more attention for the moment.

By now we should understand that eschatology and apocalyptic mark the Christian difference from the temporal political world and so also instructs Christians how to relate to this world. The "how" involves a threefold criteriology. (1) We are the Lord's. (2) The Lord's time of reign has begun, has come, and comes repeatedly by God's gracious initiative into the time of the earthly city. (3) Therefore, Christians are called to live as the very anticipations of the coming kingdom by practicing respect and mutuality *now* with each other in the spiritual kingdom and with all people in the temporal kingdom. We do this as sisters and brothers in the ecclesial *koinonia*—the beloved community—and we do so for the good health of our neighbors, including those who exercise authority in either realm. We also do all this urgently because of *what* time it is. This is a qualitatively different time that has broken into the accretional dulling of quantitative time. Being attentive to this differently dimensioned time, we recognize that we are summoned to messianic life and that when positively answered this messianic time qualitatively changes us.

---

17. Welborn, *Paul's Summons*, loc. 108 of 2549.

Messianic Time and Messianic Life: Retrieving Critical Density

Messianic time and messianic life are two key markers for how Giorgio Agamben rereads Paul's Letter to the Romans in his consequential book, *The Time That Remains: A Commentary on the Letter to the Romans*.[18] Derived from a series of seminars in Europe and North America, the book may first strike the reader as a linguistic analysis of the first ten words of Romans. The informed theological reader understands that we bring our own horizons of understanding to the reading of a text even while the text has its own sometimes inaccessible horizons of understanding (Gadamer). There can be no such thing as original intent when we read Scripture, which is also to affirm that Scripture is alive to God and to the times. Neither does Agamben avert to an inert text of but one meaning. Rather, while necessarily dressed in culturally and time-bound language, there is an aspect in the language of Scripture that points beyond itself.

Agamben goes deep into textual and literary analysis with his reading of Paul. But do not think thereby he looks to uncover a naked universal truth. Agamben discerns the horizons upon horizons to infer something quite more. Paul uses several forms of Greek based on knowledge of Hebrew so that his writing and consciousness is not quite Hebrew and not quite common Greek. Yet, Agamben discerns in Paul more than the linguistic uniqueness.

Paul's "Greek," in sum, is an evocative blend unique to him. "Being neither Greek, nor Hebrew, nor *lashon-ha qodesh*, ["the holy tongue"] nor secular idiom, is what makes his language so interesting."[19] Agamben intuits that Paul wants to say what language normally has not been able to say. Agamben, as it were, intuits an original intent in Paul that itself cannot be fixed and univocal, because the intent is to refer to a reality that is not of this world and always "new." Agamben sees that Paul's matured voice in Romans connects intimately with Paul's vibrant memory of Christ's revelation to him on the Damascus Road. Paul's born-anew (literally, "born from ahead") identity is a personal *creatio novum* from having met Christ. That occasion was an intimate immediacy, what Agamben elsewhere would call an authentic occasion of Paul's being experienced for a moment in human temporality.

"Immediacy" is important here, as it reminds that language really cannot capture experience in the present tense. We can only speak after the

---

18. Agamben, *Time That Remains* (TR).
19. TR, 5.

fact, as cognition can never be fully coincident with the experience. Even if said as a gerund, to say "I am doing a new thing" necessarily connotes that I could say such only after having begun doing the new thing. Something, then, already has passed by the time I speak of doing it. I cannot fully grasp then what God is doing, because I must admit the past tense of it all. And in admitting the past tense, I must recognize its authority in having been done. "God speaks" is only recognized by appreciating that God has spoken. *Deus dixit*.

Furthermore, when we reimage another moment of time, it is not imposed back upon that moment itself, but upon our previous imaging of it. Many verb forms of language are required for us to do this. These forms include our having grasped a time image as potentiality, as the present construction of the image, and the state of having been constructed. This is tantamount to something more than a linear sense of time. Its character is of three non-spatial dimensions. "Among other things," Agamben infers, "this would explain why the thought of time and the representation of time could never coincide. For in order to form the words in which thought is expressed—and in which a certain time-image is realized—thought would have to take recourse to an operational time, which cannot be represented in the representation in which it is implicated."[20]

In the immediacy of the Damascus Apocalypse, Paul began truly to know himself. Out of that immediacy—that moment of new creation wrought by a word—Paul's own language began to change in accord with his new person. New Pauline language communicated his new understanding of the real, of the holy domain beyond history, of temporality's fulfillment in eternity. In the time of immediacy with Messiah Paul knew Messiah in his present tense. Whatever language was spoken in that "time" was what Agamben calls the Sacrament of Language that I presented in chapter 4. When Paul then writes as hortatory in Rom 13 we could suppose he then follows the course of Agamben's Sacrament of Power (language's second and "normal" descriptive and prescriptive use). This is the language from authority spoken responsibly to guide hearers and readers toward the good in the *civitas*. It also, ideally, guides the audience to another occasion of appreciating messianic time in the spiritual domain, where the Sacrament of Language as the experience and vow of communion binds the human with the eschatological. Agamben sees that Paul's new language about his encounter on the Damascus Road conjoins eternity with history. This is a conjoining of *theos* with *polis*. Paul is theopolitical. This is why Agamben announces his desire as a self-identified not-Christian, a contemporary in

20. TR, 67.

postmodern Continental philosophy, to want "to restore Paul's Letters to the status of the fundamental messianic text for the Western tradition."[21] With this Agamben adds a fresh perspective to the many continental philosophers who also have new interest in the Pauline corpus. Two of Agamben's most distinct contributions in this conversation concern "messianic time" and "messianic life." Agamben is the author of the term "messianic time" and the first to connect "messianic life" to its metaphysical origin in messianic time.

Agamben arrives on the notion of "messianic time" by first centering on an early Pauline term from 1 Cor 7:29. The NRSV translates *ho kairos sunestalmenos estin* as "the appointed time has grown short." Agamben prefers a less conventional rendering that is closer to a literal translation: "time contracted itself, the rest is." For Agamben, this phrase "represents the messianic situation par excellence, the only real time."[22] This real time is the "radical abbreviation of time." It "is the time that *remains*."[23] One infers that this is the kernel for what becomes so winsomely and carefully explicated in the mature theology of Romans. But it is also here a term enriched by Agamben's detailed thought over the rest of the book. What follows this term is its justification, begun by positing that every term itself in the incipit—the first ten words of Romans—is a compression, a contraction within which the virtual whole of Romans is included. Paul's literary contraction, then, mimics the most important contraction that governs the whole of the letter, that time that remains.

The concept of messianic time derives from a person's momentary experience of and interpreted meaning of Messiah's "untimely" presence. Messianic time could be no more awe filled, as well as filled by a unification of the most fundamental binaries; "the particular conjunction of memory and hope, past and present, plenitude and lack, origin and end that this implies." Understanding fuses with the experience.[24] To "know" messianic time is to be both "in the now" and *aware* of being so. Agamben gives messianic time central status. He takes his cue from Paul's calling it "the now time" (*ho nun Kairos*).[25] The *nun* is emphatic and the use of *kairos* signals that Paul is not writing about the standard time by which we manage our routine needs and activities. Furthermore, because Paul's addressees "know" messianic time, expectation should be greatly heightened of Messiah's permanent return/

---

21. TR, 1.
22. TR, 6.
23. TR, 5.
24. TR, 1–2.
25. TR.

manifestation in human temporality.[26] And those who have known messianic time know too that though still mostly hidden, messianic time suffuses *chronos* "now" with gravamen, liveliness, expectation, and responsibility.

One must acknowledge that this "now time" differs from how many interpreters have understood Rom 13:11 and following. Seeing ample connection to detailed eschatological expectations (as in the Psalms of Solomon 17:32, 26, 29, 34, 44; the Testament of Levi 18:2-4; and the apocalypse of Mark 13:26-27), interpreters of Rom 13 read Paul in their same future tense. But they miss the critical difference of Paul having added the emphatic *nun*. In Paul's earliest writing (that we know of), 1 Thessalonians, his eschatology appears to have been more of the "we must wait and see" type; a time of the parousia's coming to our simple linear path that abruptly will break that path with a new reality theretofore unimaginable. By the time he wrote the letter to the Romans, however, Paul's eschatology matured dramatically. Now he looks toward no parousia. He does not even use the word. The kingdom with its time, or the time with Messiah's kingdom, is now here—*nun*—for those who know.[27]

This *now time*—messianic time—differs from the end of *chronos* and the future age. It also differs from *chronos* itself. Yet it is not outside of *chronos*, not external to chronological time.[28] Messianic time must not be confused with the eschaton, which is outside time. While within *chronos*, messianic time exceeds it. And while also part of eternity, messianic time extends beyond the end of *chronos*. Messianic time is that compressed time *between* the force of the future on the past and present. Agamben agrees that this is difficult to comprehend. In matters of spatial ordering our convention of linear symbolism (point, line, segment) may be useful representations. But they fail at communicating the *experience* of the time represented.

What is this "experience"? Consider how we "tell" time. Every representation of time includes another time that is not entirely consumed by the representation. The "other" time has not come to mind from outside. It is "there" because of the operation of our own mind; there is something there that we could not name or account for by the very process of our accounting for the otherwise. So we intuit an "ulterior" time, but must deduce that it is actually interior to my "telling" of time. That is, there is something that coheres with my connection to time, and there is yet the disconnect, a kind of positing of a real time but done so by a kind of negative profiling. By

---

26. Jewitt, *Romans*, 819. See also Johnson, *Reading Romans*.
27. Welborn, *Paul's Summons*, loc. 336 of 2549, details this nicely.
28. TR, 64.

naming what is, I also name by not naming what isn't transparent to me, but still is an experience and presence of time.

This explanation could be taken as a psychological linguistic description of Kantian critical realism.[29] But Agamben would not leave it at that. He presses further from a description of a neurolinguistic act to a reality statement, from epistemology to ontology *and then* to ethics. The sequence is as follows. If there is a remainder time interior to the time I do know, my being non-coincidental with my representation of time does not stop me in my tracks. Rather, because the remainder with which I am out of sync *is there*, there is "the possibility of my achieving and taking hold of it." This remaining time is the time that we can now take "to make time end." It is the only time we really have to "make something of ourselves," to let pass the time in which we have been impotent spectators of time, to seize the present tense so that we do not see ourselves as past tense, so that we no longer miss ourselves. This time that remains, the messianic time is our opening to seize the time "that we ourselves are." This is the only real time, the only time we actually have.[30] *Zeizetei ten hemeron* ("seize the day") is a mere greeting card shout-out that cannot ascend to the ethical call (*klesis*) that this ontological claim of *nun kairos* exhorts. Agamben does not repeat the mistaken ontological/ethical claim that "ought implies is." Rather, Agamben's argument finally is of this kind: "because there is, one ought." The announcement is declarative and hortatory. It does not have the personal and pausal distancing of syllogism. The "Being" of messianic time *immediately* calls for action. Being *is* Act and vice versa. Therefore the time that remains has the highest moral-ethical significance. The time that remains reveals itself with immediacy. Which is partly why Agamben labels it "messianic."

Again, Agamben moves from literary analysis to metaphysics, including an ontology of time, and so then to ethics. That he infers an ontology of time and then writes as much as he can from different angles toward and around the phenomenon is significant. Were he not to do so, the consequence would be little more than a complicated restating of the older anti-metaphysical existentialism that stresses only the necessity of one's choice to make oneself, to be, as one says without external reference or point of relativity, "authentic." There is a "there, there" of a different temporality convened by a different body between Agamben's move from analysis to

---

29. In simple terms, critical realism holds that our language does refer to real objects, but that our terms of reference can never be exact. In this Kant even anticipated postmodernity and the physics of Heisenberg; subjectivity always qualifies objectivity and objects are only observable according to the means we use to observe them.

30. TR, 67.

ethics while in existentialism there is not. There is a newly seen remaining time there between *chronos* and *eschaton*, and with it the one called Messiah. Only because *that* time is there and comes with Messiah does the time seized give the gift of authenticity to the person who seizes and so ends the time of dispossession of self. The self-possessed one, then, the person who has seized what is really real in the time that remains, is truly ontologically "authentic."

"Messianic" is the time "remaining" between human *chronos* and the new time of the eschaton that actually is already present and readied for rule. "Messianic" includes the presence of Messiah. *Chronos* time has no such identifiable palpable presence of another body. *Kairos* time does and a specific body at that. And *kairos* time bears with it the parousia, the very presence—the kingdom—of Christ. To regard messianic time as only a psychological "spin" on regular chronos time is only to postpone the action invited by the presentation of messianic time.[31] Postponement is actually denial of the reality of the new moment. Postponement, and so also waiting, is to discount the moment as merely one on the same temporal line of banal *chronos*. Postponement and waiting for the so-called delayed coming of the kingdom are indeed signs that those who postpone response or wait are still asleep. The import of the reality of messianic time for Agamben means that the parousia is not and cannot be a second coming. Were it really that, and therefore disconnected still from *chronos*, its human postponement would be infinite.[32] Rather than using the phrase "second coming," Agamben argues, parousia means "presence" (*par-ousia*, by-being, next to; "being is beside itself in the present").[33]

This novel definition does not contradict the doctrinal status of parousia, that God's reign has come and is coming. Rather, Agamben by being more serious about the grammar helps us to refigure our representations of time and space. The simply linear does not work when one attends to the grammar of parousia and its intimacy with *kairos*. Agamben's refiguration accords well with what we've learned of Augustine's sense of the "already" of the heavenly city. It accords with the "now and not yet" that courses through almost all the doctrinal foci of Augustinian Christianity. *Kairos* is embedded in *chronos*[34] and exceeds it. *Kairos* seizes hold of the instant and brings it to fulfillment.

31. "Postponement" is but one political tactic amidst many used in operational time to achieve or resist serving the common good. The disingenuousness goes beyond "wait and see."

32. TR, 70.

33. TR, 70.

34. TR, 70–71.

Yet (and Agamben's compound examples indicate the difficulty of expressing this insight), we *chronos*-bound human beings do not have sufficient capacity to grasp *kairos*. There is a hair's breadth between the desultory weekday and the promised eternal sabbath day, between "the sixth day" and God's completion of all on "the seventh day." There must be some way for the human to take hold of God's future. Agamben suggests it is the metaphorical "Saturday" which is messianic time, different from the eschaton, that offers human being the opportunity by its sheer and sliver-like proximity to the eternal to be grasped. Because this edge, this quality is so different from both the weekday and the actual sabbath, it can be grasped and "accomplished." Agamben concludes. "Saturday—messianic time—is not another day, homogenous to others; rather, it is that innermost disjoint-edness within time through which one may—by a hairsbreadth—grasp time and accomplish it."[35] This hairsbreadth of opportunity has been present in *chronos* for more than a little while. "The Messiah has already arrived, the messianic event has already happened, but its presence contains within itself another time, which stretches its *parousia*, not so to defer it, but, on the contrary, to make it graspable."[36]

The central importance of this "graspable" moment is in messianic time's changing of the "now" not into a chronological end of time, but giving the moment, the present, "the exigency of fulfillment, what gives itself 'as an end.'"[37] This means that *each* moment, each *kairos*, is immediate to God. Messianic time is not the end of some process. To paraphrase Gerard Manley Hopkins, "The time is charged with the gravity of God." It is another way, though Agamben never invokes the terminology, of understanding sacramentality; that immediacy to God is eternity in temporality,[38] and so not a Marxist reduction of history to materialism's dénouement. Memory is involved along with the real presence of God's future. It is the now time of messiah. In every time now "since we awakened" is the graced opportunity of sacramental seizure, when God's vow in the Sacrament of Language enraptures us and we respond with love's stewardship of the Sacrament of Power.

With this central proclamation of God's nearness comes the exigent urgency of human responsibility. The moment is graspable; ready to be achieved. It brings the call, the *klesis*, of human responsibility. It clothes

---

35. TR, 71–72.
36. TR, 71.
37. TR, 76.

38. The Christian theological tradition, of course, has long noted this as *finitum capax infinity* (the "finite bears the infinite").

human being with the call (*vocatus*) to responsibility, presuming human response-ability. Messianic time thus is poignantly ethical and political. A constellation of questions then is evoked. *How* human beings should respond and *why* should we respond becomes a matter of anthropology and law. That the questions are posed with respect to humans as plural invokes further topics of politics and the duties of government. And *why* has "accomplishing" the promise and offering of messianic time taken so long in "standard" time? That question leads us into consideration of the individual and corporate nature of sin and of the *katechon*, the "pushing back" of the eschaton's fulfillment. Finally, we must ask about what humanity can (!) and will achieve in and with the messianic moment until the full manifestation of the eschaton.

Nomos—Suspended and Fulfilled

Lutheran theology uses the terms "law and gospel" to understand how people can live fully and authentically and why we don't.[39] The "civil use" of the law properly refers to law that governs the temporal kingdom (also called the "first use" of the law). Then there is the second use, the "theological" use, which is uniquely civil and religious. It refers to the Abrahamic and Mosaic law—which has informed the civil use—which all people desirous of being righteous are commanded to follow. In the narrowest form of this, one must by intent and act follow the law so to be a good citizen.

The typically Augustinian Lutheran ironic understanding of the second use of the law tells us what to do "to be saved." But we find out we cannot do it on the law's terms, and so we experience condemnation. We must admit our inability not to sin and then throw ourselves on the grace of God. The truth is that we each are chronically (!) disabled even as our identity as

---

39. "Authentic" and "authentically" are tricky terms. In common use they can stand for almost anything a person desires. Used more carefully, they may refer to the Aristotelian virtues that were said to constitute the good life, and were reclaimed and reframed to some extent by existentialism's centrality of human autonomy and centrality of the self-knowing/self-defining person. I use them here both to pay homage to Aristotle and to tip the hat to existentialism of the Kierkegaardian sort, but also to anticipate Agamben's notion of the *Homo Sacer*, the "raw" or "authentic" human being, who may be killed but cannot be sacrificed, thus (if in Agamben opaquely) emphasizing that sovereignty can only apply to the individual human being. In my view, Agamben extends his notion erringly to an ideological extreme of libertarianism. With Žižek, I would redirect Agamben toward a more positive communitarian end. Appreciating the state's role during the COVID pandemic, Žižek sees Agamben as having turned his own theory into a reactive liberal ideology of "blah, blah, blah" ideology against the state. Žižek, *Freedom*, 193.

God's image bearers remains. As Luther writes in "The Babylonian Captivity of the Church," we are in bondage to sin through and through and can do nothing good of our own. This "essential condition" being so, we merit and can merit nothing. Any salvation to be had is by God's grace alone through faith alone in Christ Jesus, itself all grace and gift as well. This is the beggarly human condition.

Not that Agamben is interested in confirming Lutheran doctrine. But he does offer unawares surprising support of the confession that a person cannot win one's own righteousness with a perfect performance of natural/civil law. Law, *nomos*, also is not opposed to faith (*pistis*) and the gospel's promise (*epaggelia*). These three are mutually implicated, while, at the same time, law has its own seeming internal contradiction as the guide for civic behavior and its promissory character in service of the gospel. We recall that Barth defined the law as "a form of the gospel whose content is grace" while Luther and Lutheranism speak of law and gospel as opposed, complementary, and almost synonymous insofar as the gospel includes the law of love. Agamben sees similarly,[40] but from the perspective of Paul's use of the verb *katargein*. Twenty-six of its twenty-seven uses in the New Testament are in the Pauline letters, so *katargein* has a certain Pauline privilege that demands attention. The root *argeo* derives from *argos*, meaning "inactive." Agamben reads the addition of *kat* ("work" or "make") then, in Paul's first-person use (*katargeo*) as "I make inactive," or "I deactivate." The Septuagintal version refers to sabbath rest; works of the law are deactivated or suspended on Saturday. How fitting that with messianic time, then, when the proclamation of the *euanggelion* reveals the promised presence of the messiah's time in operational ("regular") time, that the normativity of the law for operational time is deactivated and the non-normativity of the law of messianic time with its own power of activation (*energeo*) thus rules "weakly." Agamben cites Rom 7:5–6 as paradigmatic. "For when we were in the flesh, the passions of sin were enacted [*energeito*] through the law in our members to bring forth fruit unto death. But now we are de-activated [*katergethemen*, 'made inoperative'] from the law."

Ah! Return to Rom 13 where the "passions of sin" had been deactivated upon awakening to messianic time and with the messianic law of love. The woke Christian here is not compelled by the normativity of law to obey Caesar. No, the Christian awakened in messianic time is deactivated from the law's normativity to be non-normatively "weak" (unusual? abnormal?) when the law of love takes charge, where and when the power of messiah is then realized. When the thorn in Paul's flesh is not removed, Paul realizes

---

40. TR, 91–97.

that in his weakness (*asthenia*) he is powerful. "God has chosen weak things of the world to shame the things which are mighty" (1 Cor 1:27).[41]

"Obedience to the governing authorities" is not then a command to submit to government's normative law. Neither is the advice and strategy to meet temporal power with temporal power. Those who have awakened to messianic time and live by its ways "weakly" respect the authorities with the volunteered love for the good of the authority, for the good of the institution, and for the good of the purposes of the institution and authority, which is to ensure the rights of life, liberty, and the pursuit of happiness. On this I suggest Agamben's goal of the *Homo Sacer* squares nicely with the law and the gospel and theopolitics. With regard to and in distinction from the temporal realm, messianic time's effect on the Christian deactivates the law. The Christian is free to be. But not only that. Messianic time makes the law inoperative *so that* the law can be restored with potentiality to be fulfilled in Christ. "As the highly original pericope in 2 Cor 3:12–13 states, the messiah is *telos tou katargoumenou*, 'fulfillment out of that which has been deactivated,' taken out of the act—namely, at one and the same time, deactivation and fulfillment."[42]

Readers may misinterpret Agamben here. Those accustomed to, shall we say, "strong" law might construe him to advocate for a kind of messianic anarchy. There are those, like the enthusiasts of Luther's day, who think the law was thus abrogated and they then celebrated anomia. But they are few. More, unlike the enthusiasts, inhabit the church and keep their heads low harboring "a secret loyalty to the antichristic rather than the christic mystery of lawlessness."[43] More yet don't "get" the christic mystery of lawlessness given in messianic time. Still in "flat time," with a rigor of pop-apocalypticism and legalistic devotion to their secular temporal construal of Christ's rule, they try to rule church and state as religious supremacists. Choosing not to be "woke," they are in Pauline terms "asleep." To be clear, the law in its temporal form is not destroyed. But in the messianic now time, when it is grasped (one infers with effusive gratitude), the law is happily "autonomically" fulfilled, its intimacy with messianic time being so complete.[44]

The temporal specification of Rom 13:11 makes clear that the *kairos* has arrived, been around for a while, and will arrive again. Its influence on

41. TR, 97.
42. TR, 98.
43. Farrow, "Engaging Agamben," 16.
44. This is indeed a consequence that L. Ann Jervis explicates, though without reliance on Agamben at this point, in her work considered below. By Christ's enfleshing of himself in human beings, Christ both abrogates the law and resituates the Christian fully to obey the law.

the present comes now from the past, even as it has come as the herald of God's future. Messianic time is the time between Jesus' resurrection and the fulfilled parousia, within but not collapsed with chronological time. Messianic time "is the time we need to make time end: the time that is left us."[45] So it is a time calling for Christian responsibility awakened to the urgency of the moment. But there is one more note of grace to announce. It is that as *chronos* or operational time is the same for residents of either of the kingdoms under discussion, we've not been discussing an ontological structure designed only for Christians. Messianic time is available to all and those awakened to it therefore belong to Christ. There is a comprehensiveness of grace offered in Agamben's salvific metaphysic which he may not even have recognized. *Kairos* is a "contracted and abridged *chronos*." Messianic time, then, is not wholly outside of our temporality; it is in "the secular world itself, with a slight adjustment," a disjointedness with regard to chronological time."[46] From such disjointedness are we purposed to engage with Caesar? Have we avoided engagement and in fact "delayed the parousia" by underappreciating messianic time's extension within *chronos*?

Lawlessness, *Katechon*, Sin

There is a larger and baser reason beyond human sleepiness for the delay. Sin still abounds, and God will have God's patient way. Final deliverance is all up to God as well. No matter how urgent the time and consequential the demand for awakened action, Christians will not usher in the kingdom by their own will. It is and will be all God's action. So Paul is concerned to provide practical advice and encouragement to would-be faithful who are both understandably anxious and more practical than inclined to abstract theory. The mature theology of Romans would be insufficient on its own for the Roman faith community. It needed some practical advice, though the ample theological reflection about the large "abstract" issues about which I have hinted in this discussion.

Paul's maturity of critical thinking and theological reflection here differs markedly from his earliest epistolic outreach to the Thessalonians. The church at Thessalonica needed concrete counsel more than deep reflection if it was to grow. With them the blindness to and even defiance of the import of messianic time was more evident than in Rome. So, with 2 Thess 2:3–12 particularly, Paul—and so Agamben—addresses the problem of the one who "restrains" the revelation of messianic time (Agamben's translation

45. TR, 67.
46. TR, 69.

differs from standard translations and is likely more accurate). Paul has just referenced the self-appointed exemplar apostate who resists the soon coming messiah:

> You know what it is that is now holding him [true messiah] back [*ho katechon*], so that he will be revealed when his time comes. For the mystery of anomy [*anomia*] is already at work, but only until the person now holding him back [*ho katechon*] is removed. Then the lawless one [*anomos*] will be revealed, whom the Lord will abolish with the breath of his mouth, rendering him inoperative by the manifestation of his presence [*parousia*]. The presence [*parousia*] of the former is according to the working of Satan in every power [*dynamis*].[47]

Can we be more precise about this *katechon*? The *katechon* is that force that holds off the coming of the antichrist,[48] the "lawless one" of 2 Thess 2:9. To hold or stave off the antichrist is a positive function; it sustains the "Now Time" even as the *katechon* may be quintessentially mundane, as a political force, so that the quality of the *chronos* may be more converted by the witnesses-agents of messianic time. Were such delay not achieved, the apocalypse with the antichrist could or would be an unwelcome destruction of the church before it felt itself ready for the parousia. Tertullian linked the *katechon* to the Roman Empire more specifically and prayed for its positive role in maintaining peace and delay of the end.[49] Carl Schmitt in turn sees here the only possible justification for a Christian doctrine of state power. It is an ironic claim that a Christian state should be sustained even as it knows of its necessary mortal terminus. Yet it is Carl Schmitt's conviction that only this sense of the *katechon* that serves rightly for "originary Christian faith."[50] It "is the only link leading from the eschatological paralysis of every human action to such a great historical agency [*Geschichtsmächtlichkeit*] as that of the Christian empire at the time of the Germanic kings."[51]

As we know, Schmitt's argument about a positive sense of *katechon* bore negative consequences. Paul does not regard *katechon* positively. Far from it. It is the mystery of lawlessness that is the problem. Whoever holds back the revelation of the ultimate agent of lawlessness sustains the problem of temporal lawlessness. This temporal non-discloser is *the katechon* [*ho katechon*]. This one must "get out of the way" ("is removed," 2 Thess 2:7)

47. TR, 109.
48. Agamben prefers the term "anti-Messiah."
49. TR, 109.
50. TR, 109–10.
51. TR, 109–10.

before the ultimate lawless one—the Satan—is annihilated by the manifestation of Messiah's full arrival. The force that holds back the revelation of lawlessness, the *katechon* that thus supports *anomos* could be a *katechon* for the Katechon. At the least, one lawless entity serves a greater lawless entity, as a Saruman to Sauron or fascist Italy to Nazi Germany, an antichrist to the antichrist. Insofar, then, as one lawless entity constitutes a "good" by staving off a worse—or the ultimate—lawless entity, Agamben nuances Paul's curation of *katechon*; in effect, Agamben mediates and has it both ways.

The same process of replacement of agencies applies to the role of the law, *except that* with the arrival of messianic time, it is the law (*nomos*) that is made inoperative and put into a state of *katargesis*. In messianic time lawlessness is a good thing, as when written on the heart rather than as an authoritarian *heteronomos*. Christ's law is lawlessness as the world of *chronos* sees it. Messianic time sees the temporal world's law as having no transcendent legitimacy. "Profane power—albeit of the Roman Empire or any other power—is the semblance that covers up the substantial lawlessness [*anomia*] of messianic time."[52]

So though Agamben earlier celebrated that the traditionally conceived apocalypse had not yet arrived, when messianic time inserts itself into standard temporality it evokes a complex set of tensions that require appropriately apocalyptic language. There are two kingdoms in the deepest tension, two parousias, one of the Messiah and one of the Satan. The *telos* of messianic time will manifest the clash of these two kingdoms, Augustine's original two kingdoms model and the victory of Christ's rule over the devil's. Then the Satan's lawless power of law will be rendered inoperative and the messianic law of lawlessness fulfilled. Then Messiah will deliver his kingdom to God the Father, who will render inoperative all temporal rule, power, and authority forever.[53] This will be the final and total annihilation of evil. In the fully manifest kingdom of God—the heavenly city—neither light nor law will be needed, so lively is eternity. In effect, this scenario amps up the spiritual stakes we've been describing in Luther's versions of Two Kingdoms as spiritual and temporal. To Agamben's apt apocalyptic description we add Augustine's counter-spiritual reign of Satan as a third kingdom that deleteriously affects the temporal kingdom. But it all, also appropriately, lands at an important theopolitical conclusion as to what can never be allowed to characterize the temporal kingdom. "*2 Thess. 2 may not be used to found a 'Christian doctrine' of power in any manner whatsoever.*"[54]

---

52. TR, 111.
53. TR, 111. See also 1 Cor 15:24.
54. TR, 111. Emphasis mine.

New Testament Exegetes Respond

Agamben's literary-critical and philosophical reading of Paul touches closely on current Pauline studies and—*quelle surprise!*—physical cosmology, though he shows no familiarity with either discipline. Studies on the subject of time and temporality began in earnest with the famous debate between Oscar Cullmann and James Barr in the mid-twentieth century.[55] Lately, New Testament scholars constructively advanced Barr's and Cullman's work by breaking apart their perseveration as to whether the "Hebrew" understanding of time was linear and the "Hellenic" view as circular.

That debate was necessary then, but it was judged insufficient when the significance of Einstein and new cosmology dawned on theologians. J. Louis Martyn recast the debate by asking whether Paul's understanding of the eternal having entered time was "linear" or—rather than "circular"—"punctiliar," as is the character of myth. By "punctiliar," Martyn signifies those occasions when God *uses* time by creating events—like the covenant with Abraham; like the incarnation, life, death, and resurrection of Christ—that do not fit *chronos* in a developmental or progressive way. Sequence does not matter.[56] Certain events matter more than others because God places them at certain times so to be significant. That is, a past event does not always of itself "flow" into the present so to add meaning to the present. Rather, God takes the past event and places it anew in the present. Likewise God does so with future events. Thus the "punctiliar." Thus, the future kingdom of God is placed by God "now" into history via the cross and resurrection of Christ and the en-spiration of God's Spirit. The future has come into the present. What evil there is of the present age does not merely bleed into the future. Neither does it merely meet the coming future, as has been the proleptic argument of Pannenberg and Moltmann. Instead the present is discretely "invaded" by the "future" event such that the old age and the new age simultaneously exist and are co-mingled. "Time" became an issue for theologians in the modern age once eschatology itself became its own locus in Pauline studies. But here we have a realized eschatology of a different sort than had been envisioned by the likes of Bultmann, Barth, or even N. T. Wright. There is no "before" followed by an "after" with this punctiliar sense of time. There rather is a *simul* of "before" and "after." The present and the future coexist. The eschaton is not something for which Christians wait. It began with the Christ event. This is what Paul reminds his readers of with his urge to awaken.

---

55. See Cullmann, *Christ and Time*; Barr, *Biblical Words*. I summarize their work and significance in Larson, *Times of the Trinity*.

56. Martyn, *Galatians*, 349.

What is also different with this notion of a "real" realized eschatology consonant with the human *chronos* is that its language is apocalyptic. I restipulated earlier the proper meaning of apocalyptic as the language necessary to bespeak truths that cannot be known in ordinary temporal ways. Such rhetoric discloses what is truly "down deep real" about the human psyche and behavior, individually and collectively. Interesting for our purposes is that apocalyptic properly understood when leashed to eschatology reveals something about our physics as well as our psyches. Agamben intuits this when he argues that messianic time is that real moment different from standard time that we can seize for personal and communal freedom.[57] We can do this because the future has come into the present. We have seen that Agamben disavows apocalyptic. His disavowal is of that kind of future that only meets the present and does not envelop it. But that messianic time is revealed as real is fundamentally in sync with what I here have described as basic apocalypticism, contradistinct from a developmental or progressivist sense of time.

With some self-differentiation, Pauline scholar L. Ann Jervis newly corroborates Agamben's argument and boldly explores the implications of "seizing" messianic time.[58] Jervis builds on the observation that Pauline scholarship regularly and unreflectively has imposed either of two suppositions about time and eternity on interpretations of Paul. The two schemes are the "salvation historical" and the apocalyptic. The former is progressive, as if human history evolves with enlightenment at the grasping of the gift of redemption and shall finally meet and yield to the fullness of the new age, even though the new age has been with and for the creation in its own unrevealed fullness since the whole of the Christ event. The latter, apocalyptic, accents more the encounter and challenge to the sinful age by the new age. Conflict ensues. From the human perspective, battles are won and lost, though the final triumph of God in Christ has already happened in God's eternity while not so in human temporality. Jervis agrees more with this latter scenario, agreeing that the evil principalities and powers are "defeated, though not yet annihilated."[59] Both interpretations, despite their differences, rely on the conviction that Paul inherited a "two-age framework" of the sinful evil age and the new age of the reign of Christ. Of the latter, Jervis underscores that being *en Christo* is a term of the strongest prepositional value; the Christian is actually and exclusively *in* Christ.

---

57. TR, 71.
58. Jervis, *Paul and Time*.
59. Jervis, "Response."

Jervis confutes the longstanding model of an overlap of the ages that typifies most Pauline interpretation—not to mention Augustine's sense of the fusing of the new city with the earthly or Luther's sense of living in both ages at once as *simul* sinner and justified. Believers live exclusively in Christ. Nonbelievers do not. We are either in or out. We do not live in a middle vector of both/and. Jervis adds nuance, however, by agreeing that though we are not corporeally or locationally *simul* in both ages or realms, we do live within the conditions of the old age's principalities and powers while we do not live under or by their conditions. So there is a kind of coexistence of the old age and the new, but they are not confused in even a partial way while one does not yet fully cancel out the other.

Jervis makes explicit here what may be inferred from what Agamben never engages: that time is never separated from space. The fourth dimension of time is never without the three dimensions of spatiality. As we know from both of Einstein's theories of relativity, time is always impacted by bodies in motion and the manifold of space itself is shaped by mass in motion (thus gravity). Jervis draws on this to say clearly what heretofore has been mostly embedded in more theoretical research. Observe the sequence. I put this in the simplest vernacular, intended literally to make these three points. (1) Bodies make their own relative time(s). (2) Christ constitutes Christ's own time. (3) Those who are in union with Christ are no longer with their own times. They are with Christ's time. And the denotation of "time" in all of Jervis' instances includes spatiality. Time is not an empty cipher or set. It is not a theoretical model. It is its own reality always relative to and specific to a body, a mass in motion. Jervis cites Martyn at length so to make the connection between her spacetime and the apocalyptic moment revealed to Paul, making clearer her differentiation (parallel to Agamben's *chronos* and *operational/messianic time*) between death-time and life-time.

Time has a spatial dimension. We know from both the theories of special relativity and general relativity that time and space are inextricably related. New Testament exegetes see something analogous, if not outrightly corroborative. J. Louis Martyn, for example, treats Paul's apocalyptic question of "What time is it?" with a spatial answer: "The characteristic of the present time is . . . that it is the juncture of the new creation and the evil age."[60] Martyn sees Paul as asserting something phenomenal and metaphysical here, as do many others.[61] They read Paul as holding that the two

---

60. Martyn, *Galatians*, 102, quoted in Jervis, *Paul and Time*, 21.

61. So also do Susan Eastman and Alexandra Brown, after the apocalyptic tradition of exegesis since Schweitzer, Barth, Käsemann, Beker, et al.

ages exist at once. These simultaneously extant ages have what I suggest as "density." Douglas Campbell[62] and many others agree.

Paul's witness to the coexistence of two ages is not an appeal to an ephemeral existential moment for self-actualization. It is a proclamatory recognition of two metaphysical horizons with content: two places each with their own time and spatial density. To speak of two ages/kingdoms for Paul, thus, is not a rhetorical tactic. Paul witnesses to a new creation. He may see it on the horizon, but that horizon is present with all its content now and reaching through the temporal world's stained sky. Terms like "new creation" and "kingdom" signify God's creative and salvific presence. Further, being "counter" terms, they signify that spacetime that exists where God's reign is not whole and manifest. But, as Jervis strives to make clear, while the ages are co-extant, in her view, the Christian does not and cannot maintain Christian integrity in both; that is, we may reside in deathtime, but we only really *live* in Christ-time. We are not "of" two ages. Christians are of Christ's time; we are *of* lifetime. Consciously to manage one's life by deathtime's terms in this time-place is neither to live nor to be Christian at all.

So goes Jervis's reading of Paul on the life to which he implores our awakening. To so awaken is also to live in, with, and from God. And God Trinity, as revealed in Christ, is temporal too, though with the tenses of past, present, and future as nonsequential. I have written of this elsewhere as God having and living in time amidst the fullness of all temporalities.[63] Christians, per Jervis, live in Christ's time, which is in God's time. Though Christian bodies are mortal, to live in Christ's time even while mortal is to live in lifetime (Rom 8:2 and 8:11), the time in which death no longer is the normative organizing power. So set free from the "present evil age" (Rom 1:4), Christians are united with Christ in Christ's lifetime. Indeed, we live in Christ's always present tense and Christ's future—his parousia—to us will be the full unveiling of his present tense. It will be, as it were, the full apocalypse of what we already know partially of the apocalypse of Christ's rule. First Corinthians 15:20–57 and Rom 8 both support this conviction.

Paul does not present the parousia exclusively in the indicative mood in the Corinthians text. Jervis emphasizes that Paul's unusual play with language is deliberate. The verbal moods and tenses are mixed, as if Paul describes the parousia from Christ's time perspective rather than from a human sequential view. "The strange paucity of future indicatives in 15:22–28

---

62. The modern and postmodern interest in time is large and well beyond these authors I here cite as markers of the movement that I believe corroborate Agamben.

63. Larson, *Times of the Trinity*.

appears to be Paul's way of signaling that here he has his gaze primarily fixed on Christ's time."[64] Having his eyes so fixed, Paul can then state with pure conviction in Rom 8 that the human present tense of physical death is inconsequential. Already "all things [of Christ and his resurrection] are yours" (1 Cor 3:21) as the spirit of God who raised Christ now lives in Christian's mortal bodies and will give resurrection life to our mortal bodies. Mortal death, now being destroyed with the passing of the present age (1 Cor 7:31). All "inimical powers, including death are [already] in submission." Thus, neither "the event of Christ's handing his rule to God nor his subjection to God changes Christ's situation. Christ's future actions reveal his present tense."[65]

Current Scientific Theory on Temporality

While Jervis's strong and provocative analysis goes beyond Agamben's notion of messianic time by specifying implications he does not, her vision coheres well with his. She appears to support his proposal, though she may be more interested (of course) in his support for her position than the converse. She is a most recent affirming voice among many New Testament scholars who value and add value to Agamben's philosophical literary interpretation of Paul. The remaining question presently concerns the "reality claim" Agamben leaves to the reader. Postmodernists generally are as indisposed toward metaphysics as they are to sweeping statements (!). But Agamben clearly means to marshal Scripture and high literature with much classical philosophy, ethnography, psychology, the arts, and more to make a reality claim. So the question is raised and must be answered. Might theories held by those fields devoted to understanding the nature of reality and its ultimate origin cohere with Agamben's articulation of temporalities? Could they, even as they necessarily are tentative, ally with Agamben so to yield an adequate and compelling imagination about our human origin and future in which spirit, mind, and matter cohere?

Coherence is all we can ask for, as nowhere in his voluminous work does Agamben engage theoretical physics and cosmology, much more the less speculative empirical sciences. A philosophy of science, as distinct from science itself, can ask reasonable questions about correspondence or coherence. But no philosophy of science argues for strict relationships of causality without significant caveats. This is evident in the present conversations as

64. Jervis, *Paul and Time*, 97.
65. Jervis, *Paul and Time*, 106–7.

to what kind of relationship exists, if any at all, between religion and natural science. The qualified character of any relationship is amplified when the discussants are theology and science. Agamben does not specify that he writes theology per se, but his addresses to audiences of religion experts show that he is clearly aware of the implication of his thought for the church. He also would not write as artfully and capaciously as he does were he not interested in disclosing what is really real to his audiences. So here, in a most summary way, I propose cosmological warrants—let's humbly call them "resonances"—for his argument that messianic time is a reality statement.

The broad brush of the history of ideas has led us to think in two allegedly opposite ways about time. The question always at hand has been whether reality changes or not. Does time stand still, finally, even as we experience it as present, allow that it has passed, and expectantly await it? As Parmenides charted it, does time as past-present-future eternally exist in what we now call a "block universe"? Or, as we received from Heraclitus, is time dynamic? Does it come and go, flowing like a river into a sea that is physically nowhere? Either there is temporal passage or there isn't. Either answer prompts significantly theological iterations. To pose the question for our purposes in this raw way is a fruitful heuristic so to assess whether "in the grand scheme" of things—whether Parmenides or Heraclitus!—there *still* would be coherence between Agamben's and stargazers' visions. In any case, eschatology is involved.[66]

If time comes and goes, appears and disappears, if time is fully dynamical, we can well predict when "all time" will disappear with the fate of the universe. In about fifteen billion more years the universe will either dissipate like the river into a sea of nowhere or it will collapse into the fiery furnace of an infinitely dense sun. The universe will either freeze or fry. All depends too upon whether the universe is one particle too short in its composition or one too many. So far, scientists who are Christians find this mathematical balance to be a remarkable instance of Divine Providence.

"But what if the open universe therefore freezes or fries?" the Parmenidean asks. What would be left for resurrection? How would eschatology be anything other than the prediction of only bad days ahead? Would not eschatology, with all the substance of Christian faith that centers with 1 Cor 15 on the promise of the objective resurrection of the body then be compromised? Doesn't theology require physicality, and so temporality? This is the major implication for theology of time as passing from somewhere into

---

66. In other words, for many reasons not necessary to discuss here, I take Heraclitus for the win. Agamben and Jervis, Martyn, and Paul et al. would win too. They also do if Parmenides wins. In this eschatology, everybody wins.

nothingness. But note this. "Nothingness" is a cipher here, if not the marker of a loaded argument. The universe will be either unimaginably dense or more imaginably dissipated. But energy particles still populate somewhere, and only the really "cold" ones, like cold human hearts, would be imaginably purposeless. And we have no cause to suppose that a supra-temporal dimension of time like Agamben's messianic time would be as dispersed. If eschatology and thus the "otherness" of God as *the* primal causal agent independent of and yet intimately related to an open universe as the universe's inserter and reframer of energy *ex vetere* is the big X factor, that only increases the mystery of the different messianic time-dimension that all the witnesses cited in this chapter propound.[67] It does not mitigate Paul's keener eyesight and still requires apocalyptic signification to communicate what he sees.

On the other hand, a block-universe model of spacetime would give God something still physical to resurrect. Physicist theologians like Emily Qureshi-Hurst evidently prefer this model, perhaps because it more respects the divinely imputed value to the physical/*temporal* character of what Christians expect to be resurrected. Yet, Christians are promised "new creation." We are not promised recreation, but resurrection, yet resurrection with a difference as a "spiritual body" (1 Cor 15:42–44). This spiritual or "glorified body," we expect, is itself different from the different body I have presently, my being a wholly different molecular composition than I was many years ago. But I am more my identity now than I was decades ago or even last year. So perhaps it is not so much our physical bodies that will be resurrected but our *identities* that carry with them their changed and changing physical composition.[68]

There is promise and coherence with Agamben in this interpretation of time and our communal human being too. My life is not a solo performance in an empty hall. I am we, and we are I's. It is (almost) taken for granted now that human identity is communally-relationally in-formed. We cannot be fully-formed individuals without responsibly and response-ably being communitarian. This of course is *the* ontology beneath the natural law of the Golden Rule. Furthermore, we are mindful of these relations. They are cognitively embedded in us and our cognition is embodied. Cognitive scientists increasingly assert that we cannot even have minds without a body. "In light of work in embodied cognition, then, individuals are increasingly

---

67. Outstanding more exhaustive accounts of all the theological and physical implications are offered by Russell, "Eschatology"; Russell, "Bodily Resurrection"; Russell, *Time in Eternity*. For a most recent summary of these discussions, see Qureshi-Hurst, *Problem of Spacetime*.

68. Qureshi-Hurst, *Problem of Spacetime*, 52.

understood as fundamentally and irreducibly situated in wider contexts of cultural, intellectual, and spiritual meaning. Our minds, and therefore (arguably) our identities, cannot exist apart from the physical bodies that inhabit these contexts."[69]

In short, real bodies enjoying intersubjective relations already are the good "stuff" of citizenry in the passing age of temporality and the already arrived and further graspable age of messianic time. We can respect, even prefer, Parmenidean permanence. It allows for family reunions, after all! But a Heraclitean view of time is no less consonant with the point of messianic time. Eschatology is the theological penumbra for both classic understandings and above eschatology is always the one God. Agamben's linguistic literary comprehensiveness appears to go hand-in-glove with an ontology fancied in serious contemporary physical theory today, no matter the temporal differences of the models. In it, all God is hidden but active; the eternal manifests itself in time and, where human temporality is broken or fractured, reaches through to grasp us with a holy word to bring us from death to life.

Summary

We began this chapter with Rom 13 and learned that it cannot be followed rightly without awakening to Paul's eschatological urgency. Agamben's very close reading disclosed the cause of Paul's urgency, that God has inserted an ontologically other dimension of time, messianic time, into the banal human timeline. To communicate this requires a different sort of language adequate to eschatological otherness. That language is apocalyptical, which should be understood first as the positive and faith-encouraging discourse about spiritual reality, not as fear-inducing news of destruction and damnation. Agamben's deep analysis is supported by current Pauline scholars. It also resonates with contemporary physical theory. Obedience to messianic "now time" includes with it the personal transformation of the aspiring believer into the more complete be-liever. This is because with messianic time there is Messiah, the Christ. Christ, who was crucified and raised in our temporal time for all time(s) takes up life in the be-liever and in the Church. Awake to and grasping the significance of the now time, we individually and together as the body of Christ poignantly confess that temporal power can never legitimize the state above the eschatological. Nor can equivalence between the temporal and the eschatological be granted. Such equivocation would indicate that messianic time was not personally grasped, but

---

69. Qureshi-Hurst, *Problem of Spacetime*, 54.

only used for temporal ideology. In other words, just as eschatology cannot be coequal with temporality, so also "Christian" cannot be coequal with "Nationalism" or any other kind of secular enthusiasm. Thus, there is an internal delimitation in Rom 13 about obedience to the state. That delimitation is eschatological. Romans 13 is read rightly when the Christian is awake to God's eschatological immediacy in the spiritual kingdom and awake with gracious patience and purposes in the temporal kingdom. We will see in the next and concluding chapter what this further means for a reclaimed Doctrine of Two Kingdoms.

6

A Future for the Doctrine of Two Kingdoms?

"This is what gives poetry its governing power. At its greatest moments it would attempt, in Yeats's phrase, to hold in a single thought reality and justice. Yet even then its function is not essentially supplicatory or transitive. Poetry is more a threshold than a path, one constantly approached and constantly departed from, at which reader and writer undergo in their different ways the experience of being at the same time summoned and released."
—Seamus Heaney[1]

EDWIN ABBOTT ABBOTT'S NOVELLA *Flatland* satirized his shallow and prejudiced culture of 1884 with an extended parable featuring live geometric forms. Women were figured as line segments, often invisible but also stabbingly dangerous. Men were variously sided polygons. The more sides men had and could gain (which only men could do) the higher their status and the more they evolved toward the "perfect" Platonic ideal of a circle. The narrator in the novella is a square and properly named so. Square is visited by Sphere, but being only two-dimensional, Square is unable to see Sphere as anything other than a disk. Still, because Sphere presents to Square's view the perfect form of a circle, Square is compelled to listen. To prove its own reality, Sphere levitates to various heights so that Square sees him assume different sizes as a circle. But Square still cannot understand what he sees until Sphere takes the Square to the larger context of Spaceland constituted

---

1. Heaney, *Government of the Tongue*, 108.

by three dimensions. From that higher dimension Square can see the whole of Flatland. Thus Square is converted to Sphere's perspective and is then appointed as an apostle to Flatland. Square is not very successful in converting his fellow Flatlanders to a more spacious perspective. Many more like Square would have to be appointed as apostles over many years to make any impact of Flatlander consciousness.

The parable gets more complicated. Drama happens. For our purposes it is enough to observe that the characters with lesser dimensionality cannot of their own capacities understand the apostles of greater horizons. The Flatlanders cannot imagine anything other than what they can describe only from "inside" their own limits while not recognizing, of course, that they are limited. Such knowledge would and could only come from an unimaginable "outside." Properly termed, they required an apocalypse, and then would need a rich new language to imply, not directly refer, their "threshold," as Seamus Heaney depicts such a situation.

Like his parable, Abbott's criticism of Victorian society did not go far in his lifetime. It drew new attention when Einstein published his general theory of relativity, as Abbott's imagination of higher dimensions was strikingly prescient of the new physics that Einstein revealed. The parable suggests still how language must be tapped deeply, insistently, exploringly, and creatively to reveal, like apocalyptic, the deeper and transcending architecture of reality. The parable is relevant today as a critique of the popular flat interpretation of eschatology and trivialized apocalyptic language. It also serves as an apt imagining of Agamben's interpretation of messianic time in Paul's letters. A larger reality is now "here and there," imminent, in and beyond our narrower dimensions. Eschatological reality is present and transcending in all directions. Its temporality is not just linear, like a single arrow of time. The eschatological is not simply "the end of the line," not merely what happens when this train finally runs out of fuel. Chronos, who devours his children, signifies the default perspective of the parable's Flatlanders and our society's fundamentalists. The spiritual kingdom is of an infinitely larger and multiply dimensioned topology than the secular temporal kingdom. And having seen and heard the gift of the spiritual kingdom necessarily repeatedly, lest fickle human memory grow dim, Christians and especially Christian "leaders" speak and serve insistently, resolutely, enticingly, gracefully, graciously, evocatively, imaginatively, intimately. In response, we commit to speak apocalyptically so to encourage each other and those of the "flatland" to stand and live at Seamus Heaney's "threshold" of "reality and justice," *knowing* in that trans-Kantian way the experience of being "summoned and released."

In this final chapter I seek to bring the parts together into a reconstrual of the spirit and politics of the Two Kingdoms doctrine. Having considered new perspectives after reading Agamben, I will suggest implications for two-kingdoms thinking and for how the church must proceed anew with its work. Insights inspired by Agamben and Pauline studies underscore the urgent need for the church itself to recenter and reclaim the priority of eschatology and apocalyptic imagination for its own proclamation and teaching. This simply must be done if the church authentically is to understand, live, practice, and inspiringly communicate—actually, mediate—the sparkling power of the word in messianic time. Only as the immediate consequence of encounters in messianic time does the Christian be-liever serve with faith's activated love in the temporal kingdom; only when stirred by spirit is the work of lasting justice in daily life possible. In Agamben-inspired phrasing, the Two Kingdoms are not just here to be noticed. We discern their distinction and their relation when the apocalypse of messianic time intervenes in our lives, like a thief breaking into our strongly built and secured homes to bind us and expose us so to plunder our goods (Matt 12:29). In this case, though, the intruder is Messiah, and the consequence is our freedom.

But the church has a theological "method," too, that the church much ignored until the latter twentieth century. That method is the Theology of the Cross. The Theology of the Cross is the distinctive and central theological method that informs the spiritual epistemology of the be-liever and guides the believer's ethics in the secular world. The Theology of the Cross also correlates the Christian's ethics with the secular world's centering of law for the alleviation of suffering, the agenda advocated by H. L. A. Hart. Dietrich Bonhoeffer is a paradigmatic figure who recovered the Doctrine of Two Kingdoms by linking it with the Theology of the Cross.[2] Thereby, it happens that he anticipated Hart's thinking by linking Two Kingdoms with the mandate to relieve suffering by employing the Theology of the Cross as the Christian's epistemology and ethical "system." Where there is suffering, there is God. Know God in the act of redressing suffering. And in redressing suffering, know both God and the "new" natural law that bids all people to practice compassion. Bonhoeffer's linkage further argues (against Luther) for the realizable practicality of the Beatitudes. We saw that Luther's "realism" brought him up short when he could not accept "the clear and present meaning" of Jesus' words from the mount (or plain) as doable. But we have seen, thanks to eschatologically aware Pauline scholars like Jervis, that Jesus' words as the kind of positive apocalyptic speech that the church needs to

---

2. DeJonge, *Bonhoeffer's Reception*, 74–75, 116–22.

recover as an expression of the benevolence of the spiritual kingdom directed to life in the temporal kingdom.

It is helpful to recall here that "apocalyptic" means the distinctive genre of language that speaks to the positively gracious eschatological reality of the spiritual kingdom. "Apocalyptic" may necessarily be imaginative, given the finitude of human being and compression of rational Enlightenment thought (which rationality of course must be taken up again with urgency in a "post-truth" era, but not again totalized). But the imaginative impulse of apocalyptic must not again itself be reduced to the totalitarianism and spiritual impertinence of fundamentalist caricatures. "Apocalyptic" means a gospel good that is literally incomprehensible. Thus the immeasurable good must employ positive faith-filled imagination, as did the apostolic sages of the early church. Poetry *makes* something new of the poet and the poetized. Poetry is true while never only literal.

Cruciform Sovereignty and Service

I've argued that the notion of sovereignty, like natural law, came to be so conflicted that its applicability to nation-states philosophically had no good end. Still, of course, there is no other legal term by which to respect the integrity of other nations. Giorgio Agamben with his career-long theme of *Homo Sacer* restated the point of individual human sovereignty as of such autonomy that no human being any longer could be "sacrificed" for the totemistic religious purposes of the state, though it still happens that humans kill each other. "Murdered, but not sacrificed" for Agamben philosophically and descriptively speaks to the autonomous sacrality that every human has. I do not read Agamben as accepting "half a loaf" here. Rather, his project is to reclaim all individual human integrity and to serve as prophet against the State (which to him is still all government, all the time) that arrogates to itself the status of "State of Exception" so fully that exception includes the "right" to murder at will. *Homo Sacer* serves as the cipher that simultaneously uplifts human dignity and condemns chronic sovereign state indignity.

On its own, the posture of *Homo Sacer* is vulnerable to being extended into libertarian ideology, which Agamben himself has had occasion to advocate and for which he has been criticized. Agamben's description of messianic time, however, ameliorates the ideological threat by asserting (like Martyn, Jervis, and scores more) Jesus' and Paul's proclamation of "present eschatology," for which gracious (!) apocalyptic language discloses the intimacy of the one Sovereign God with the reconciled community of be-lievers. What Agamben proposes as his "Sacrament of Language" at the same time, I suggest, reveals God and binds hearers with God and each other in beloved communion. Properly apocalyptic language best befits Agamben's intuition here and should be part of the church's recovery project of being its true self again in a two-kingdoms declension. Agamben's further (still developing) idea of a Sacrament of Power, as it were, names the more desultory nonapocalyptic speech that guards temporal life together, with perhaps an inchoate aim, but aim still, of preserving and guiding common life toward the gift of the Sacrament of Language. It is, I think, a helpful further illumination of the exhortative function of language and, even, could serve as a linguistic template for the functions of government. It coheres with the temporal realm's necessary and characteristic discourse (though Agamben's naming will not receive popular acclaim).

This would be my compact theological reframing of Agamben for a further reframing of the Two Kingdoms doctrine itself. And Agamben has provided good rhetorical and philosophical clues about "where" God speaks from and how to "know" it. "Knowing" our whence and so what God speaks, inspires and guides our ethics. Theology is knowledge of God, or it is nothing. Knowledge of God necessarily entails reference to the world and so also a knowing of the world as the Two Kingdoms would offer. Rightly knowing from the spiritual realm informs right politics in the temporal realm. Formal philosophical logic argues that "is" does not imply "ought." But the theo-logic of the spiritual kingdom does mean that "knowing" implies "ought" in a way that is commensurate with the moral-political logic of the temporal kingdom. The Christian strives to see more clearly and compassionately what still should hold morally true of the solely political. For the latter, just law no matter how positivistically written—or perhaps precisely because it must be positivistically written—must serve the suffering neighbor. It must do so at least for no more transactional, selfish reason than that no pragmatically reasonable person would want unnecessary and unjust suffering for oneself.

Still, minimal self-serving transactionalism is not the only driver of the temporal world's Golden Rule. I assume the affection of compassion, too. Compassion is the pre-reflective partner of sensing what is "fair." Compassion may begin with empathy, the ability to enter into the situation of another, but compassion goes further by identifying with and acting for the alleviation of the suffering of the other. This may require abstract and experiential learning about oneself, as well as about people generally. Compassion is a serious, painful, non-blaming, and presently attentive trained emotion. It also practices patience in faith's view that those to whom one is compassionate are as valued as the one who is moved by compassion. The "knowing" of compassion, then, is egalitarian and eccentric, the opposite of the intentional ignorance that drives the sociopathy of the narcissist.[3]

This is, at the least, the compelling moral logic beneath H. L. A. Hart's theory of law freed of higher accountability. Hart's logic hints that he recognizes compassion as the one unquestionable essential driver of good law, genuine justice, and legitimate government. If sovereignty and natural law have been excused from the halls of law schools and government, compassion is an apt replacement. And because compassion is less abstract and still circumstantially "universal," it is therefore more humane, therefore even more fitting for the purposes of the temporal jurisdiction. Compassion as a formal category is not an alien and unwelcome term in sophisticated political theory, after all.[4] It appeals even to the best of people's common sense.

This brings us to a crucial point. I've chronicled the de facto loss of natural law in the temporal kingdom and asked about its replacement, if any. If compassion may so serve, and I propose that it can, then Luther's Theology of the Cross is its correlate and amplification in the spiritual realm. Thus a trifecta is won in this rethinking of the Two Kingdoms doctrine. First is the reality of compassion as a humanly "internal" natural law for which language as power acts as external guide and force (Agamben's "Sacrament of Power"). Second is that we regain what had been absent in Luther's political theology that he had before described as essential to theological method. Third, this regaining actually correlates strongly both with the law of love in the spiritual realm and the purpose of civil law in the temporal realm. The Theology of the Cross, we find, has all that is needed to complete Luther's Two Kingdoms principle as, indeed, a "Theory of Everything."

Luther's "Heidelberg Disputation," anticipating his later "The Bondage of the Will," begins with his well-known recognition that human works to fulfill God's law will not advance the human into righteousness. Such efforts, however successful to mortal eyes, will further hinder persons from attaining righteousness and even increase sinful pride. The works of God,

---

3. See Nussbaum's excursus on compassion, *Political Emotions*, 142–55.

4. See also Nussbaum, *Upheavals of Thought*; Snow, "Compassion." Snow argues that compassion is a "rational emotional response" (195) and proceeds to build "a compassion-based theory of political and civil society" (198–99) in contrast to the common Hobbesian account, which, like Kant's, is a "narrow conception of rationality" (201–2). Advocates for what I'll call this "Nussbaum School of Political Ethics" are many and growing. They constitute a ready alliance for the broader concept of reason advocated by Hamman and Leibniz. Furthermore, a compassion-based theory of justice goes far in countering not only Hobbesian absolutism, but also improves on the individualism that remains in Rawlsian liberalism, thus contributing to a better vision of a democratic communitarian postliberalism in which we otherwise still founder as a society bereft of either.

however, though appearing "unattractive" and even "evil" to human being, are really "eternal merits."[5] Because all people are in thrall to sin, even a person's good works are mortal sins unless that person feared they would be mortal sins, so apposite are human works to God's works. Free will for human being so conditioned is an oxymoron. No eternal righteousness can be obtained by any human work, not even in part. Righteousness can only be imputed and received by the grace of Christ. And Christ's grace comes from the incursion of messianic time that is in-conceivable by human imagination apart from a knowledge imparted by God. And so Luther arrived at his famous maxim of the Theology of the Cross. "That person does not deserve to be called a theologian who looks upon the invisible things of God as though they were clearly perceptible in those things which have really happened [Rom 1:20]. He deserves to be called a theologian, however, who comprehends the visible and manifest things of God seen through suffering and the cross."[6]

There are three major implications of these two theses. The two theses are in part further exegeted by Luther's subsequent theses, particularly the first two that I here will discuss. The third implication, however, is not further explicated by Luther, but attains a "Lutheran imprimatur" when it is read in light of Luther's "Freedom of a Christian." The first two are construals of the (1) cruciform "metaphysical" character of God, and (2) the crucified epistemological character of the theologian. The third construal is about the ethics that touch most directly on two-kingdoms thinking.

As to the first, the Theology of the Cross is about who God reveals God to be on the cross. To paraphrase Moltmann's recapitulation of Luther, God the Father suffered the death of the Son on the cross.[7] This reveals God as the "fellow sufferer" (Bonhoeffer). God is not in any Hellenic sense simply immutable and unaffected. God is neither allergic to time[8] nor unwilling to enter into all of history's vicissitudes while taking it all in. Yet, to accept death and to defeat death by resurrection is to reveal also that the most powerful dynamic at the heart of the universe is the power of divine love. The weakness of God reveals the foolishness of human conceits of power.[9] The weakness of God, so unsurpassingly powerful in the most unexpected of places, as of an excruciating executioner's device for simultaneous

---

5. "Heidelberg Disputation," in Lull, *Basic Theological Writings*, 30.

6. "Heidelberg Disputation," theses 19 and 20, in Lull, *Basic Theological Writings*, 30.

7. Moltmann, *Crucified God*.

8. Jenson, *Unbaptized God*.

9. Caputo, *Weakness of God*.

shaming and killing, sneaks in so unexpectedly as to shock a centurion into messianic confession (Mark 15:39). Thereafter, slowly, patiently, even surreptitiously, the "weakness" of God nurtures and in-spires a fledgling prayer group of young disciples into a universal church's confession of God's love and solidarity with sinners.

Not only does the cross reveal God as the lover who will save as sufferer.[10] The cross reveals too that God in the crucified and resurrected Christ chooses to be in solidarity with all who suffer, especially those who suffer, as human legal imagination puts it, unjustly. The Theology of the Cross means that God is on the side of those who do not get to choose sides. What could be more universal and more powerful than such love? What proof of a solidarity better than neutral omnipresence than willful solidarity with the unjustly suffering who bemoan the paucity of promised abundant life? The truest *apocalypse*, the primal revelation, here is of the character of God. God reveals God's character in Jesus Messiah as the fellow sufferer. This also makes the apocalyptic medium of the cross the *sine qua non* of divine communion with history. The cross is God's definitive chosen intersection of eternity and temporality. This doesn't cancel out any of God's "previous" or subsequent self-revelations, certainly not the incarnation; certainly not God's raising Israel out of Egypt and then Babylon; certainly not the resurrection; and certainly not the Pentecost sending of God's Spirit. The cross does give all these divine acts the "theo-psychic" predication for how and why God does so act. God suffers and wills to suffer our human predicament. In other words, God's character is cruciform. God is *so* God, *so* other than sinful human being can imagine, that the transcendent shows and proves itself in the counterintuitive apocalyptical sign of the cross and in cruciform loving care again and again. God *will be* God even and especially in and with those who suffer. And because *God* raised Jesus from the dead and delivered Israel from Egypt is so relating, redemption will be the final and full eternal gospel word.

Further, it is rarely noted that the Theology of the Cross is the only way to state the ubiquity of God and so also God as the final and universal "explanatory principle" of all things. Only by including what is typically excluded of God in the usual philosophy can the profundity of transcendence even be signaled. No human "typically" expects to see God assassinated on a torture device. Only a revelation of God thereafter overcomes the prideful

---

10. Any number of different theories of atonement could be entered into discussion here. Mine would integrate Abelard with both the Christus Victor motif and the ethical mandate consequence of Girard's "no more scapegoats" model. But whatever the theory (and atonement models are only that), it isn't germane to the discussion here. Most any could fit.

human delimitation of God's presence and power. Only a religion which grasps that God suffers could know the joy and abundance of life granted as a grace. In this the problem of a sovereign God or a finite God is overcome. Slavoj Žižek makes this point against the inadequacy of the secular humanist response to human catastrophes like the Holocaust. Only with reference to God can anyone begin to grasp the scope of events like it; "the fiasco of God is still the fiasco of *God*."[11] The Theology of the Cross is a *whole* word about God yet capable of more detail given that there is a future for us yet of God to be revealed. The Theology of the Cross, therefore, is the necessary starting point for anything that is and can be said of God as the revealed God. This is also to say, as I will continue to say in different ways, that the Theology of the Cross is apocalyptic and requires apocalyptic language of God.

The second implication, as Luther stated, is that the Theology of the Cross describes the necessary epistemic state of the theologian. I do not privilege only professional theologians on this point. Luther, of course, wrote the "Disputation" theses as a provocation to other theologians to debate him. But there is no reason to suppose that the epistemic element here would not or should not apply to all be-lievers in Christ. There is a kind of "knowing" *in Christ* claimed in Luther's explanation of his twenty-first thesis. "This is clear: He who does not know Christ does not know God hidden in suffering. Therefore he prefers works to suffering, glory to the cross, strength to weakness, wisdom to folly, and, in general, good to evil. . . . It is impossible for a person not to be puffed up by his good works unless he has first been deflated and destroyed by suffering and evil until he knows that he is worthless and that his works are not his but God's."[12]

As for the third implication: the Theology of the Cross is *the* Christian social ethic and informs how Christians are to understand and relate to the temporal order. Because God aligns with the suffering, Christ in Christians meets Christ where suffering people are. When the suffering is unjust, this is where the church reminds the state of its vocation. Conscientious obedience to authority in Rom 13, thus, is ultimately to God's institution. This likewise entails conscientious dissent—including conscientious disobedience—when the state betrays its vocation to care for all people and not just a tribe's people, which includes when Christians theologically unknowing of this two-kingdoms implication would assert the state need only care for "their" or "its" tribe. When the state is so self-justifying by claiming itself as a state of exception and does not attend to unjust suffering, it betrays

---

11. Žižek and Gunjević, *God in Pain*, 158.
12. Theses 19 and 20 in Lull, *Basic Theological Writings*, 44.

its mission. As do Paul and the Gospels, Augustine's *City of God* prescribes resistance to empire or nation when the state has lost its way.

The church is best resourced to do this when it lives from faith for faith, strengthening its inner life with the praxes of prayer, sacramental mysticism, intentionally intense life together, and focus on language. These are essential for a political program based on Jesus' vision and expectation of a community of radical equals. Theologian Boris Gunjević, for example, comes to this conclusion after exegeting the Gospel of Mark's rejection of empire and embrace of equalitarianism. It is also a rejection of any populist apocalypticism and religious nationalism, with which Žižek concurs.[13] These three implications—the Theology of the Cross is theocentric, epistemic, and constitutive of *the* Christian ethic—shape the manner and mode of how Christians should relate to our everyday temporal conditions.

Were the Theology of the Cross *not* integral to Christian life in "the world" . . . well, we know how that looks. It should be no surprise that the Theology of the Cross's absence in Christian proclamation and teaching could easily allow the Two Kingdoms doctrine's capitulation to fascism, to its echoes in Christian Nationalism, its adaptation today by Catholic integralism, and more. One does not find the Theology of the Cross in liberal theology's on-ramp to the Third Reich.[14] Rather, one finds sermons and teaching more devoted to a Christian identitarian triumphalism. For example, the earliest institutionalization of the German Christian movement was the League for a German Church (*Bund für Deutsche Kirche*) established in 1921. It emphasized the "heroic" Indo-European, not Jewish, Christ and dismissed any accent on the suffering Christ. It called for de-judaizing Christianity and celebrated the anti-Semitic Luther as the "German prophet."[15] Above all, the *Deutsche Christen* effusively proclaimed their own ascendancy as a theology of glory that included the German people's own heroic suffering and sacrifice to liberate suffering and oppressed Germany. If there were any likening to the Theology of the Cross in this, it was a co-option of it to justify German martyrdom. The absence of faithful proclamation and teaching of the Theology of the Cross in the German Church was not the sole causal agent for the rise of German fascism. But it was an integral one. It is surely telling that the Theology of the Cross became the "go to" theme in the angst and guilt-driven pursuit of trying to answer the harrowing question of theodicy after the Holocaust.[16]

13. So suggest Žižek and Gunjević, *God in Pain*.
14. Steigmann-Gall, *Holy Reich*; Hinlicky, *Before Auschwitz*.
15. Solberg, *Church Undone*, 13.
16. I'd also argue that early interpretations in the return to the Theology of the Cross then were not yet a correct understanding of Luther, but they were a start.

Because Luther first posed it as a matter of academic debate on the limits and ultimate insufficiency of the received philosophy of his day for theology, one could have the impression of the *theologia crucis* as only about Luther's epistemology. Even if it were only about that, it would still improve on the delimitations of later Enlightenment rationalism. It would do us well to accent this theology as an improved theological epistemology while also attending to its empowerment of a particular ethic. But we add knowing's apocalyptic predicate, too. The epistemology is not one of a certain rational cognition only. There is a "knowing" from the cross that is deeper and broader than, shall we say, post-Luther apologetical orthodoxy or the restriction of reason to critical and practical. Nor is theological knowing merely the counterreaction to Enlightenment's reasoning. The knowledge revealed and given from the cross is not romanticism, contra Kant; not only Schleiermacher's feeling of absolute dependence on an inchoate transcendental presence as protest against tired and tiring expositions of competing logics. Nor is theological knowing a last-ditch leaping effort of the will to believe because all else is absurd.

The "knowing" given under the cross is a revelation of the fact and significance of the crucified God through a unity of inferential cognition and feeling (a synthesis of the classic supposed binaries of Barth and Schleiermacher). The ontological meaning of revelation and the "sense and taste of the infinite" are wedded in the Theology of the Cross. The sincere theologian "knows" this in the same sense (if partial!) as God "knows" what and whom God loves with intimate presence. The believer "suffers" God, because God is Other and in suffering—being com-passionate, *com-patior*, being-with-patience, being with and receiving from the suffering of the other—the believer, the one who lives in God, suffers (again partially) the suffering of God. Luther anticipates Hamann and Leibniz when Luther states that the person who would be a theologian will herself suffer the cross. What is of the "old Adam," the pride of having done good works and having thought big ideas: all this is destroyed by the cross. The cross subtracts from the believer all her preconceived notions of merit, progress, and self-righteousness. The cross adds to the being of the believer the capacity of a deeper knowledge suffused with patience, humility, gratitude, intellectual and personal hospitality, and receptivity to how God will be God by not playing to or by the world's rules. The would-be be-liever experiences and so *knows* this.[17]

Furthermore, those who meditate on Christ's passion and death recognize their own complicity in the deicide. "We say without hesitation that he

---

17. "Heidelberg Disputation," thesis 21.

who contemplates God's sufferings for a day, an hour, yes, only a quarter of an hour, does better than to fast a whole year, pray a psalm daily, yes, better than to hear a hundred masses. This meditation changes a man's being and, almost like baptism, gives him a new birth. Here the passion of Christ performs its natural and noble work, strangling the old Adam and banishing all joy, delight, and confidence which man could derive from other creatures, even as Christ was forsaken by all, even by God."[18] Change in one's being is no small thing. It encompasses all of a person's heart, mind, and spirit. And it causes all speech to pause for reconsideration, discernment, authenticity, then to issue forth in halting yet trusting and trusted words, because the experienced knowledge of the cross put into words belongs to the Sacrament of Language ringing in and from messianic time.

The Apocalyptic Language of the Cross

Considering that God suffered the darkest effects and affects brought into action by human being is a curriculum that goes deep. This course of study is not a prescription for dramatically sober piety. It is a lifelong course to nurture the self-knowledge that comes with faith. It frees the believer for confidence in God's grace and widens the personal aperture to see and act in the world more congruently with the gospel and the teaching of Jesus. If the Theology of the Cross is Christian epistemology learned in the spiritual realm, it is then the Christian theological method for moral and ethical service in the temporal realm. It serves most profoundly for what is often called Christian formation. It shapes and defines the mature Christian who is "sanctified" by the crucifixion of the old Adam. As well as epistemology and ethic, the Theology of the Cross is also the character marker of the be-liever who has been transformed by the presence of the Spirit of the crucified and raised Christ in the eschatological experience of Messianic Time. Apocalyptic language is integral to this transformational experience. Transformation is not a smooth and seamless process. It is epi-occasional. But the "more" than occasional that apocalypse is spoken, the more the "non-identical repetition"[19] of eschatology is taught and caught, the more one draws breath and new life and promise from the air of messianic time, the more then that the beatitudes are known as true rather than a "Lutheran" trick unto grace. Further, the more one is the be-lieving Christian marked by the cross, the more the be-liever situates herself in and redresses concrete conditions

---

18. Luther, "A Meditation on Christ's Passion," in Lull, *Basic Theological Writings*, 169.

19. David Ford's wonderful term for sacramental experience.

of human suffering in whatever ways she is so gifted. Not all are called to embed themselves in places of war, but each Christian is uniquely gifted to care for the victim and alleviate the circumstances that cause suffering.

The Beatitudes are among the most poignant apocalyptic present indicatives of Christ for the life of the believer. The Beatitudes themselves cannot be "achieved" without having personalized the Theology of the Cross. We regard them as impossible to obey when we think of them as absolute principles, so generalized then that though they may be cross-stitched on linens and minds, they have no particularity for the human heart. Bonhoeffer did not so regard the Beatitudes as general principles. In asserting the Beatitudes as reality—and therefore as real possibilities—he equally asserted their applicability to the *concrete conditions* of life. Just as the Theology of the Cross reveals a God who enters into the concrete conditions of human suffering rather than one who acts "generally" from distant heavens, so also the Beatitudes are specifications of where the Theology of the Cross is practiced concretely. Bonhoeffer could and did say, then, that in the concrete situation of the looming Nazi war against the world, "the cross does not want it."[20] It could be the case, however, that the beatitude for peace might not concretely apply, as war might be required to preserve fallen creation, and so maintain the possibility of gospel revelation. Such is a circumstance when Bonhoeffer envisioned government positively as the *katechon*. But to confess also is to be situational. The same self-giving love commanded of the Christian to obey the authorities, as I have underscored, also intrudes with one's cheek rather than turn it so to defend the victim from the perpetrator. Peace making, as with any beatitudinal action, is work in concrete conditions, where listening to and being with the victim is as important as secular expertise and political savvy.

As did Luther, we do "settle" for the impossibility of fulfilling the Beatitudes. I've come to conclude that as impossible as they are on one's own merit and strength to fulfill, surrendering to the presumption of the impossibility only expresses the insistent influence and standards of the temporal non-eschatological zone in which we also reside. Surrender expresses the truth of our bondage of human will, too, and so underscores that wholeness (*salus*—salvation) indeed is only by grace, free from the law (as when Agamben's Sacrament of Power is misused). Yet, by the sheer grace of the apocalyptic moment of speech in and from messianic time, the Beatitudes are also sublime instances and evocations of the Sacrament of Language. Recall, again, that the Sacrament of Language both signifies the reality of God *and* enacts human and divine intimacy. The Sacrament of Language

---

20. Cited in DeJonge, *Bonhoeffer's Reception*, 165.

is the poetry that "does" (creates) unity from plurality.[21] Agamben's Sacrament of Power more concerns the protocols that sustain the conditions for the "doing" of the Sacrament of Language. One might extrapolate that the Sacrament of Language is the very speech of God Trinity that unites the Persons eternally (!). They identify those who live in Messiah as they also signal the residence of Messiah in be-lievers. The Beatitudes thus mark the Christian aspirations that Christians can live and will incarnate. Bonhoeffer, again, is famous for his consoling counsel that the Christian is bidden by the cross to "come and die." Obedience to the cross shaped and evoked a humility that then invoked the courage of faith and dedication of love to the neighbor's world. There is, so wonderfully and graciously, no other way for the Christian to be and act, unless the eschatology that framed Jesus, the disciples, Paul, Augustine, Luther, and the whole Christian movement is but temporal fiction.

Bonhoeffer's Reframing of Two Kingdoms

Not so long ago the Doctrine of Two Kingdoms was arguably the most important and relevant theopolitical ground for Bonhoeffer's witness against both the church and the state. This, of course, was not his only or even central theological theme. His central theme, synthetically put, is that Christ, whose body is the church (!), rules the kingdom of God that is present also in the state while transcending both church and the state. Immanence and otherness bespeak the presence and rule of God over God's kingdom. Immanence and otherness (my terms), both understandable only to eyes and minds of Spirit-given faith conforming to Christ, help us to imagine the size and place of God's rule. Bonhoeffer is dedicated to the Doctrine of Two Kingdoms to explicate this.

In "Thy Kingdom Come," Bonhoeffer's 1932 essay on how to think about God's kingdom, he warns about and observes the effects of "otherworldliness" and "secularism." "Otherworldliness" refers to the purported Christian desire to separate fully from the world's unrighteousness (as if this were indeed possible). "Secularism" in Bonhoeffer's use is to pledge one's life by default fully to the world's machinations, believing in no spiritual influence. Both of these forms of piety have had deleterious effects on Christian prayer and political action. Neither are responsible ways of explaining two-kingdoms framing. If we are otherworldly, we flee the world's real challenges

---

21. The word "poetry" derives from the Greek *poeisis*, to do. Poetry "does" something and adds to the knowledge for and between the writer, hearer, and referents that literalism cannot do.

to and infliction of suffering on all lives, illusorily instead thinking we can construct our own peaceable eternity with "church only." Those who try this escapism inevitably are shocked to discover "politics in the church" and may find themselves repulsed by both the spiritual and the political. This disposition today is likely also with those who would abandon "religion" for "spirituality."

On the other hand is a Christian embrace of secularism. Having "reasonably" concluded that religion is about things that do not "really" exist, Christians can easily become secularists, thinking that our concerns should *only* be about this material realm that God created and called good, and that therefore we should also enjoy and let live in a happy "seize-the-day" spirit. This kind of secularism is not that of which Augustine spoke. The attitude here that Bonhoeffer rightly criticized is a privileging of the material over the spiritual, the concrete over the eternal. Psychologists know well of this concrete operational mind that presents unique challenges to teachers of theology and poetry. Concrete operational minds easily become literalist when reading texts. They also easily can adapt to a secularity that conforms to Enlightenment rationalism while rejecting a spiritual realm predicated by dogma and doctrine.

Bonhoeffer recognizes that these two dispositions of otherworldliness and secularism[22] are related. They are not binaries. They signal the root crisis of lack of faith in God's kingdom, which is to say, lack of faith in Christ himself and where he chooses to be and speak. So Bonhoeffer: "We are other-worldly or we are secularists, but in either case this means that we no longer *have* faith in God's kingdom."[23] Faith instead sees Christ in the neighbor and sees the kingdom of Christ in the opposite of how humans imagine a glorious reign; faith sees the kingdom in the suffering temporal world. For purported Christians to attempt to convert the secular world into their image of kingdom by controlling it, like the enthusiasts of Luther's day, is not to have faith. They fail to see that God's kingdom is on earth, as the secularist does not see that it is *God's* kingdom that is on earth. To have faith would mean *serving*, not "converting," the suffering neighbor in daily life *and* to see that Christ is in those who are served. The secularist might be moved to consider the neighbor compassionately as a bearer of the image of God, or, at least, dignity. But the Christian is supposed to *know* better, having had one's eyes opened at least epi-occasionally to God's kingdom come and spoken. To have faith active in love within the temporal kingdom

---

22. Again, he treats both terms in regard to their "Christian" use. Bonhoeffer is not addressing the meaning of secularism in the larger non-religious manner as contemporary culture regards it.

23. Quoted in DeJonge, *Bonhoeffer's Reception*, 108.

would mean to advocate for and shape a political order that preserves and enhances life.

Bonhoeffer saw this as God's holy work of preservation, which is tasked to government, in which the Christian with all others is to be active. Bonhoeffer even says that Christ after his crucifixion is only recognized in twofold form as church and state, reigning from the left and right hands of God; in other words, as one lord of one kingdom broken into two realms, to be united again in Christ's own time of eschatological fulfillment when the temporal has been fully transformed into the spiritual.[24] Only then by God's purposing will the spiritual kingdom's vocation as the proclaimer of miracle and redemption finally blend fully with the temporal kingdom's priority of protection. Only then too will the temporal state even turn inside-out Paul's negative valuing of the *katechon*, because the state that acts rightly will resist (acting as *katechon*) all attempts either to destroy life or force the coming of God's full kingdom. "Forcing the kingdom" indeed would be but a religious ideological wish dream, the violent imposition of subjectivity, which too would be tantamount to the world's destruction. Bonhoeffer's recognition against his malevolent state of exception is that God would prefer the righteous nation to resist the onslaught of forced religion, while righteous religion would resist the onslaught of absolutist politics. Turn history's page to today and people of faith must similarly confess-instruct that the righteous state, per a proper following of Two Kingdoms, should resist Christian Nationalism and that the faithful church would nonviolently advocate and partner in this resistance.

The church has no life other than to be active in the world and in coordinated collaboration with the state, for the church is dedicated to God's action of *preservatio* too. But this dedication is a consequence of the church's priority function of proclaiming the gospel message of justification. The proclamation of the gospel—which is a dutiful apocalyptic act—then evokes the two-kingdoms distinction. It leads the believer to plead that God's kingdom would come and God's will be done as in heaven; spiritual kingdom first, temporal second. It is on the apocalyptic good news of justification that the church stands or falls. On this basis Bonhoeffer described the church's work as declaring the redeeming miracle of God and the state's work as the protective ordering of God.[25] The spiritual and temporal jurisdictions neither interfere with nor fully separate from one another. Both work together

---

24. Bonhoeffer, "Christology," DBWE 12:326–28.
25. Bonhoeffer, "Thy Kingdom Come," DBWE 12:292–93.

and never either alone. Thus they point "to the kingdom of God, which is here attested in such splendid twofold form."[26]

Bonhoeffer thus mitigates the complaint of some against Two Kingdoms as biblically unfaithful enumeration. More importantly he clarifies how the divinely charged tasks of the spiritual and temporal governments are constitutively important. "Common sense" does not always appreciate this. "Common sense" complains about what it sees as unnecessary complication. "Why can't theologians just say that we should bring our faith to our politics and just love the neighbor?" Of late the complaint is a refrain in all political campaigns. But in the perceived all-encompassing relevance of "just bring your faith to your politics" is the question of the existence of and the nature of faith itself. Bonhoeffer's complaint is addressed to both church and state; to both the presumptive dominance of the "otherworldlies" and the secularists, as well as to the *Deutsche Christen* or any identitarian-predicators of Christianity who add their preferred perversion to the faith. The first two collapse the distinction of Two Kingdoms and neglect their proper roles. The third is a form of the prior two that idolatrously adds imagined transcendence of identity politics to the enmeshment of religious enthusiasm and ideological secularism.

These options have served as supposedly positive and ready answers to the desire that people should bring faith into politics. But the long experienced destructive consequences of blithe "faith solutions" in our fractious politics have made many temporal voters hostile to any collaboration of faith and politics. Religious justifications for war are chief among reasons for the public dismissal of religion in politics. Other contemporary negative responses to religion in politics are similar. The re-birthed religious ideology that women should be baby makers and homemakers in a "complementarian" relationship to the supremacy of their husbands has not done well for politics. A purportedly religious commitment to the abolition of women's bodily autonomy and against all abortion does not account for the religious freedom of faithful Jews who believe differently about the beginning of human life. Prescribed prayer in public schools, mandated posting of the Ten Commandments in all classrooms, and insertion of untrained religious chaplains on school staffs after removal of trained school counselors all work more in the long run more like an anti-religion anesthetic than cultivation of spiritual sensitivity. Religion as heteronomy for the multi-religious and a-religious public does not evoke faith. The Reformation insight still holds. The law positively enforces public order (first-use). But when law is used to forcibly march people toward particular virtues of a hegemonic

---

26. Bonhoeffer, "Thy Kingdom Come," DBWE 12:294.

faith, only three responses are possible: (1) despair at not actually achieving the virtuous/religious end; (2) the false pride of having "saved" oneself; or (3) rebellion against religious overreach. Government speech that would enforce faith would exemplify the severe misuse of what Agamben called the Sacrament of Power.

Ironically, politicians who persevere with the agenda of forced moralism are in league with the liberalism that morphs into pronounced anti-religiosity.[27] Consider how the French Declaration of the Rights of Man and the Citizen invited the Reign of Terror, or how initial righteous protest of a state's egregious maltreatment of Palestinians metastasized into anti-Semitism. Such extreme liberalism rehearses the Enlightenment consensus that reduced spirituality to moralism and faith's knowledge to sequestered subjectivity, restricted from intercourse with "real" reason. The counter-punch of conservatism yields no better, relying on the same "rational" economy. Real religion, however—the spiritual tissue that re-ligaments head and heart and active hands—has its own legitimate warrants for living with a coherence of differently dimensioned temporalities. Contemporary cosmology; Pauline eschatology as both a Presence and a Not-Yet; the rediscovery of the meaning of apocalyptic; the creative power of language and the reality of messianic time as expressed by the deep literary archeology of Agamben; the more expansive understanding of reason offered by Hamman, Leibniz, and many more; the Theology of the Cross itself marking the nexus of enjoying eternity with the suffering of human temporality: all this feeds into the "complicated" answer of a political theology that carefully delimits the roles of church and state while also stating when and why they must hold the other to account. But in the end, it is not all *so* complicated. It is enough that the spiritual and the temporal are delimited and yet correlative, separate and mutually accountable.

It is also enough, and challenge enough, for the person of faith to see in the neighbor the face of Christ while graciously and humbly serving him or her with no sense of superiority. To rejoice in one's freedom as a liberated suffering servant in Christ is not to lord it over the neighbor who does not see himself or herself in the same way. This is the exact antidote for the malady of faith gone wild in and overwhelmed by politics. Politically determined faith in the end is unfaith. It is ironically secular in its lack of eschatological consciousness. Robert Jenson recognized this problem early in his career. His diagnosis still holds: "The believer's social involvement must not be an attempt to 'Christianize' the social order, or to achieve churchly domination

---

27. I have in mind the ideological heirs of Bentham, opposed to any hint of religion in the public space.

of culture or state. For this attempt assumes that Christ is not already lord of all human community—which is the assumption of unbelief."[28]

There is more to say about Bonhoeffer's example on this matter. It impinges on how the faithful Christian "knows" what she is about as a thoughtful person. The church is constituted by the proclamation of the presence of the crucified and risen Christ, forgiving sin and bestowing life abundant. In *Act and Being*, Bonhoeffer conceptualizes revelation (which I interpret here as the received knowledge of God) under the mode of being. This too is a necessary implication of the Theology of the Cross. God is what and how God is revealed! God is revealed as the crucified one, and God is revealed in the creative act of language. *Deus dixit*. Indeed, the clearest and most definitive word about who God is is spoken from the cross. *Deus dixit ex cruce*, and that contextualizes all else that God has spoken to both the spiritual and the temporal. Because God's inexhaustible compassion is spoken from the cross—"today you will be with me in paradise!"—at the very nexus of eternity and history, the cross conjoins the spiritual and temporal kingdoms. There God speaks from and for suffering humanity which is all humanity, and God speaks as the Sacrament of Language so to bring and preserve people in intimacy with God. Those who have heard follow the shepherd's voice.[29] Those who live in and from him, who "heard" him and so be-lieve in him, are gathered to where he speaks as church, and they go to where God in Christ speaks as fellow sufferer. "Feed my sheep."[30] Love my sheep. Jesus identifies with his sheep and with the caregivers of the sheep. And Jesus, the Christ, gives all that is necessary, himself, to his appointed caregivers to think and do this work.

Bonhoeffer's own mystical appreciation then elides with a proper literalism. The church *is* "*Christus praesens*." The church then receives and acts from and with all that Christ gives in communion with the church. The church is and is to be, then, the spiritual kingdom's expression of Christ's attributes in the temporal order. The church lives in and from the shared attributes, the *communicatio idiomatum*, of Christ, including Christ's bearing/forgiving of sin so to bestow righteousness. How eschatologically different the church would appear to a wondering and wandering temporal "seeker" when the church so intentionally would receive and manifest its Being from and as Christ and accordingly act! How much more, even in banal terms, would and should the church be the evident eschatological presence for Flatlanders.

28. Jenson, *God After God*, 5.
29. John 10:27-28.
30. John 21:15-25.

The church and the people of Christ so seen would be known (that word again) as revelation of holy presence, word, and act that together inspire direct human action of neighbor love. The beloved is *acted upon* by the lover to love. The action of love then is not a "considered response." It is not an afterthought. The action of love, of self-giving, is an action of self-knowledge, knowing that one is a person "only in the act of self-giving" while still free from the one to whom one gives oneself.[31] The action of love unreflectively impelled by the announcement of the gospel in spoken and visible words (sacraments) is itself then also a mode of knowing that Kant would not know.[32]

The impetus for the enthusiast and ideologue who would forcefully make government over in a theocratic image or a secular Leviathan is power lust, not compassion for the neighbor. Zealots of secularity are problem enough. But zealots for religio-political utopianism by force of personal will and law are not in-formed by anything near as profound as the Theology of the Cross. I do not discern Bonhoeffer as having appealed to the *theologia crucis* explicitly in arguing how the church should relate to the state. But the theology is evident there even so. The themes of Christ as "fellow sufferer," Christ in the neighbor, God in the "form of the opposite" bespeak Bonhoeffer's cruciform orientation. Bonhoeffer's developed Christology and ecclesiology of Christ as tangibly present, the *Christus praesens*, is a full retrieval and elaboration of Luther's Theology of the Cross. In being so, Bonhoeffer's Christology and ecclesiology demonstrate that the Theology of the Cross is not only a matter of knowing God, though that is rather a large matter in itself! Because it extends to the act and being of Christ in the believer, for Bonhoeffer and for Luther the Theology of the Cross is a matter of the believer's being and then acting as a member of the body of Christ. The believer *knows* who she is by so being. And so knowing and being, the be-liever then *acts* unreflectively in and with love for the neighbor. Further, the knowing, acting, and being are not "sequential." Like the experience Agamben intends to illumine in his terms of Sacrament of Language, knowing-acting-being are mutually related and simultaneous; they are immanental. Choose one and you get the whole deal.

This is a knowing, a positive gnosis, different than the knowing that is more reductively defined as critical and practical reason. This is the kind of knowing that is distinctive to the Christian. It is neither unreasonable nor unprovable. By its fruit it is known. Faith as a gift of simultaneous being

---

31. Bonhoeffer, *Act and Being*, DBWE 2:128.

32. For a fine excursus on Bonhoeffer's development of the Theology of the Cross in answer both to Barth and Heidegger, see de Keijzer, "Revelation as Being."

and acting is a kind of holy pragmatism. It proves itself by its motivation and movement toward the good. It does not dismiss critical reason. It is not embraced in a leap of faith because it is absurd. This knowing is revealed and responsive. This knowing is an immediacy of receiving and reciprocating. In that respect, this knowing is the immediate consequence of what Agamben calls the Sacrament of Language. God "acts" in the proclamation of the word. In that moment of the recognition of messianic time the "being" of both God and human in communion is revealed. Apocalypse happens. Then act happens again, this time in love's service to neighbor. Critical reason on its own still is paramount for the strategic thinking necessary to identify the systemic dynamics that cause suffering and then effectively to address them in the work of temporal government. The gift of faith, an event of giftedness again and again, moves the whole person into acting for the neighbor without losing, but even gaining, oneself. And in the gaining of oneself the gift of faith inspires the desire for discipline in the faith.

This dynamic activity marks God's love in the believer and the church together. It marks the uniqueness of the spiritual kingdom and the work of the church, even as it then stretches to serve and connect with the hidden crucified Christ in the secular world. After all, Christ has given himself in love to and for all the world already and gives still. The person of the spiritual kingdom *knows* this and *knows* in a very personal and differently rational way that she is so loved distinctly, just *as* she knows too that Christ loves all the world. If I do not act as if Christ loves all the world, which is to say every person in it, then I do not recognize Christ's love being for and in me. If I do not recognize and live from Christ's love for me as a distinctively gifted individual with a particular voice and vocation, then I cannot say with integrity that Christ loves the world or is even in the world "generally." But to confess such love and commitment is immediately to identify myself with all humanity in its suffering and joys and thus to act on my catholicity under the cross of the crucified and risen Lord of all.

To confess *Christus praesens* in me, in the church, in the church in the world, is to assert with Luther that Christ is in solidarity with, indeed in-with-under, the neighbor. If Luther's definition of a sacrament is that which Christ is "in-with-and under," then not only is Christ our sacrament, so also is the church a sacrament for the world, and so also (if not consistently recognized!) those who be-lieve are themselves sacraments. We who live in Christ, which is to be-lieve, are sacred events on the earth, works of the Holy Spirit, apostles to Flatlanders. These statements may seem to be mere syllogisms. But syllogisms under both pure *and* faithful reason illumine the fullness of knowing and so inform also how to act. The Theology of the Cross is epistemology with the immediacy of ethics. It is its own moral spiritual disposition just as it is realized in its own ecclesiology. It *necessarily* identifies the citizens of the spiritual kingdom and *necessarily* enjoins and inspires Christ's citizens to act for the fullness and justice of life in the temporal kingdom.

The Sacrament of Language Is Apocalyptic

I take Agamben's discussion about the Sacrament of Language to refer to God's speech act of creation and promise. I also connect it with the positive understanding and role of apocalyptic as the language of a church with an eschatological consciousness. By God's utterance, order is brought from chaos, meaning from confusion, and with the consequences of God's speech act, God's Word creates words. God's words vivify. They bring forth life. The point of God's first speech acts is human being itself, what the psalmist called the very "crown of creation."[33] By speaking creative words, by speaking the temporal into existence, God not only or even merely creates. God binds human beings to God and each other by this divine gift of language itself. And by creating human being in God's own image, God thus enables "God-in-the-human" (in the humus) to speak "God" back to God. *That* God enables words to be uttered from the human is the original promise of solidarity from and with the only true Sovereign, God with relatively sovereign individual human beings.

The first words of the Hebrew Bible are a revelation *in speech*. They are, in the most proper sense of the word, apocalyptic. What do they reveal? What truth do they disclose? Several themes converge and connect here. Language is sacramental, as Agamben puts it, because by its very offering it promises a positive binding relationship. We cannot speak until God first speaks to us. The first word is from and about transcendence. In the Urmyth, God creates by speaking a word. *Ish* and *Ishah* are created, each and together in God's image, each sacred human, each *Homo Sacer*, each created for joy in relationship, each created and bound in relationship with their Creator and each other.

What is the first thing that God does for them? God speaks. *Deus dicit.* God speaks a first word of further creation, blessing the sacred humans bearing God's image with the vocation of birthing more sacred humans as stewards of world of abundant life. Every subsequent event of creation and stewardship—the managing act not of violent domination but of enacting God's goodness—is contingent on the fact that God spoke, *Deus dixit*,

---

33. Ps 8:5.

personally to human being. That God has spoken undergirds our creaturely communication. With that, the charge to human beings to steward the creation extends the purpose of God's speech to preserve and sustain the creation with the goodness of words, even by human beings first naming the elements of creation. Contra Derrida's rather grand claim, stewardship by words is not necessarily to exercise domination. It is not that at all in Agamben's parsing of language's sacramental/vow character. It is to speak and act so to distribute God's words through human words with their intent of communion. By God's first speaking, God gave the gift of community and the capacity to speak for communion. Language is a communion service that reveals God and Human Being together as the Alpha and Omega of language. With the Sacrament of Language, God created the community that God intends to transcend Agamben's ironic *Homo Sacer*[34] that is repeatedly called again to hear and speak the point of the Sacrament of Language, and charges in language to preserve the peaceable community, all of which God spoke into being. The Sacrament of Language, then, is revelatory. It is apocalyptic. Apocalyptic reveals the truth of all truths and draws people into truth's purpose of relationship that fulfills individual integrity. Apocalyptic language is truth telling and truth inviting.

I put a finer point on it. Apocalyptic speech is not against the Enlightenment's canons of reason. Rather, it supports and fulfills them, not unlike Christ's declaration that he came not to abolish, but to fulfill the law. Apocalyptic language is just as counter to the cynical nihilism of today's intellectual fad of social constructivism as is critical realism. The difference is that apocalyptic language is more capacious than critical realism even as apocalyptic language can use and ally with critical realism for apocalyptic speech's purpose of inviting the hearer into messianic time. Reality is not just what anyone makes of it. Reality is not the epistemic *tohu wabohu* (chaos and confusion) of aggregated "my truths" to which today's undergraduates unreflectively subscribe. This lazy side of postmodernity indeed is the totalitarian's tool for lying with such consistency so as to cult-ivate followers who believe whatever the autocrat says, because finally they've been convinced by the autocrat's dependence on their own intellectual lassitude that nothing

---

34. A full systematic theology in an Agamben form would require much elaboration and qualification of his key theme of *Homo Sacer*. As I noted earlier, I read the term as an emphasis on the dignity and integrity of the human being who, sovereign of one's own life, will not be sacrificed by others or the nation for its own political purposes masked by religious pretensions. But, being political, the unjust state murders/kills humans, innocent as well as criminal. Thus the *Homo Sacer* is a sacred (unto oneself) human who may be murdered but not sacrificed. I think Agamben takes this theme, however, in a direction that is too libertarian and, finally, even ideological, such that he betrays his better original intentions.

is true. So apocalyptic speech does not hesitate, as the Theology of the Cross requires, to tell the truth. Temporal reality is temporally real, though conditioned by sin and requiring appropriate suspicion. Temporal reality has its opaque integrity, but integrity nonetheless. It therefore deserves the regard in language first charged, to be stewarded with the disposition of overseers in the temporal peaceable kingdom who are knowingly responsible with the power of language.

And a finer point yet. Apocalyptic speech tactically should blend with the prosaic without losing itself in whatever way necessary to tell the truth. Apocalyptic speech will state the real without pulling punches and without itself becoming violent. Apocalyptic speech also avoids the counter-extreme of being so gentle and merely suggestive that it lacks the authority of faith's conviction. It helps to reveal the eternal/eschatological within the temporal. Sometimes apocalyptic language must defy the conventions of daily life and strain to counter the trappings of habit and boredom. But apocalyptic speech does not swing so far as to invent and entice with spectacle, as with a surplus of national flags around the largest gilded cross over which an F-15 flies and the national anthem is sung . . . all "in worship." Apocalyptic perseveres against the anti-truth of both boredom and spectacle by being more prayerfully diligent with the power of language. Apocalyptic language clarifies the nature of God's power in history against the power of evil, naming evil outright (!) and the good even more emphatically,[35] as apocalyptic language also will and often must use compelling and poetic imagination suffused by the eschatological *Christus praesens* to achieve its ends. Apocalyptic language is truth telling, nothing more and nothing less. Apocalyptic language may need imagination to evoke attention. So many Sundays even in the purported spiritual realm have only been temporal, misusing language as power to make ears partisan and to dull them with desultory rationality.

Luther himself, as Ulrich Duchrow attests, was in this "apocalyptic New Testament Augustinian tradition," believing that God will defeat all evil and fully establish God's kingdom on earth.[36] Apocalyptic speech as truth telling is documented as part and parcel of the eschatological consciousness of the church fathers, as well. The primary event for the telling of truth by the early church was its own keen attention to word and sacrament. So said Hippolytus, "For neither is a mere place able to be called a church, nor a house which is built with stone and clay, nor a man himself able to call

---

35. Consonant with and required by the Theology of the Cross.
36. Duchrow, *Lutheran Churches*, 23.

himself a church.... What therefore is a church? A community of saints participating in truth."[37]

What then of the necessary words *after* the Sacrament of Language? Not all, not even a small fraction, of speech carries the full forceful inspiration of its eschatological origin, and the memory of its intended future inevitably grows faint when we return as we must to the desultory experience of *chronos*. This is why believers have sabbath, so that real eschatological knowing might be fired "again for the first time" in the event of messianic time. Of course, the delights of temporality (which we should enjoy and be grateful for!) can and do impinge on and compromise messianic time. This is why language becomes "after" messianic time more prescriptive than ecstatic and gracious. Again, Agamben called this the Sacrament of Power, when language is used to describe, protect, preserve, extend, and adjudicate human action as to its degree of coherence or incoherence with the original and originative sacrament.[38] He calls it a "sacrament" because, again, an oath is involved. This time the oath is somewhat more voluntary. It is not as immediately implied and rather involuntary, as is the matter of using language at its and our origin. Agamben's "Sacrament of Language" terminology, in other words, accents the grace of God Creator.

Agamben's terminology of "Sacrament of Power," on the other hand, accents human responsibility. This declension of language provides a helpful means to understand anew the obligations embedded in the two-kingdoms typology. In the spiritual realm, God revealed God's Being by acting (creating) originatively with language. God speaks. Human beings respond with understanding that God has spoken. *Deus dixit*. That human beings are given the capacity to speak and that we do speak in return to God and to each other is an implicit, if initially unrecognized, acceptance of God's oath of solidarity in language and the human obligation in return to speak for the cause of communion with God and each other. The term "Sacrament of Power" describes our human speech subsequent to and increasingly distant from the originative sacrament. This subsequent speech must serve and preserve the original and originative purpose of the "Sacrament of Language" to enjoy and "be" God's community of diversity. This "Sacrament of Power," subject to and constructing of history, can be used and is intended by God's institution of temporal authority to be used for the preservation and amplification of community. This is when the administration of law is and must be for communal justice and individual equality.

---

37. Hippolytus, *Commentary on Daniel* 1.18.5–6. Thanks to Michael J. Svigel for the reference.

38. This also describes doctrinal theology as second-order discourse.

This "sacrament" can be misused for self-servingness (most commonly preferred) at the expense of community, or for communitarian totalitarianism at the expense of individual integrity. Greed for personal power marks Agamben's negative "second use" of linguistic law. The misuse of power is evident when unnatural suffering occurs. Unnatural suffering is unjust suffering. It happens because someone of power as physical and mental force inflicts domination and cruelty. Any of these actors may enjoy the support too of legal philosophy that reads history eisegetically.[39] Here is where the school of Hart recognizes that just law and just law enforcement must alleviate the problem. Hart-theory holds that there is no such "thing" as natural or higher law. With everyone in a "common sense" way except sociopaths, Hart-theory recognizes when something is not fair, and unjust suffering is just that. In its way in the spiritual jurisdiction, the Theology of the Cross agrees, because it also sees that God is with those who suffer. So being in solidarity with the sufferer, God pleads for the believer's aid in alliance with temporal authorities. The Theology of the Cross holds its own spiritual trump card, that *natural* suffering too requires Christian compassion. "All creation groans with eager longing for the revelation of the children of God."[40] The state may and does respond helpfully to that too. We are thankful when government responds as best as it can to natural tragedy with its limited resources. But prayer has its own holy etiology, and miracles cannot be legislated. They are of the transcendent domain.

In sum, the duet of compassion and common sense of fairness together replace what political philosophy and Augustinian Christianity had regarded as common natural and higher law in the temporal kingdom. Per the Hart tradition, that duet should be and has been serving as the criterion for making, adjudicating, and enforcing law. But the duet is not always sung clearly. Lately, dissonant voices again praise that power that inflicts unjust suffering. This is precisely that point when authorities in the spiritual jurisdiction must step in and restore sonority. At just such a time all who knowingly live their lives primarily from the graces of the spiritual kingdom are charged to salve the wounds and redress the wrong-doers in the temporal kingdom. All Augustinian Christians who daily claim the gift and promise of their baptisms are called to cross the soft boundary between the spiritual and the temporal, to advise or even chastise secular "thought influencers" for their injustice and to aid the suffering neighbor in whatever

---

39. Noted in ch. 3. See also Gienapp, *Against Constitutional Originalism*. Gienapp shows how current Supreme Court justices have projected their unspoken assumptions onto the original document, not recognizing that eighteenth-century constitutional thinking was foundationally different than their own.

40. Rom 8:19.

way possible. The believer's rationale is related to but more specific than the rationale for resistance of compassionate nonbelievers. Nonbelievers follow what is still recognized as the basic universal expectation of fairness for and imputation of dignity to all human beings. Believers act on that basis and because by such oppression any consequence of the freedom of the gospel, which is to say the gospel itself, is suppressed. Any suffering calls for compassion from neighbor to neighbor. The Christian obligation additionally is to bring the more personalizing love of God along with the right physical care to the suffering neighbor. The disciples not only healed the sick and saw to the care and feeding of the marginalized. The disciples brought to suffering humanity the eschatological word of the new future begun.[41] They simply announced the good news in word and deed and left outcomes to the mercy of the Spirit. They did not model some hackneyed evangelical tactic of preaching a conversion sermon before feeding the hungry or healing wounds. It is to advocate such personalized and attentive care with evident hospitality that the helper should act in such a non-performative humane way that the helped cannot but ask why the helper is helping. The answer is that the love of God and the love of neighbor are inextricable.

When the Church Declares a State of Exception

Any of us who *know* suffering know that much disinterest rules the reasoning of government. There are those in temporal government who will not provide Medicaid for the medically helpless or meals for hungry school children even if resources were freely offered. Governing authorities emplace unfair law to enhance their own interests over the good of the people. History tells repeatedly of state leaders of nations anywhere who play neighbors against neighbors and groups against groups to divert attention from their personal agendas and covert schemes. Political opponents weaponize what they can of the institutions to denigrate the authority and his followers. Church officials collude to hide and protect sexual abusers within their own ranks and publicly scapegoat victimized women so to secure their male-dominant subculture. Any and every group of like-minded self-interests, no matter the political or religious orientation, can fall to these machinations. For any and every such political or religious group self-identified Christians have strenuously stated their justifications. None of them have succeeded or ever will, because none of them at such times have regarded the neighbor

---

41. Cf. Acts 3:1–10.

above self. None gave themselves to even a Hart-sense of legal compassion, much more to seeing Christ in those who suffer.

When temporal and spiritual authorities refuse calls for accountability and fail to correct themselves, one can make the case that the freedom of the gospel itself is being suppressed. Then spiritual resistance of individuals in prayer, political activism, and nonviolent action are appropriate for the believer. One could add the argument that such occasions mandate a church response of public resistance. The original Lutheran policy, as we recall from chapter 2 in our conversation about Article 10 of the Formula of Concord and the use of the so-called Doctrine of the Lesser Magisteria, was that a declaration of a state of confession (*in statu confessionis*) was required when the freedom of the gospel itself was at stake. Charles V's attempted suppression of new Lutheran worship practices and publications was judged by the Lutherans to be just such an occasion to require this resistance. Likewise prompted were the Christians who signed onto the Barmen Declaration. Two-Kingdoms thinking further instructed that the church itself, being of the peaceable spiritual kingdom, could not engage in violent resistance. But given this particular "state of exception," the temporal authorities could employ violence under the rules of just warfare. And so they did.

An argument against current immoral and unfaithful practice could go further (and to which I am not committed to a final answer). Why would immoral practices by the "state" as exemplified above not be subject to the church's declaration of a state of confession? Is there not a point in the oppression of the neighbor that the neighbor is so constrained as a victim as to be denied the right to life, the right to liberty, the right to the pursuit of happiness, including the right to religious freedom, the latter of which would be the right to hear the proclamation of the gospel, to hear God speak? Is that not a suppression of the freedom of the gospel itself? If so, many occasions of suffering then may be situations for confession that require the additional response of nonviolent Christian resistance as well as what should be expected as simply human compassion.[42] Christ's solidarity with the suffering commands no less.

There are cases, however, when the suppression of the gospel is even more explicit, and so the call for resistance must be even more formalized. I've noted this with respect to church vs. state. Bonhoeffer's denunciation of the Nazi regime and his call for the church nonviolently to resist by keeping to the purity of the gospel still exemplifies the proper response. But what of occasions today when the matter is both an ecumenical and a religion/government relational problem? What of when a movement within the church

---

42. And so the witness of William Stringfellow again comes on stage.

would go against the church itself, and the former doing so in alliance with sectors of government?

This is when recurring movements like Christian Nationalism must be faced head-on. The "Seven Mountains Mandate" articulation of Christian Nationalism,[43] to which one poll concludes that 41 percent of Christians subscribe,[44] is such a case. Seven Mountains Dominionism theology takes its title from Rev 17:1–18 with focus on v. 9: "This calls for a mind that has wisdom: the seven heads are seven mountains . . ." The interpretation claims to be literal. It is a classic case of eisegesis, of imputing subjective ideology onto and into a text and then claiming the interpretation as the text's originalist meaning. This belief system holds that Christians must assume authority and lead in all seven primary areas of culture: family, religion, education, media, arts and entertainment, business, and government. The theological agenda now infuses ultraconservative government policy. Policy examples include the aims of: rerouting funds from public school systems to private schools, including religious schools, with the long-range goal of privatizing public schools; teaching and enforcing male hierarchy in the family and church; and maximally legalizing the freedom of religious business owners to refuse services to certain populations. The eschatology of this form of Christian Nationalism is of the flat, linear sort I've referenced often. The movement's followers train in and practice "spiritual warfare" to exorcise the mountains of their secular demons. Seven Mountain believers allow that violence may be necessary to actualize God's kingdom. They believe they are following Isa 2:2 ("the mountain of the Lord's house shall be established as the highest of the mountains") and will thus by their actions initiate the end times. This belief system is actually ironic: its eschatology depends on human action. It contradicts the proper eschatology of God's kingdom now and "coming again." It is also "anti-katechonic" (a peculiar inversion of the *katechon*, being katechonically anti-katechonic) and so proving itself as a clear and present threat to the gospel because it presumes to hasten by human hands the destruction of God's creation and people, rather than to delay the linear end of history so that the freedom of the gospel may yet prevail.

Here may well be the occasion when the faithful church must declare its own state of exception to its usual church practice of being ecumenical, precisely because (given the "rules of exception") Christian Nationalism suppresses the gospel by falsely teaching it. I proposed with youthful bravado and naivete some years ago that the whole church catholic was

---

43. Johnson and Wallnau, *Invading Babylon*.
44. On this poll by Denison University, see Butler, "Christian Nationalists," para. 19.

long past due for convening an ecumenical council to publish its conviction on proper biblical interpretation and the nature of the gospel. Official ecumenical conversations progressed well on those issues. But they do not and will not "trickle-down" into popular consciousness. And it is unlikely that we'll ever see another attempt at a truly global ecumenical council. So, for church traditions like Lutheranism, the question must be asked: Is this time of religious and political fracture and outright false teaching one, like the Barmen Declaration, when we should declare again a case of confession, *in casu confessionis*? The Two Kingdoms doctrine, renewed by the Theology of the Cross and rekindled by proper eschatology with appropriately apocalyptic speech, urges our prayerful discernment.

The Urgent Work of the Church

The reader may now see the structure and consequences of my reimagining of the Two Kingdoms doctrine as influenced by Agamben and many others. I turned to them to illumine what the church has practiced from old and should attend to again: the centrality of the spiritual so then to support a healthy and just temporal polity. This includes the hosting of worship services, education for faith formation and service, prayer groups, and joyful togetherness in community. The pastoral aim is for all this experience to resonate with eschatological consciousness, responsibly employ apocalyptic language, and welcome that extraordinary moment when the gift of Christ is immediately known as "for you" rather than merely framed as words *about* God.

It all starts with messianic time. If we are convinced of messianic time's insertions into human temporality, if we also are convinced that this is an oft repeating apocalypse of the present transcending eschaton "all around us" as our larger dimensional manifold, then the church is only so when we are defined by this experience of messianic time and are one with it.[45] The church lives by its consciousness of messianic time and is church only insofar as it inheres in messianic time. This gives the church a quintessentially different character than that world which lives only in historical, linear time. A religious community is unfaithful to the true scriptural witness if that community lives by the secular notion of linearity and so construes eschatology as that deliverance awaiting us merely at the end of our ride on the arrow of time. This is *the* critical point. Eschatology is about the inbreaking of the time of the end, not an extrapolated end of time. Christ's church then does not lament "the delay of the kingdom." It does not look

---

45. This, admittedly, requires so much more to be taught and learned.

to the past merely to fashion a flatlandish future. And it certainly does not then reduce highly symbolic archetypal scriptural and poetic imagery to the caricatures of novellas and comic tracts. As Agamben clarified in a direct address to French prelates and theologians, "Because there is no place in messianic time for a fixed and final habitation, there is no time for delay." Citing 1 Thess 5:1–2, Agamben defines the spiritual sensibility of the church as being always attuned to Christ's coming, because "he who comes" is "he who never ceases to come."[46] Messianic time transforms chronological time from within. The church is only so when it is so grasped, proclaiming, and hosting of this time. And so the church also, when so grasped and "hosting," can only be church when its words befit both the eschatological and apocalyptic energy of the repeatedly irrupting messianic moment. In this, Agamben's messianic time coheres, if not identifies, with Bonhoeffer's *Christus praesens*. Then Agamben offers a prophetic word: "Where do we find such an experience of time in today's Church? . . . An evocation of final things, of ultimate things, has so completely disappeared from the statements of the Church that it has been said not without irony, that the Roman Church has closed its eschatological window."[47]

Agamben speaks of the church he knows in Italy and France. He criticizes what he finds as an absence of awe. I'm grateful for Catholic and Protestant colleagues alike whose spiritual disposition is not so "non-mystical." But surely we know too of mainline and, increasingly, evangelical churches with few of the eschatological windows that faith requires. So inured to the claims of "he's coming soon" after waiting thousands of years on a time line never meant for such weight, many persons admit they believe eschatology is no more than a fictional device, more about the meaninglessness of *Waiting for Godot* than spiritual extrasensory perception.

On the other hand, some evangelical theologians are returning to the early church fathers, like Irenaeus of Lyons, to retrieve their eschatology of "already but not fully yet."[48] They are retrieving a more responsible vision of a world gradually being transformed into the City of God, like Augustine's vision. But they still accent unnecessarily the unidirectionality of a temporal arrow heading in the direction of "premillennial eschatology." Not so many religious leaders of the Great Tradition, it seems, speak now in excitedly convicted tones of Christ being "really present" in sermons built on the grammar of poetry and directed in the second-person plural. Not so many speak evocatively and preside invitationally in and from the qualitatively different

---

46. Agamben, *Church and the Kingdom* (CK), 5.

47. CK, 27.

48. Cf. Svigel, *Fathers on the Future*.

messianic time by which holy transcendence reverberates in the event of church. Not so many priests and pastors speak with the Sacrament of Language so that fellow communicants, imbued with sparkling-eyed courage might again with their own customized expertise go meet neighbors in their needs. Not so many are charged by God's suffering grandeur, like Hopkins' world, to move from being in messianic time's event as church to acting from such divine immediacy for the good of banal history. And many still preach and teach, as with children's sermons meant for all, that we should be good; better, be like Jesus; better yet, do what Jesus would do, with the fatal implication that "we," with Jesus cheering us from a distance, can. And then remember that no matter what, and no matter how we don't do those things, God loves us, as if church really is little more than the piling of Enlightenment moral imperatives atop moral imperatives, then by a few words to be liberated of those burdens by the declaration of God's love. "Never mind! God loves you anyway!" It all true enough in the temporal kingdom's terms. But it is not enough at all in the spiritual kingdom's purposes. There, whence "apocalypse happens," the poetry of a real and realizing eschatology means to change our clocks with worship within messianic time.

Human words have limits. Of course preaching can never with critically aware reasoning state definitively and fully *how* the presence of the spiritual kingdom is present when preaching comes, as it should, from life in messianic time. But it can and must use all figures of speech, much compounded imagery as is the stuff of the best poetry, to communicate *that* the kingdom of God is present. Even Jesus knew as much, for his references were always stipulated with the word "like." Apocalyptic speech is simile more than metaphor, a learning the unfamiliar by comparison with the familiar. It is a distinction always worth preaching and teaching. The kingdom of God is *like* an old woman finding a lost coin. It is *like* a mere mustard seed gone full bush. It is *like* finding a treasure in a field and then loosing oneself of all else so to secure that one thing. As Kierkegaard intimated through his avatar Johannes Climacus's story of the king in love with a lowly maiden, "No human situation can provide a valid analogy, even though we shall suggest one here in order to awaken the mind to understanding the divine."[49]

The point is "to awaken," to reveal, as is the purpose of apocalyptic language. The prayer leader and the worship presider are called to "think cruciform revelation" in the choice of words and the manner of their delivery. Apocalyptic imagery does more than "help" the second-person plural declarative task here. The proclaimer with gentle and convinced eyes, not wild ones, diligently seeks just the right words, again often poetic, to make

---

49. Kierkegaard, *Philosophical Fragments*, 31–32.

the point that God's majesty in suffering solidarity is present "for you" at just this time of speaking and hearing. It does not help, indeed it detracts, if the bearer of words gets in her or his own way, as if they are but worship "leaders" who perform for the sake of other aspiring worshipers. In that case, no one worships, no one is open to the prospect of messianic time's arrival into the prescribed sixty minutes of script, even when liturgical.

For all together to be invited into such holy time, into a sense and taste for the eschatological "now," it doesn't help if the person praying looks up from the written prayer and surveys the audience as if he were speaking at a Rotary luncheon or political rally. Instead, just pray! Look at the text or look to heaven. Do not look around as if it is "your" responsibility to "connect" with an audience. *Be in* worship. Don't just lead it. In that the presider shortchanges herself and all the gathered. Be in the moment. Don't be the moment. The same goes for the Great Thanksgiving in whatever longer eucharistic rite is used. Thank God, not the "audience." It is appropriate to declare the Words of Institution, with body and eye language directed to the fellow worshipers holding high the elements while stating the "for you." But all the rest, all of it, is prayer, for and in which the presider's affect invites the same from all fellow pray-ers. Above all else, as hosts and presiders—vicars and evocateurs of Christ in such time!—live in, be-lieve in, the eschatological timbre of the gifted moment. This is not a plea to return to liturgical rigorism for the sake of form and aesthetics only. It is a plea to see in ancient or contemporary forms of worship the participatory respect for the Living Word that transcends performative, prescribed, or manipulative and manipulated behaviors. It is a plea for evoking a truly communal response to the sincere expectation that God and not "leaders" is stirring in the gathered be-lieving community, that Spirit and not temporal habit has reframed everything in grander dimensions of space and time.

The apocalyptic character of speech ringing from the nave of messianic time with its sweet eschatological air differs from the secular domain's "controlling" words (Agamben's Sacrament of Power) precisely because it freely invites, entices, and engages the hearer with the mystery of the messianic moment. In other words, the fulsomeness of revelation is not merely oral and aural. As Pierre Bourdieu has illumined, the whole new communicative act is a unique and non-identically repeated habitus of words within the context of architecture, sensory experience, newly raised anxieties, consolations, and gratitudes; in short, the sacramental word comes with liturgy that in messianic time simultaneously binds history, purpose, and eschatology in a single moment. So Jean Daniélou: "The Christian faith has only one object, the mystery of Christ dead and risen. But this unique mystery subsists under different modes: it is prefigured in the Old Testament, it is accomplished historically in the earthly life of Christ, it is contained in mystery in the sacraments, it is lived mystically in souls, it is accomplished socially in the Church, it is accomplished eschatologically in the heavenly kingdom."[50]

Daniélou's ordering is not sequential. It is an "all or nothing" offering in the messianic moment. His is a riff on an implication of the early maxim of the church that the rule of prayer is the rule of faith; *lex orandi, lex credendi*. Further, this means that the *lex credenda*, the very *words about the Word* (theology), is embedded in the whole life of prayer, the whole work of the people, liturgy and what I'll name here as liturgical knowing, *gnosis* beyond simple critical reasoning. The church's classical and correct term for this is "mysticism." Mysticism properly understood is participatory knowledge and the participation happens to be by Christ the Word's offering and knowing of himself as of the Father, Son, and Holy Spirit. Mysticism is the "knowing" of relational communion and the apocalyptic character of speech in messianic time is indeed mysticism conveyed liturgically. If the church is going to be the church of the spiritual kingdom, it will attend to its vocational identity with sincere desire for and sensitivity to the mystical presence of the eschatological. Protestantism goes amiss when the Word Alone, the Word with the enabling Spirit or the Father's presence, is taken as a trope for nothing but naked literalism. Scripture itself attests that when the Word comes it is accompanied by choirs of angels. Shepherds are not lazy about their words when the eschaton comes to fields, cribs, naves, shanties, barrios, and wherever else two or more are gathered.

The church urgently must refocus on its eschatological origin and hope. The church claims its reason-for-being with apocalyptic language rightly taught and spoken that will not be broken down to components of sociological measurement, cultural criticism, or political theory. These disciplines and more have their proper roles for understanding partially what the church is and how it came to be insofar as it, with all other institutions, is temporal as well as spiritual. The world needs this distinction, too. We traditionally have called the church's primary work the Ministry of Word and Sacrament. Recharging and rethinking this central work of the spiritual kingdom does not separate it from works of love or demote the church's insistence on justice. The eschatologically alive church also knows deeply that temporally viewed "justice first" dies of inertia when it does not first

---

50. Quoted in Fagerberg, *Liturgical Mysticism*, 15. Fr. Alexander Schmemann writes compellingly about the separation of eschatology and theology, and especially rues the divorce (his word) between eschatology and liturgy. Proper eschatology, he says, is fundamental to Christian experience and worship. See Schmemann, "Liturgy and Eschatology." For a similar argument, cf. Rausch, *Eschatology, Liturgy, and Christology*. Thanks to Samuel Torvend for the references.

proclaim, teach, and live from its eschatology. When ignoring the gracious offering of apocalypse or by or couching it with the ordinariness of temporal speech, the church may survive as a temporal institution. But it will not be of the spiritual kingdom.

As Agamben argues for the utility of his Sacrament of Power—that such language should protect, serve, and anticipate the communion and community given in the Sacrament of Language—the church also regularly uses discursive and "controlling" language for the same purpose. This includes doctrinal theology. Most of the extended argument of this book is of this kind. It is the church's responsibility and inescapable task to draw from other ecumenical and non-Christian religions firstly to continue to make "better sense" of itself and more effectually to do its spiritual and temporal work. Having been so long in an ecumenical winter that one is justified to conclude that ecumenism has wearied and fallen to its own devastating climate change, the ecumenically enervated church dismisses ecumenical and interfaith dialogue at its mortal institutional peril. Some traditions just might be more "tuned in" to the eschatological and could help revivify the essential vocal chords of denominational traditions like Lutheranism or, even, the larger chorus of Augustinianism. Ecumenical rapprochement enriches denominational thought, protects against the dulling of routine, and, above all, reminds that just as the church *is* the body of Christ, so also we as parts are not the whole body. As ecumenical it is paramount that the church catholic learn from its members wherever possible how to live more profoundly from its ontologically distinct spiritual ground. There is no question, for example, that the Orthodox and Pentecostal traditions can teach and inspire much of us in the "mainline" about the eschaton and the real presence of the Holy Spirit when the church itself is realized in messianic time.

Of course, not all of the church's speech is apocalyptic, nor should it be. The church is both of the spiritual kingdom and the temporal because the church is also in and for the good of the temporal while not of it. The church as institution did and does still well with sponsorship and governance of hospitals, social services, psychological counselling, community organizing, justice advocacy, homeless shelters, day schools, federal chaplaincies, college and university campus ministries and postsecondary education (though, regrettably, these latter two are declining). These and more all stand with traditional congregational ministries as diaconal agents to serve needs beyond the primary Ministry of Word and Sacrament. But this larger work, too, suffers when eschatological vision and memory dim. Wise commentators who do not identify as religious speak to the benefits of faith communities for culture including their witness to transcendence.

They also lament the devolution of religious institutions because of the moral corruption, intellectual paucity, financial greed, and extremist political partisanship of religious leaders.[51] These commentators do not shout "tax the churches!" as so many from the fully secularized public now do. But the commentators understand why. Their charges of hypocrisy and earthly greed are tragic but acceptable secular synonyms for willful eschatological blindness.

The Urgent Work of Government

My primary addressees have been religious discerners who with me want to live robustly in the spiritual kingdom while hoping with more joy than sorrow to abide in the temporal. We do not seek escape from "the world." We love it. And we wish our love to be more effectual for its preservation and redemption. Luther and Lutheranism, with all Augustinian Christianity, believed similarly, though they differed from us in believing that their larger secular constituency held the same general political philosophy as did self-identified Christians. "Two Kingdoms" then addressed a mostly shared worldview, even if the eschatological component was not so "democratically" known. The secular pluralism of our day does not allow any such presumption of a shared worldview. Apocalyptic is not a worldview. It is a "God view."

Yet, if one seeks to commend a "new and improved" version of an old doctrine that once addressed both church and government, what might or should one say to government, having said plenty to the church? It is likely that the less one says, the better, given that religion does not enjoy a good public reputation. But to practice renewed two-kingdoms thinking, silence toward government is not an option. We must start with expressing good will. We'd best begin with lament and confession for the wrong the church has done. Say without fudging that the church has betrayed its own confessions, that repeatedly we have traded integrity for position, privilege, and power by taking up partisan platforms and practicing transactional politics, even identifying some political positions as the one and only true "Christian" place to stand. In sum, wherever we are on the political spectrum, lament that we have not followed our own Christian Doctrine of Two Kingdoms. Say, too, that even if we knew our purportedly confessional position, we have not cared.

---

51. Rauch, *Cross Purposes*, states just this, that society needs the goodness of the institutional church, but immoral and politically ideological clergy have nigh destroyed the church's viability for the secular public.

After clearing our throats and our consciences (without expecting the "state" to forgive in return), then we honor the good of government. We translate the actions of God's providence into the language of politics, law, and more, thanking government when we can for securing personal and national liberty so that suffering people anywhere can pursue life, liberty, and happiness. Along the way we help government define what personal and corporate happiness is by involving ourselves in public and private education, supporting freedom and fullness of information, and—being well-informed ourselves (!)—advising government as to what would seem to be the best policies and legislation for society as a whole, and not just "church" interests, though we do remind that government is duty bound to protect freedom for all religious traditions and freedom from religion.[52] Only in this way is space preserved for the freedom of the gospel and its proclamation.

The institutional mediation of government care for its citizens and residents, however, has significantly devolved over recent generations. This devolution has been and continues to grow as an unnamed crisis. Journalists write of this as the "disintermediation" of our liberal institutions.[53] I discussed in previous chapters how classic liberalism led to the aporia of freedom, that freedom becomes self-canceling when not moderated. Classic political liberalism founded the notion of institutions that would mediate freedom so that the opposing interests among individuals would not destroy the praxis of freedom when the ideal is impossible to meet. Thereby Enlightenment liberalism preserved freedom with a system of checks and balances including guarantees of minority rights. Institutions like democracy, the legal establishment, NGOs, unions, universities, nonprofit charitable institutions including religious communities, etc. "mediated" relations between individuals and interest groups so that freedom could remain as the ideal. Tax incentives and breaks were given to many of these private institutions precisely because they were integral to the preservation of the (classically) liberal order that when measured by economic and fairness indices unquestionably has outperformed every other political order.

But we Americans developed an antipathy to intermediating institutions. "Freedom," whether sung by left-wing rockers or a right-wing country music star, was newly defined as the absence of any mediations between individuals and group interests. Anything that inhibited individual choice was demonized as antidemocratic. Into the newly exorcised space once

52. Cf. the still recent inspiring example of "Die Wende" in former East Germany, of the church as the zone of freedom there, congregations hosting civil discourse and debate that avoided partisan co-optation.

53. E.g., Rauch, "Spontaneous Order."

taken by liberalism came rushing the neoliberal alliance of global corporate capitalism, the defense and security industries, and their incentivizers at all levels of government. The rationale was that the consumer is always right. This adage itself attests to the reduction of the sovereign individual to a mere walking bag of appetites to be put, actually, at the defining disposal of the corporatists. Every institution, including religion, is damaged by the new authoritarianism of corporatism. What sorts of hospitals will serve rightly, having once been founded and run by churches, when they have been recast as corporations and corporations then legally declared to be "persons," though now monetized so their voices overwhelm all other voices in the once real public commons? What philosophies for constitutional interpretation must we have so that "originalism" is not the final cipher for any law being what its interpreter wants it to mean? What law must be advised, written, and administered so that—if the principle indeed is like the once highest obligation to natural law—relief of suffering is core to jurisprudence? What institutional guards, renewed or created *de novo*, must we have to support and re-provide *social* capital so that individual interests cohere with a commitment to a *common* good? No individual human being can live with relative sovereignty if there is no communal relative sovereignty extensive through time, just as no Christian can be so without a realized sense of herself as a member of the body of Christ, in the Great Tradition, accompanied by the great cloud of witnesses, *all* the saints. But also, because we know of the beauty and transcendence in which we are ensconced, we advocate too for the beauty and transcendence that citizens can achieve through good government in its temporal way, as with support for education, the arts, architecture, parks, and hospitable public places.[54] Government too in its expected prosaicness can turn to art to realize government's work of justice. As the poet Zbigniew Herbert writes, "Everything that can be achieved / by so-called art / is contained in the concept of reconciliation."[55]

This compact critique of current government is of the sort that the church as an institution in the temporal kingdom is itself "instituted" to conduct. In my critical retrieval I've taken for granted our context of democratic governance in a pluralistic culture. Government polities differ between nations and even within nations. A constitutional federal republic, for example, wherein the individual states have their own rights, also then may have a heightened duty to criticize or resist federal overreach, as when the national government might block interstate travel for women seeking

---

54. Martha Nussbaum's arguments for these in her *Political Emotions* are so compelling and winsome.

55. Herbert, *Reconstruction of the Poet*, 189.

health care in another state. A state may enforce laws that violate minority rights, so that the federal system is obligated by the same constitution to correct the state. Responsible reflection about how Two Kingdoms theology may identify what is at stake in constitutional or "republican" democracy would require another book. But we do know that the church, being of the spiritual kingdom, is both transnational and pointedly local. The church, being of the spiritual kingdom, is not identical with any governmental polity, while yet the church must be able to communicate effectively, given the same Two Kingdoms principle, to any temporal authorities about their duty to ensure the public good whether the public is global or local.

This suggests that ecclesiology should be of a similar character so it can speak and act effectively in the largest and most poignant ways. This requires ecumenical zeal and expertise at all levels, something for which leadership education and financial support has waned. The church's ways and means, being of the spiritual kingdom, are not and should not be stuck with historical form. Obsession with miters prioritizes neither the mission of the cross nor aptly addressing the fluctuating rhetoric and form of varied secular polities. In fact, it only echoes the earliest attachment of the church to Caesar's fashion preferences, and by this I mean far more than elite clothing. Paul's "when in Rome" reflects the Two Kingdom point of distinction with communication. And communication requires something common. But the church's witness will not be effective in any place if it does not first follow the cross and its theology into the most particular conditions of suffering, of the woman in the pew nigh despair and the worker in the barrio nigh deportation. There the apocalypse of God is most acute. There the binding love of the word of God, the spiritual kingdom's Sacrament of Language, come first in speech and act. To that the fancies of ecclesial management must adjust themselves.

Practicing Two Kingdoms is difficult in any temporal polity. It will be harder yet when the polities themselves are but masks for the newer corporate powers and principalities dedicated to pretending honor of the common good when their actual goal is their overwhelming of the commons. Their intent is plutocratic oligarchy and their tool used in all directions is the machinery of language in direct defiance of the Sacrament of Power's purpose. At this point the Doctrine of Two Kingdoms demands the church's defiance in return, a clear "Nein!" to the Fascist Medusa 2.0 beta version. In that space, the church may be a minority more than any other. Our task then all the more is to be prophetic with a clearly evident love for all God's creatures. And so God's church may find itself outside itself as well as alien to a particular polity. A Two-Kingdoms conviction would call for the church's louder voice anyway. In the name of Christ and because every

Christian is Christ's and every human being is God's, even from a distance with a different accent the church speaks to other governments for the sake of the extended common good.

It must also be said that for the church *as church* to presume superiority and mandated divine agency to compel a government's "conversion," even to the church's "just" policies, is as fraught as any fascist, authoritarian, or "biblical" Dominionist impulse. The proper humble, peaceable, and eschatological disposition of the church advises and (occasionally) consents and dissents with regard to governmental policy and action. The church must resist when the gospel is threatened. This applies to the church's relationship to other churches and religious movements as much as it might to governmental relations. Resistance must be nonviolent. The church is ultimately under the eschatologically present power of God, after all, and so its character and representation is thus quite unlike the flatter dimensionality and aptitude of temporal powers. The church will stay cruciform, according to the character of God. When Christian individuals cannot do the same given the circumstances of the vilest injustice and their extension, we act still with love, but also faith, hope, and repentance as we ask for forgiveness for the sin we from love must do.

Conclusion

I have argued that Martin Luther's doctrinal reconstruction of Augustine's Two Kingdoms and naming of them as the spiritual kingdom and the temporal kingdom were quickly confused, misunderstood, misused, and practically ignored. More devastating was the failure of subsequent interpreters to appreciate the eschatological consciousness of Paul, Augustine, Luther, and innumerably more. This was exacerbated by the Enlightenment's narrowing of the canons of reason and the redefinition of reasoned ethics as true "natural" religion. Thinkers like Leibniz and Hamman fought the sublimation, but Kant won. Religious conviction was effectively driven into privacy and subjectivity, denied authority to make a difference in the public political space. Kant's critical realism, which has its proper good due, along with the rise of the natural and human sciences, garnered public respect for their authority. The questioning of all other authority had already begun even before postmodernity.

Washed over in this generally described sea change more specifically were the concepts of natural law and sovereignty. Natural law and higher law for a long while before were the temporal kingdom's clear correlates to Christ's law of love in the spiritual kingdom. But with Enlightenment liberalism they were declared as fictions. Other bases for rights were sought. The notion of individual human sovereignty was clearly aligned with the spiritual kingdom's celebration of the human as the image of God, innate with dignity and free. Princes and then nation-state leaders were legitimized as receiving the "loan" of sovereignty from "the people." But then the step to autocracy and authoritarianism was short indeed. Because "sovereignty" is a synonym for "freedom," we traced how sovereignty and freedom could and did self-cancel when absolutized. The "sovereign" came to be defined as the one who could declare a "state of exception." The nation-state and/or its leaders were thus immunized against any differing will of the people and accountability to them. In all other respects, and for all other political purposes, the notion of sovereignty was declared useless. Simultaneously, language and political philosophers strained over the loss of referentiality, given the demise of once-agreed upon "trans-rational" facts (like God, higher law, etc.). All this transpired in what we've called the temporal order, while faith's reasoning in the spiritual order could not, as it cannot, surrender reference to and knowledge of God. The consequence was the total separation of the spiritual and the temporal, of the personal from the public.

Because of and furthering the separation, philosophy became positivistic and the practice of law went "positive." Law could be written only "to the facts" and once general principles of interpretation no longer could apply. Only the most minimal of justifications for law could be constructed. I identified H. L. A. Hart's principle that law must be addressed to "unnatural suffering" as the both minimal and yet currently most comprehensive of rationales for how to write, read, and apply law. Still, when law is "posited" and time passes, memory misbehaves and subjectivity, including outright personal ideological interest, can run wild. A definitive qualifier in a Bill of Rights is ignored and corporations are defined as persons. Just as, for example, biblical literalism interprets so wrongly when "higher laws" do not obtain, so also constitutional "originalism" has proven to be but a mask. If "all of us are originalists now," then really no one is originalist now. Opinion is spun as facts, and facts have options. Fascists routinely claim to be revolutionaries, but even they—especially they?—must pretend to claim the most primal originalist principles ("Blood and Land!") as their warrants. The worst possible outcome is that law is "what you make of it": when ideology meets opportunism and self-aggrandizement to satisfy power lust that can never be satisfied (Augustine!); when the increase of personal power and partisanship enter in to every calculus, as always happen when the spiritual kingdom with its vision of the Beloved Community is rendered irrelevant for the temporal; when also religionists lose true eschatological inspiration and pay obeisance without awareness then of captivity to Chronos.

The most damage done to the Two Kingdoms doctrine itself was the secularized worldview imposed on it, its interpreters having been bereft of the eschatological vision and apocalyptic language with which it was first articulated. Christ's birth, life, death, and resurrection marks—note the present tense!—is the apocalypse of Christ's eternal spiritual kingdom now and is how God presents the holy to us. As I said, apocalyptic originates from and is God's view and vibrates with holy terms, not temporality's. But temporality distorts human imagination by temporalizing eschatology. This reduced eschatology on the theological side was paralleled by the loss of ultimate ethical norms on the political side. The new work of Pauline scholars and the unexpected corroboration by Agamben offer a promising way to reclaim the Doctrine of Two Kingdoms. It also is no small thing that physical cosmology adds its supporting evidence with its observations of eternity's love of time. All this not only brightens Paul's eschatological sensitivity and apocalyptic imagination in Rom 13 as if with a thousand suns. The coming together of these different perspectives robustly reinvigorates a two-kingdoms vision for political theology. Luther's Theology of the Cross then completes what was lacking in the Two Kingdoms doctrine, providing also a theological-ethical counterpart to Hart's helpful legal principle of redressing suffering.

Finally, we are reminded by Agamben of language's sacred origin. Words matter. The event of language itself witnesses to God having bonded human being to God and each other; that in the gift and grasping of messianic time we know and speak language as sacrament anew and repeatedly so; and that in our intended right stewardship of speech as a Sacrament of Power, our civil discourse on one side and our doctrinal theology on the other should and could lovingly and selflessly, with our own suffering along the way, speak church and state into Messiah's remaining time.

The relationship of Christian life and Christian knowing to public and political life is a relationship of the eschatological to the temporal. This is how we are to understand and employ the protocols of the Two Kingdoms model. We in the spiritual kingdom do have our apocalyptical language in the spiritual kingdom to proclaim God's presence. And we have our positive power language too for secular goodness. It is not as if Christians are binary about our speech and personhood, one temperament for Jerusalem and another for Athens. With God and by God we care passionately for the world, our eyes sparkled by God's grandeur everywhere, speaking the best of the world's terms for its nurture toward messianic time and the eternity it presages. In that respect we are evangelical.

The spiritual kingdom and the church with it is not to be the separate and non-interfering "other." The church and state are distinct but carefully involved with each other. The spiritual domain and the temporal domain attend to the good of each other by respecting each other's space. This is God's prescription, if not a description of present circumstances. The authorities of these domains are instituted to serve as checks and balances so that inattention and oppression in one's own domain or trespassing oppressively into the other's domain are corrected. Instead, they advocate for each other's good.

The two-kingdoms framework underscores that the beloved civil order in which God's rule is indirect will elide with the beloved spiritual order in which Christ rules directly. The predication is the word "beloved" throughout. Its accompanying adjectives are not the cartoonish images of flat apocalyptic, but the language that reveals the ground of all language as the sacramental presence of messiah. His agency is of the one Sovereign manifested in his relative non-dominating sovereigns, whose citizenships in the spiritual kingdom and temporal residences are as neighbor to neighbor.

And what is the manner of agency that the we ideally as sacred humans, *homines sacri*, citizens of heaven on earth, would practice? It is only cruciform, as of Messiah in, with, and for us. Our agency is "weak," of Christ, as neighbor without dominion to neighbor, vulnerable, transparent, firmly faithful, without hubris. This is an enigma to the merely temporally ordered mind. But to live so is wonderfully to be fully human and blessingly political. This is what it means to be and act from the shared being and acting of Christ. God has spoken to the greater spiritual kingdom and to God's loved temporal creation. God has spoken and still speaks through God's Two Kingdoms with promise of their marriage that only God in God's own ways will arrange and celebrate finally as Presider. In this twofold mode of communing and binding language from and for "Two Kingdoms," God has spoken and still speaks. Would that we attune to the beautiful words in their different accents. Would that from Messiah's time and for the world's time, *ubi Deus dixit*, we train our voices.

Bibliography

Abbot, Edwin A. *Flatland: A Romance of Many Dimensions*. Overland Park, KS: Digireads.com, 2017.
Adkins, Brent, and Paul R. Hinlicky. *Rethinking Philosophy and Theology with Deleuze: A New Cartography*. London: Bloomsbury, 2013.
Agamben, Giorgio. *The Church and the Kingdom*. Translated by Leland De La Durantaye. London: Seagull, 2012.
———. *The Coming Community*. Translated by Michael Hardt. Minneapolis: University of Minnesota Press, 1993.
———. *Homo Sacer: Sovereign Power and Bare Life*. Translated by Daniel Heller-Roazen. Stanford: Stanford University Press, 1998.
———. *Means Without End: Notes on Politics*. Translated by Vincenso Binetti and Cesare Cassarino. Minneapolis: University of Minnesota Press, 2000.
———. *Potentialities: Collected Essays in Philosophy*. Edited and translated by Daniel Heller-Roazen. Stanford: Stanford University Press.
———. *The Sacrament of Language: An Archaeology of the Oath*. In *The Omnibus Homo Sacer*, 295–362. Stanford: Stanford University Press, 2017.
———. *State of Exception*. Translated by Kevin Attell. Chicago: University of Chicago Press, 2005.
———. *The Time That Remains: A Commentary on the Letter to the Romans*. Translated by Patricia Dailey. Stanford: Stanford University Press, 2005.
Aho, James. "Christian Dominionism and Violence." *Oxford Research Encyclopedia*, Aug. 31, 2021. https://doi.org/10.1093/acrefore/9780199340378.013.732.
Alison, James. *Raising Abel: The Recovery of the Eschatological Imagination*. New York: Crossroad Herder, 1996.
Alonso, Llano, and H. Fernando. "Cicero and Natural Law." *Archives for Philosophy of Law and Social Philosophy* 98 (2002) 157–68.
Althaus, Paul. "The Kingdom of God and the Church." *Theology* 14 (1927) 290–92.
Arendt, Hannah. *On Lying and Politics*. New York: Literary Classics of the United States, 2022.
August, Eugene R. "Mill as Sage: The Essay on Bentham." *Proceedings of the Modern Language Association* 89 (1974) 142–53.
Augustine. *City of God*. Translated by R. W. Dyson. Cambridge: Cambridge University Press, 1998.
———. *Confessions*. Translated by Henry Chadwick. Oxford: Oxford University Press, 1991.

———. *Letters*. In *Letters 100–155*. Edited by Boniface Ramsey. Translated by Roland Teske. The Works of St. Augustine: A Translation for the 21st Century. Hyde Park, NY: New City, 2003.

———. *On Free Will*. In *On the Free Choice of the Will, On Grace and Free Choice, and Other Writings*. Edited and translated by Peter King. Cambridge: Cambridge University Press, 2017.

Barnett, Mary. "The Poetic Space of the Liturgy." *Christian Century*, August 21, 2024. https://www.christiancentury.org/features/poetic-space-liturgy.

Barr, James. *Biblical Words for Time*. London: SCM, 1962.

Barth, Karl. *Anselm: Fides Quaerens Intellectum; Anselm's Proof of the Existence of God in the Context of His Theological Scheme*. London: SCM, 1960.

Bayer, Oswald. *A Contemporary in Dissent: Johann Georg Hamann as Radical Enlightener*. Translated by Roy A. Harrisville and Mark C. Mattes. Grand Rapids: Eerdmans, 2012. Kindle.

Bentham, Jeremy. "Anarchical Fallacies; Being an Examination of the Declaration of Rights Issued During the French Revolution." In *Nonsense upon Stilts: Bentham, Burke, and Marx on the Rights of Man*, edited by Jeremy Waldron, 46–69. Routledge Revivals. London: Routledge, 2014.

Bodin, Jean. *On Sovereignty: Four Chapters from "The Six Books of the Commonwealth."* Edited and translated by Julian H. Franklin. Cambridge: Cambridge University Press, 1992.

Bolman, Lee G., and Terrence E. Deal. *Reframing Organizations: Artistry, Choice, and Leadership*. Baltimore: Jossey-Bass, 1991.

Bonhoeffer, Dietrich. *Act and Being: Transcendental Philosophy and Ontology in Systematic Theology*. DBWE 2. Translated by H. Martin Rumscheidt. Edited by Wayne Whitson Floyd Jr. Minneapolis: Fortress, 1996.

———. "Christology." In *Berlin: 1932–1933*. DBWE 12:258–62, 299–360. Translated by Isabel Best and David Higgins, with Douglas W. Stott. Edited by Larry Rasmussen. Minneapolis: Fortress, 2009.

———. *Dietrich Bonhoeffer Works* (DBWE). Edited by Victoria Barnett et al. 17 vols. Minneapolis: Fortress, 1996–2013.

———. *Life Together; Prayerbook of the Bible*. DBWE 5. Translated by Daniel W. Bloesch and James H. Burtness. Edited by Geffrey B. Kelly. Minneapolis: Fortress, 1996.

———. *Sanctorum Communio: A Theological Study of the Sociology of the Church*. DBWE 1. Translated by Reinhard Krauss and Nancy Lukens. Edited by Clifford J. Green. Minneapolis: Fortress, 1998.

———. "Thy Kingdom Come." In *Berlin: 1932–1933*. DBWE 12:285–98. Translated by Isabel Best and David Higgins, with Douglas W. Stott. Edited by Larry Rasmussen. Minneapolis: Fortress, 2009.

Bornkamm, Heinrich. *Luther's Doctrine of the Two Kingdoms in the Context of His Theology*. Translated by Karl H. Herz. Philadelphia: Fortress, 1966.

Brooks, Richard O., ed. *Augustine and Modern Law*. London: Routledge, 2019.

Butler, Judith, and Gayatri Chakravorty Spivak. *Who Sings the Nation State?* Oxford: Seagull, 2011.

Butler, Kiera. "Christian Nationalists Dream of Taking Over America: This Movement Is Actually Doing It." *Mother Jones*, Nov.-Dec. 2024. https://www.motherjones.com/politics/2024/10/new-apostolic-reformation-christian-nationalism/.

Caputo, John D. *Cross and Cosmos: A Theology of Difficult Glory*. Indianapolis: Indiana University Press, 2020.

———. *The Weakness of God: A Theology of the Event*. Indianapolis: Indiana University Press, 2006.

Carty, Jarrett A. *God and Government: Martin Luther's Political Thought*. Toronto: McGill-Queen's University Press, 2017.

Cloud, Morgan. "Pragmatism, Positivism, and Principles in Fourth Amendment Theory." *UCLA Law Review* 199 (1993–94) 200–301.

Cohen, Elizabeth. *The Political Value of Time: Citizenship, Duration, and Democratic Justice*. Cambridge: Cambridge University Press, 2018.

Congdon, David. *Who Is a True Christian? Contesting Religious Identity in American Culture*. Cambridge: Cambridge University Press, 2024.

Corwin, Edward. *The "Higher Law" Background of American Constitutional Law*. Indianapolis: Amagi, 2008.

Costa Lopez, Julia. "*Merum Imperium* and Sovereignty in the Later Middle Ages." In "Forum: In the Beginning There Was No Word (For It): Terms, Concepts, and Early Sovereignty." *International Studies Review* 20 (2018) 498–502.

Cullmann, Oscar. *Christ and Time*. Philadelphia: Westminster, 1950.

Davies, Jamie P. *The Apocalyptic Paul: Retrospect and Prospect*. Eugene, OR: Cascade, 2022.

DeJonge, Michael P. *Bonhoeffer's Reception of Luther*. Oxford: Oxford University Press, 2017.

de Keijzer, Josh. "Revelation as Being: Bonhoeffer's Appropriation of Heidegger's Ontology." *Journal of Religion* 98 (2018) 348–70.

Denker, Angela. *Red State Christians: A Journey into White Christian Nationalism and the Wreckage It Leaves Behind*. Minneapolis: Augsburg Fortress, 2020.

Dickinson, Colby. *Agamben and Theology*. London: Bloomsbury Academic/T&T Clark, 2011.

Duchrow, Ulrich, ed. *Lutheran Churches: Salt or Mirror of Society? Case Studies on the Theory and Practice of the Two Kingdoms Doctrine*. Geneva: Lutheran World Federation, 1977.

———. *Two Kingdoms: The Use and Misuse of a Lutheran Theological Concept*. Geneva: Lutheran World Federation, 1977.

Duchrow, Ulrich, et al. *Liberating Lutheran Theology: Freedom for Justice and Solidarity with Others in a Global Context*. Minneapolis: Fortress, 2011.

Du Mez, Kristin Kobes. *Jesus and John Wayne: How White Evangelicals Corrupted a Faith and Fractured a Nation*. New York: Liveright, 2020.

Ebbeler, Jennifer V. "Religious Identity and the Politics of Patronage: Symmachus and Augustine." *Historia: Zeitschrift für alte Geschichte* 56 (2007) 230–42.

Evangelical Lutheran Church in America (ELCA). *Draft of a Statement on Civic Life and Faith*. https://elcamediaresources.blob.core.windows.net/cdn/wp-content/uploads/Civic_Life_and_Faith_Draft.pdf.

Fagerberg, David W. *Liturgical Mysticism*. Steubenville, OH: Emmaus Academic, 2019.

Farrow, D. B. "Engaging Agamben on 'The Time that Remains.'" *Journal of the School of Religious Studies* 50 (2023) 165–205.

Forde, Gerhard, O. "Justification and This World." In *Christian Dogmatics*, edited by Carl E. Braaten and Robert W. Jenson, 445–69. Philadelphia: Fortress, 1984.

Fortin, Ernest L. "St. Thomas Aquinas." In *History of Political Philosophy*, edited by Leo Strauss and Joseph Cropsey, 248–75. 3rd ed. Chicago: University of Chicago Press, 1987.

French, David. "Neil Gorsuch Has a Few Thoughts About America Today." *New York Times*, Aug. 4, 2024.

Gagne, André. *American Evangelicals for Trump: Dominion, Spiritual Warfare, and the End Times*. New York: Routledge, 2023.

Gienapp, Jonathan. *Against Constitutional Originalism: A Historical Critique*. New Haven: Yale University Press, 2024.

Golanski, Alani. "Why the Rule of Law Demands Extralegal Change." *Capital University Law Review* (2024). https://ssrn.com/abstract=4644368.

Gordon, Peter E. "The Place of the Sacred in the Absence of God: Charles Taylor's 'A Secular Age.'" *Journal of the History of Ideas* 69 (2008) 647–73.

Gorsuch, Neil, and Janie Nitze. *Over Ruled: The Human Toll of Too Much Law*. New York: Harper, 2024.

Gregory, Eric. *Politics and the Order of Love: An Augustinian Ethic of Democratic Citizenship*. Chicago: University of Chicago Press, 2020.

Gritsch, Eric W., and Robert W. Jenson. *Lutheranism: The Theological Movement and Its Confessional Writings*. Philadelphia: Fortress, 1976.

Gunther, Gerard. *Learned Hand: The Man and the Judge*. New York: Knopf, 1993.

Harrill, J. Albert. "St. Paul and the Christian Communities of Nero's Rome." In *The Cambridge Companion to the Age of Nero*, edited by Shadi Bartsch et al., 276–89. Cambridge: Cambridge University Press, 2017.

Hart, H. L. A. "Are There Any Natural Rights?" *Philosophical Review* 64 (1955) 175–91.

———. *The Concept of Law*. Oxford: Oxford University Press, 1961.

Heaney, Seamus. *The Government of the Tongue: The 1986 T. S. Eliot Memorial Lectures and Other Critical Writings*. London: Faber and Faber, 1988.

Hedges, Chris. *American Fascists: The Christian Right and the War on America*. New York: Free, 2008.

Herbert, Zbigniew. *Reconstruction of the Poet: Uncollected Works of Zbigniew Herbert*. Edited and translated by Alissa Valles. New York: Ecco, 2024.

Hinlicky, Paul R. *Before Auschwitz: What Christian Theology Must Learn from the Rise of Nazism*. Eugene, OR: Cascade, 2013.

———. *Beloved Community: Critical Dogmatics after Christendom*. Grand Rapids: Eerdmans, 2015.

———. "Luther on Ecclesiastes: Nature in the Light of Grace." *Word and World* 43 (2023) 31–42.

———. *Paths Not Taken: Fates of Theology from Luther Through Leibniz*. Grand Rapids: Eerdmans, 2009.

———. Review of *Law and Protestantism: The Legal Teachings of the Lutheran Reformation*, by John Witte Jr. *The Sixteenth Century* 35 (2004) 534–36.

Hippolytus. *Commentary on Daniel*. In *Hippolytus: Commentary on Daniel and "Chronicon."* Translated by T. C. Schmidt. Gorgias Studies in Early Christianity and Patristics 67. Piscataway, NJ: Gorgias, 2017.

Holm, Minda. "Conclusion: What, When, and Where, Then, Is the Concept of Sovereignty?" In "Forum: In the Beginning There Was No Word (For It): Terms, Concepts, and Early Sovereignty." *International Studies Review* 20 (2018) 513–16.

Holmes, Oliver Wendell. *The Common Law*. Boston: Little, Brown, and Co., 1881.

Hunt, Bruce A., Jr. "Lock on Equality." *Political Research Quarterly* 69 (2016) 546–56.
Ingersoll, Julie. *Building God's Kingdom: Inside the World of Christian Reconstruction.* Oxford: Oxford University Press, 2015.
Jenkins, Jack, and Emily McFarlan Miller. "Lutheran Church-Missouri Synod President Calls for Excommunicating White Nationalists." *Religion News Service*, Feb. 22, 2023. https://religionnews.com/2023/02/22/lutheran-church-missouri-synod-president-calls-for-excommunicating-white-nationalists/.
Jenson, Robert. *God After God: The God of the Past and the God of the Future, Seen in the Work of Karl Barth.* Philadelphia: Fortress, 1969.
———. *Unbaptized God: The Basic Flaw in Ecumenical Theology.* Minneapolis: Fortress, 1982.
Jervis, L. Ann. *Paul and Time: Life in the Temporality of Christ.* Grand Rapids: Baker Academic, 2023.
———. "Response: Review Panel of Ann Jervis, *Paul and Time* (Baker Academic, 2023)." Paper presented at the Society of Biblical Literature/American Academy of Religion Annual Meeting, San Antonio, TX, Nov. 20, 2023.
Jewitt, Paul. *Romans: A Commentary.* Minneapolis: Fortress, 2007.
Johnson, Bill, and Lance Wallnau. *Invading Babylon: The 7 Mountain Mandate.* Shippensburg, PA: Destiny Image, 2013.
Johnson, Luke Timothy. *Reading Romans: A Literary and Theological Commentary.* New York: Crossroad, 1997.
Kant, Immanuel. "The Doctrine of Right." In *Groundwork of the Metaphysics of Morals, a German-English Edition*, 15–41. Edited and translated by Mary Gregor and Jens Timmerman. Cambridge: Cambridge University Press, 2011.
———. *On the Miscarriage of All Philosophical Trials in Theodicy.* Translated by George di Giovani. Cambridge: Cambridge University Press, 2001.
———. *Religion Within the Limits of Reason Alone.* Translated by Theodore M. Greene and Hoyt H. Hudson. New York: Harper & Row, 1960.
———. "Toward Perpetual Peace: A Philosophical Sketch." In *Toward Perpetual Peace and Other Writings on Politics, Peace, and History*, edited by Pauline Kleingfeld, 67–109. New Haven: Yale University Press, 2006.
———. "What Is Enlightenment?" In *Political Writings*, 54–60. Translated by Hugh Barr Nisbet. Cambridge: Cambridge University Press, 2011.
———. *Works in Practical Philosophy.* Translated and edited by Mary J. Gregor. Cambridge: Cambridge University Press, 1996.
Käsemann, Ernst. *Church Conflicts: The Cross, Apocalyptic, and Political Resistance.* Edited by Ry Siggelkow. Translated by Roy A. Harrisville. Grand Rapids: Baker Academic, 2021.
Kaurin, Pauline Shanks. *On Obedience: Contrasting Philosophies for the Military, Citizenry, and Community.* Annapolis, MD: Naval Institute Press, 2020.
Kaylor, Brian. "When a Dictator Quotes the Bible." *A Public Witness*, Aug. 29, 2024. https://publicwitness.wordandway.org/p/when-a-dictator-quotes-the-bible.
Kierkegaard, Søren. *Philosophical Fragments.* Originally translated by David Swenson. Revised translation by Howard V. Hong. Princeton: Princeton University Press, 1974.
Kirk, Russell. *The Conservative Mind: From Burke to Eliot.* Washington, DC: Regnery, 1987.

Kolb, Robert, and Timothy J. Wengert, eds. *The Book of Concord: The Confessions of the Evangelical Lutheran Church*. Translated by Charles Arand et al. Minneapolis: Fortress, 2000.

Lamb, Michael. *A Commonwealth of Hope: Augustine's Political Thought*. Princeton: Princeton University Press, 2022.

Lapiana, William P. "Thoughts and Lives." Review of *Justice Oliver Wendell Holmes: Law and the Inner Self*, by G. Edward White. *New York Law School Law Review* 607 (1994) 607–10.

Larson, Duane. "Theology Confronts Wrongdoing in Eagle Pass." *Word and Way*, Feb. 7, 2024. https://wordandway.org/2024/02/07/theology-confronts-wrongdoing-in-eagle-pass/.

———. *Times of the Trinity: A Proposal for Theistic Cosmology*. New York: Peter Lang, 1993.

Latham, Andrew. "IR's Medieval-Sovereignty Debate: Three Rival Approaches." In "Forum: In the Beginning There Was No Word (For It): Terms, Concepts, and Early Sovereignty." *International Studies Review* 20 (2018) 494–98.

Lewis, Sinclair. *It Can't Happen Here*. New York: Signet, 2014.

Lindbeck, George. *The Nature of Doctrine: Religion and Theology in a Postliberal Age*. Philadelphia: Westminster, 1984.

Locke, John. *The Second Treatise of Government*. Edited by C. B. Macpherson. Indianapolis: Hackett, 1980.

Luther, Martin. "The Bondage of the Will." LW 33:3–295. In *Career of the Reformer III*. Translated by Philip S. Watson and Benjamin Drewery. Philadelphia: Fortress, 1957.

———. "The Freedom of a Christian." LW 31:347–77. In *Career of the Reformer I*. Edited by Harold Grimm. Philadelphia: Fortress, 1957.

———. "Lectures on Genesis." LW 1–8. Edited by Jaroslav Pelikan. St. Louis: Concordia, 1958–65.

———. "Lectures on Romans." LW 35. *Word and Sacrament I*. Edited by E. Theodore Bachmann. Philadelphia: Fortress, 1960.

———. *Luther's Sermons I*. LW 51. Edited by John W. Dorbenstein. Philadelphia: Fortress, 1959.

———. *Luther's Works*. Edited by Jaroslav Pelikan and Helmut T. Lehman. St. Louis: Concordia, 1958–.

———. *Martin Luther's Basic Theological Writings*. Edited by Timothy Lull. Minneapolis: Fortress, 1989.

———. "On the Councils and the Church." LW 41. *Church and Ministry III*. Translated by Eric W. Gritsch. Philadelphia: Fortress, 1968.

———. "The Sermon on the Mount and the Magnificat." LW 21. Edited by Jaroslav Pelikan. St. Louis: Concordia, 1956.

———. "Temporal Authority: To What Extent It Should be Obeyed." LW 45:77–129. In *Christian in Society II*. Edited by Walter I. Brandt. Minneapolis: Augsburg Fortress, 1962.

———. "Treatise On Good Works." LW 44:15–144. In *Christian in Society I*. Edited by James Atkinson. Philadelphia: Fortress, 1966.

———. *Weimarer Ausgabe*. Weimar: Böhlaus, 1883.

Marion, Jean-Luc. *God Without Being*. Chicago: University of Chicago Press, 1991.

Maritain, Jacques. "The Concept of Sovereignty." *American Political Science Review* 44 (1950) 343–57.

Marshall, Ruth. "Destroying Arguments and Captivating Thoughts: Spiritual Warfare Prayer as Global Praxis." *Journal of Religious and Political Practice* 2 (2016) 92–113.

Martyn, J. Louis. *Galatians: A New Translation with Introduction and Commentary*. Anchor Bible 33A. New York: Doubleday, 1997.

McNeil, John T. "Natural Law in the Thought of Luther." *Church History* 10 (1941) 211–27.

Meckled-Garcia, Saladin. "Sovereignty." *The Oxford Guide to Philosophy*, edited by Ted Honderich, 886. Oxford: Oxford University Press, 2005.

Milbank, John. "Natural Law; Natural Law and Natural Right Revisited." In *Christianity and Constitutionalism*, edited by Nicholas Aroney and Ian Leigh, 410–31. Oxford: Oxford University Press, 2022.

Mill, John Stuart. *On Liberty and Other Essays*. Oxford: Oxford University Press, 1991.

Moltmann, Jürgen. *The Crucified God*. Translated by R. A. Wilson and John Bowden. New York: Harper and Row, 1974.

Nelson, Robert H. *Lutheranism and the Nordic Spirit of Social Democracy: A Different Protestant Ethic*. Aarhus: Aarhus University Press, 2017.

Nessan, Craig L. *Free in Deed: The Heart of Lutheran Ethics*. Minneapolis: Fortress, 2022.

———. "Reappropriating Luther's Two Kingdoms." *Lutheran Quarterly* 19 (2005) 302–11.

Niebuhr, Reinhold. *Faith and History*. New York: Scribner, 1977.

———. *Moral Man and Immoral Society: A Study in Ethics and Politics*. 2nd ed. Louisville: Westminster John Knox, 2013.

———. *The Nature and Destiny of Man*. New York: Scribner's Sons, 1943.

Norris, Andrew. "Giorgio Agamben and the Politics of the Living Dead." *Diacritics* 30 (2000) 38–58.

Nussbaum, Martha C. *Political Emotions: Why Love Matters for Justice*. Cambridge: Belknap, 2013.

———. *Upheavals of Thought: The Intelligence of Emotions*. Cambridge: Cambridge University Press, 2001.

Nygren, Anders. "Luther's Doctrine of the Two Kingdoms." *Journal of Lutheran Ethics* 2 (2002). https://learn.elca.org/jle/luthers-doctrine-of-the-two-kingdoms/.

Obgar, O. "The Concept of Legal Language: What Makes Language 'Legal'?" *International Journal for the Semiotics of Law* 36 (2023) 1081–107. https://doi.org/10.1007/s11196-023-10010-5.

O'Scamlin, Diarmuid F. "'We Are All Textualists Now': The Legacy of Justice Antonin Scalia." *St. John's Law Review* 91 (2017) 303–13.

Osiander, Andreas. *Before the State: Political Change in the West from the Greeks to the French Revolution*. Oxford: Oxford University Press, 2008.

———. "Sovereignty, International Relations, and the Westphalian Myth." *International Organization* 55 (2001) 251–87.

Passavant, Paul A. "The Contradictory State of Giorgio Agamben." *Political Theory* 35 (2007) 147–74.

Pasternak, Lawrence, and Courtney Fugate. "Kant's Philosophy of Religion." *The Stanford Encyclopedia of Religion*. https://plato.stanford.edu/archives/sum2022/entries/kant-religion/.

Perry, Samuel, and Andrew Whitehead. *Taking America Back for God: Christian Nationalism in the United States*. Oxford: Oxford University Press, 2020.

Petit, Philip. "Liberalism and Republicanism." In *Cicero and Modern Law*, edited by Richard O. Brooks, 543–72. London: Routledge, 2017.

Qureshi-Hurst, Emily. *God, Salvation, and the Problem of Spacetime*. Cambridge: Cambridge University Press, 2022.

Raeder, Linda C. "Mill's Religion of Humanity: Consequences and Implications." *Humanitas* 14 (2001) 3–26.

Rauch, Jonathan. *The Constitution of Knowledge: A Defense of Truth*. Washington, DC: Brookings Institution, 2021.

———. *Cross Purposes: Christianity's Broken Bargain with Democracy*. New Haven: Yale University Press, 2025.

———. "From Spontaneous Order to Ordered Spontaneity." *National Affairs* 63 (2023). https://nationalaffairs.com/publications/detail/from-spontaneous-order-to-ordered-spontaneity.

Rausch, Thomas. *Eschatology, Liturgy, and Christology: Toward Recovering an Eschatological Imagination*. Collegeville, MN: Liturgical, 2012.

Rilke, Rainier Maria. *Rilke's Book of Hours: Love Poems to God*. Translated by Anita Barrows and Joanna Macy. New York: Riverhead, 1996.

Russell, Robert John. "Bodily Resurrection, Eschatology, and Scientific Cosmology." In *Resurrection: Theological and Scientific Assessments*, edited by Ted Peters et al., 3–30. Grand Rapids: Eerdmans, 2002.

———. "Eschatology and Physical Cosmology: A Preliminary Reflection." In *The Far Future Universe: Eschatology from a Cosmic Perspective*, edited by G. F. R. Ellis, 266–315. Philadelphia: Templeton Foundation, 2002.

———. *Time in Eternity: Pannenberg, Physics, and Eschatology in Creative Mutual Interaction*. Notre Dame: Notre Dame University Press, 2012.

Scalia, Antonin, and Bryan A. Garner. *Reading Law: The Interpretation of Legal Texts*. St. Paul, MN: West Group, 2011.

Schelia, Arnulf von. "Die 'Zwei-Reiche-Lehre' im deutschen Protestantismus des 20. Jahrhunderts: Eine kritische Sichtung." *Zeitschrift für evangelisches Kirchenrecht* 59 (2014) 182–206.

Schmemann, Alexander. "Liturgy and Eschatology." *Eclectic Orthodoxy*, June 18, 2013. https://afkimel.wordpress.com/2013/06/18/liturgy-and-eschatology-by-alexander-schmemann/.

Schmitt, Carl. *Die Diktatur: Von den Anfängen des modernen Souveränitätgedankens bis zum proletarischen Klassenkampf*. Munich: Duncker and Humblot, 1921.

———. *Political Theology: Four Chapters on the Concept of Sovereignty*. Translated by George Schwab. Cambridge: MIT Press, 1985. Kindle.

Schofield, Malcolm. *Cicero: Political Philosophy*. Oxford: Oxford University Press, 2021.

Sigmund, Paul E. "Jeremy Waldron and the Religious Turn in Locke Scholarship." *Review of Politics* 67 (2005) 407–18.

Snow, Nancy E. "Compassion." *American Philosophical Quarterly* 28 (1991) 195–205.

Solberg, Mary. *A Church Undone: Documents from the German Christian Faith Movement, 1932–1940*. Minneapolis: Fortress, 2015.

Springer, Carl P. E. *Cicero in Heaven: The Roman Rhetor and Luther's Reformation*. St. Andrew's Studies in Reformation History. Leiden: Brill, 2017.

Steigmann-Gall, Richard. *"The Holy Reich": Nazi Conceptions of Christianity, 1919–1945*. Cambridge: Cambridge University Press, 2003.

Stout, Jeffrey. *The Flight from Authority: Religion, Morality, and the Quest for Autonomy.* South Bend, IN: University of Notre Dame Press, 1981.
Stringfellow, William. *Conscience and Obedience: The Politics of Romans 13 and Revelation 13 in Light of the Second Coming.* Waco, TX: Word, 1977.
Svigel, Michael J. *The Fathers on the Future: A 2nd-Century Eschatology for the 21st-Century Church.* Peabody, MA: Hendrickson Academic, 2024.
Taylor, Charles. "The Meaning of Secularism." *Hedgehog Review* 4 (2010) 23–32.
———. *A Secular Age.* Cambridge: Harvard University Press, 2007.
Tillich, Paul. *Systematic Theology, III.* Chicago: University of Chicago Press, 1963.
Tomaszewska, Anna. "Kant's Reconception of Religion and Contemporary Secularism." *Roczniki Filozoficzne* 64 (2016) 125–48.
Tyler, Amanda. *How to End Christian Nationalism.* New York: Broadleaf, 2024.
Vatter, Miguel. "The People Shall Be Judge: Reflective Judgment and Constituent Power in Kant's Philosophy of Law." *Political Theory* 39 (2011) 749–76.
Waldron, Jeremy. *God, Locke, and Equality: Christian Foundations in Locke's Political Thought.* Cambridge: Cambridge University Press, 2002.
Wallace, David Foster. "Authority and American Usage; Or, Why 'Politics and the English Language' Is Redundant." In *Consider the Lobster, and Other Essays*, 64–128. New York: Little, Brown, and Co., 2005.
Webster, John. "Principles of Systematic Theology." *International Journal of Systematic Theology* 2 (2009) 56–71.
Welborn, L. L. *Paul's Summons to Messianic Life: Political Theology and the Coming Awakening.* New York: Columbia University Press, 2015. Kindle.
Westhelle, Vitor. "God and Justice: The Word and the Mask." *Journal of Lutheran Ethics* 3 (2003). https://learn.elca.org/jle/god-and-justice-the-word-and-the-mask-2/.
———. "Power and Politics in Luther's Theology." In *The Global Luther: A Theologian for Modern Times*, edited by Christine Helmer, 284–300. Minneapolis: Fortress, 2009.
———. *The Scandalous God: The Use and Abuse of the Cross.* Minneapolis: Fortress, 2006.
Whitford, David M. "'Cura Religionis' or Two Kingdoms: The Latter Luther and the State in the Lectures on Genesis." *Church History* 23 (2004) 41–62.
"Why America Is a 'Flawed Democracy.'" *Economist*, Mar. 21, 2024. https://www.economist.com/graphic-detail/2024/03/21/why-america-is-a-flawed-democracy/.
Wilder, Amos N. *Early Christian Rhetoric: The Language of the Gospel.* Cambridge: Harvard University Press, 1971.
Witte, John, Jr. *Law and Protestantism: The Legal Teachings of the Lutheran Reformation.* Foreword by Martin E. Marty. Cambridge: Cambridge University Press, 2002.
Wittgenstein, Ludwig. *Philosophical Fragments.* Oxford: Blackwell, 2009.
———. *Tractatus Logico Philosophicus.* New York: Dover, 1998.
Yoder, John Howard. *The Politics of Jesus.* Grand Rapids: Eerdmans, 1972.
Žižek, Slavoj. *Freedom: A Disease Without Cure.* London: Bloomsbury Academic, 2023.
Žižek, Slavoj, and Boris Gunjević. *God in Pain: Inversions of Apocalypse.* New York: Seven Stories, 2012.

Index

Abbot, Edwin A., 223
adiaphoron, 62
Adkins, Brent, 223
Agamben, Giorgio, xxvi–xxix, 26n, 34, 102–9, 134–44, 158–76, 182–84, 197–204, 209–11, 214, 221, 223
Aho, James, 28n, 153, 223
Alison, James, 152, n223
Alonso, James, 94, 223
Althaus, Paul, 88, 88n, 89, 134, 223.
apocalyptic, xxiii–xxvi, xxix, 4–14, 64, 70–72, 108, 118, 127, 141, 144, 147–57, 170, 172–215, 221, 222, 225, 227
Arendt, Hannah, 137, 140n, 143, 223.
Aquinas, Thomas, 78–81, 87, 91, 100, 106, 109, 119n, 226
Augsburg Confession (AC), xii, xix, xxiv, 8, 31, 38–45, 117
August, Eugene R., 223
Augustine, xix, xxii–xxv, 6, 13, 19, 33, 73, 78–81, 91, 98, 106, 118, 145, 193–194, 219–20, 223–25
authority, xxii, 9, 11, 33, 40, 46, 47, 51, 74, 95, 114, 228, 231
   civil authority, 31, 40, 41, 45–47, 51, 52, 60, 113
   spiritual authority, 42, 45, 59
   temporal authority, 9, 11, 33, 40, 46, 47, 51, 74, 228

Barnett, Mary, 38n, 224
Barr, James, 171, 171n, 224

Barth, Karl, ix, 1, 2, 18, 18n, 20, 142, 166, 171, 173n, 190, 199n, 224, 227
Bayer, Oswald, 89n, 102n, 224
beloved community, xxvi, 16, 25, 156, 220, 226
Bentham, Jeremy, xxvi, 89, 89n, 90–93, 95, 106, 126–29, 140, 197n, 223, 224
Bible, xxiii, xxiv, 2, 30, 32, 131, 201, 224, 227, 229
beatitudes, 64, 67, 182, 192, 193
Bodin, Jean, 113n, 115, 119, 120n, 224
Bolman, Lee G., 21n, 224
Bonhoeffer, Dietrich, xi, xvii, 22, 45, 45n, 142, 182, 186, 192–99, 224, 225
Book of Concord (BC), ix, xxii, 30, 38, 43, 228
Bornkamm, Heinrich, 47n, 51n, 60n, 148n, 224
Brooks, Richard O., 79n, 224, 230
Bultmann, Rudolf, xxi, 72, 171
Butler, Judith, 143, 143n, 224
Butler, Kiera, 208n, 224

Caesar, 26, 42, 149, 150, 166, 168
Caputo, John D., 138, 138n, 152n, 153n, 186n, 225
Carty, Jarrett A., 225
Charles V, 64, 115, 117, 150
Christian nationalism (see nationalism)
chronos, see time
civil authority (see authority).

INDEX

Cloud, Morgan, 95n, 225
Cohen, Elizabeth, 225
compassion, 50, 101, 184, 185, 231
Congdon, David, 97, 97n, 98, 225
conscience, 35, 39, 45, 47, 50, 52, 75, 77, 79, 94, 101n, 106, 147
Corwin, Edward, 77n, 78n, 94, 225
Costa Lopez, Julia, 113n, 114n, 225
Cross, Theology of the, xxiii–xxvii, 6, 60, 64–67, 71, 80, 152, 182, 185–192, 197–200, 203, 205, 209, 221
Cullmann, Oscar, 171, 171n, 225

Davies, Jamie P., 225
Deal, Terrence E., 21n, 224
DeJonge, Michael P., 182n, 192n, 194, 225
De Keijzer, Josh, 199n, 225
democratic, 88, 225, 226
Denker, Angela, 225
Dickinson, Colby, 143n, 225
doctrine, definition of, 31–33
doctrinal theology (see theology).
dogma, definition of, 29
dogmatic theology (see theology)
domain, 32
Dominionism, 28n, 31n, 43n, 118, 208, 223
Dominionist, 5, 14, 218
Duchrow, Ulrich, 8, 203, 225
Deutsche Christen, xxiv, 3, 8, 189, 196
Du Mez, Kristin Kobes, xxii, 225

Ebbeler, Jennifer V., 78n, 225
ecumenical, xii–xxv, 8, 14, 20n, 28–30, 40, 69, 87n, 118, 207–9, 214, 218, 227
empire, 2, 21, 26, 94, 112, 114, 117, 119, 145–49, 169, 170
Enlightenment, xii, xiii, xviii, 4, 5, 36, 81, 89, 90, 97, 98, 110, 123, 125, 134, 140, 141, 183, 190, 194, 197, 202, 216, 219, 220, 227.
enthusiasts, 55n
epistemology, xxv, 96, 139, 141, 162, 182, 190, 191, 200.
eschatological, xxvii, 3, 4, 104, 145, 181, 223, 230

eschatological imagination, 4, 7, 12, 37, 88, 144, 146, 152
eschatology, xxiii, xxiv, xxvii, 4–6, 14, 61, 64, 72, 133, 141, 144, 146, 154, 155, 157, 161, 171, 172, 176–79, 181–183, 191, 193, 197, 208–14, 221, 230
Estates, Three, 56–58
eternity, xxvii, 71, 119, 144, 159, 161, 164, 170, 172, 187, 194, 197, 198, 221
evangelical, 1, 2, 15, 206, 210, 221, 225, 226.
Evangelical Lutheran Church in America, 7, 225

Fagerberg, David W., 213, 225
Farrow, D. B., 167, 225.
fascist(s), xxii, xxvi, 29, 170, 219, 220
Fernando, H., 94n, 223
Flacius, Matthias, 62, 63, 117
Forde, Gerhard O., 225
Formula of Concord (FC), xxiv, 39, 116, 207
Fortin, Ernest L., 80n, 226
Freedom, 62, 82, 85, 100, 110, 126, 130, 134, 138, 165, 186, 217, 226, 228, 232
French, David, 95n, 226
friendship, xvi, 98–101, 109, 110
Fugate, Courtney, 85n, 230

Gagne, André, xxiin, 226
Garner, Brian A., 95, 95n, 230
Genesis, 12, 74, 75, 83, 228, 231
Gienapp, Jonathan, xxvin, 205n, 226
Golanski, Alani, 226.
Golden Rule, 16, 22, 28, 50, 61, 126, 139, 148, 178, 184
Gordon, Peter E., 226
Gorsuch, Neil, 95, 95n, 226.
Gospel, 42, 116, 152, 184, 189, 231
government, 18, 70, 75, 125, 127, 151, 180, 197, 215, 217, 225, 226, 228
Gregory, Eric, 226
Gritsch, Eric, 30n, 226, 228
Gunjević, Boris, 188n, 189, 189n, 231

Hart, H.L.A., xxvi, 93, 93n, 101, 107,
    182, 185, 205, 207, 220, 226
Heaney, Seamus, 180, 189n, 181, 226
Hedges, Chris, xxiin, 226
Herbert, Zbigniew, 217, 217n, 226
higher law, xxvi, 76–78, 82, 94–97,
    107 116, 124, 127n, 148, 205,
    219, 220
Hinlicky, Paul R., xi, xii, xiv, xv, xviii,
    56, 75n, 88n, 141, 141n, 156n,
    189n, 223, 226
Hippolytus, 203, 204n, 226
Hitler, Adolf, xi, xii, xxiv, xxviii, 3, 7,
    22, 127, 133, 134, 141
Hobbes, Thomas, 82, 83, 113n,
    118–23, 128, 131, 132
    Hobbesian, 13, 122, 133, 185n
Holm, Minda, 115n, 226
Holmes, Oliver Wendell, 92, 93, 226,
    228
Homo Sacer, xxiv, 103n, 135, 135n,
    139, 165, 167, 183, 201, 202, 223
Hunt, Bruce, A., 84n, 227

Ingersoll, Julie, xxivn, 227

Jenkins, Jack, 32n, 227
Jenson, Robert, 30n, 186n, 197, 198n,
    225–227
Jervis, Ann L., 69, 118n, 167n,
    172–176, 182, 183, 227
Jewitt, Paul, 161n, 227
Johnson, Bill, 28n, 208n, 227
Johnson, Luke Timothy, 161n, 227
just war, 38, 40, 54, 68, 115, 116, 207

Kairos, see time
Kant, Immanuel, xxvi, 6, 84–90, 94,
    96–98, 102, 106, 119, 122–28,
    139–41, 162, 181, 190, 199, 219,
    227
    Kantian, 96, 103, 139, 143, 153,
        162, 181
Käsemann, Ernst, xx, xxi, xxin, 173n,
    227
Katechon, 132, 133, 151, 165, 169,
    170, 192, 195, 208
Kaurin, Pauline Shanks, 101n, 227

Kaylor, Brian, 227
Kierkegaard, Søren, 165, 211, 228
kingdom (see spiritual kingdom and
    temporal kingdom)
Kirk, Russell, 90n, 228
Kolb, Robert, 43n, 228

Lamb, Michael, 228
language, 95n, 102–5, 112, 140, 191,
    202, 229, 231, 232
    sacrament of, 104–8, 137, 138,
        142–44, 159, 164, 183, 184,
        191–93, 198–204, 211, 214, 218,
        223
Lapiana, William P., 92, 93n, 228
Larson, Duane, 116n, 171n,
    228
Latham, Andrew, 113, 113n, 114,
    114n, 127, 228
Lewis, Sinclair, xx, 228
liberal, 16, 70, 76, 82–84, 90, 97, 98,
    110, 125–29, 165n, 189, 216,
    217, 228
liberalism, 12, 70, 82, 88, 125–27, 132,
    141, 142, 185, 197, 216, 217, 220
Lindbeck, George, 20n, 228
literalism, xx, 1, 2, 12, 13, 37, 71,
    193n, 198, 213, 220
liturgy, xx, 212, 213, 224, 230
Locke, John, 82–86, 89, 90, 93,
    99–102, 106, 119, 121–23, 228
Logos, 105, 135, 137
love, xiii–xxix, 1, 2, 13, 14, 16, 24, 25,
    36, 48–51, 59–62, 65, 66, 74, 82,
    83, 97, 101, 134, 147–49, 154,
    156, 157, 164, 166, 167, 182, 185,
    187, 190, 195, 196, 199, 200, 206,
    211, 213, 215, 218, 219–22
Luther, Martin, xxiii, xxvi, 4–6, 46, 13,
    16, 19, 21, 22, 33–35, 38, 46–62,
    65, 66, 68, 69, 71, 74–84, 97, 100,
    102, 106, 112, 113, 118, 128, 145,
    149, 150, 166, 182, 186, 188–93,
    199, 200, 203, 215, 219, 225, 226,
    228

Lutheran, xi, xiv, xvii, xxi, xxii, xxiv,
    xxvi, xxviii, 7–9, 11, 14, 18, 27,

28, 31, 34, 36, 38, 41, 43, 45, 53, 56, 58, 63, 64, 67, 69, 70, 76, 81, 85, 86, 88, 108, 112–18, 128, 139, 152, 165, 166, 186, 191, 203, 207, 225–29, 231, 232
Lutheranism, xii, xxiii, xxv, 7, 13, 15, 30, 31, 40, 58, 58n, 59n, 64, 69, 81, 82, 92, 113n, 118, 141, 166, 209, 214, 215, 226, 228, 229

MAGA, 16, 100
magisteria, 114, 116, 118
  lesser magisteria, 2, 207
Marion, Jean-Luc, 104n, 228
Maritain, Jacques, 119, 119n, 120n, 122, 129n, 229
Martyn, J. Louis, 118n, 171, 171n, 173, 173n, 174, 176n, 183, 229
Marx, Karl, 25
McNeil, John T., 77n, 116n, 229
Meckled-Garcia, Saladin, 111n, 229
messianic time, see time
Melanchthon, Philip, 38, 41–47, 52, 56, 56n, 62, 63, 77, 81
metaphysics, xxvii, 108, 138–41, 162, 175
Milbank, John, 97n–101, 109, 110, 125, 229
Mill John Stuart, 90, 91, 93, 106, 119, 125–28, 223, 229
modern, x, xi, 3, 49, 67, 79, 113, 114, 119, 122, 122n, 127, 131, 136, 139, 144, 153, 171, 174
  modernism, 15
  modernity, xi, 4, 16, 36, 37, 97, 134, 137, 153
  postmodern, xxiv, xxvi, 6, 15, 19, 28, 37, 89, 96–98, 143, 160, 174
  postmodernity, 11, 15, 16, 20, 36, 84, 92, 97, 110, 162, 176, 202, 219
Moltmann, Jürgen, 138, 171, 186n, 229
mystical, 89, 141, 157, 198, 210, 213
mysticism, 189, 213

nation (nation-state), xii, 2, 13, 23, 32, 44, 50, 81, 97, 109–17, 119, 120, 123, 124, 128, 130–33, 137, 138, 183, 189, 195, 202, 220
national, xi, xx, 145, 203, 216, 217
nationalism xxii, 2, 3, 28, 117, 146, 189, 224
  Christian Nationalism, xxiv, 2, 3, 5, 8, 16, 56, 189, 195, 208, 225, 230, 231.
natural law, xxiii–xxvi, 4, 6, 11, 14, 28, 36, 37, 50, 51, 57, 59–61, 64, 72–109, 115–21, 128–31, 138, 139, 148, 177, 183, 185, 217, 219
nature, 7, 30, 57, 58, 61, 65, 73, 76–83, 86, 89, 91, 93, 98, 104, 119, 124n, 125, 131–34, 147, 154, 165, 175, 196, 203, 209
Nelson, Robert H., 58n, 59n, 229
Nessan, Craig L., 34n, 229
New Testament, xxvi, 3, 26, 46, 52, 70, 150–54, 166, 171, 173, 175
Niebuhr, Reinhold, 7, 70, 88, 88n, 133, 229
Nitze, Janie, 226
Norris, Andrew, 137n, 229
Nussbaum, Martha, 138, 138n, 185n, 229
Nygren, Anders, 7n, 8, 229

obedience, 44, 59, 60, 66, 68n, 69, 71, 74, 88, 94, 100n, 101n, 105, 120, 128, 149–51, 155, 179, 188
Obgar, O., 95n, 229
objective, 11, 19, 25, 49, 55, 88, 89, 91, 97, 98, 176
  objectivity, xxi, 96, 162n
ontological, 18, 19, 32–34, 34n, 102, 106, 162, 168, 190
ontology, 18, 34, 34n, 35, 50, 102, 136, 138–41, 162, 177, 178
originalism, xxvi, 94–96, 102, 106, 131, 140, 217, 220
O'Scamlin, Diarmuid F., 229
Osiander, Andreas, 113, 113n, 229

Passavant, Paul A., 229
Pasternak, Lawrence, 85n, 229

Pauline, xiii, xxiv, 5, 8, 28, 37, 69, 70, 108, 118, 147, 148, 159, 160, 166, 167, 171–73, 178, 182, 197, 221
peace, 3, 17, 21, 33, 39, 40, 48–50, 54, 60, 68, 75, 78, 82, 86, 87, 93, 101, 117, 120, 125, 143, 169, 192
Perry, Samuel, xxiin, 230
Peter, Letters of, xxiv, 3, 48, 148, 150
Petit, Philip, 230
philosophy, xxi, xxii, xxiv, xxv, xxvi, 4, 5, 11, 25, 37, 61, 74, 82, 87, 92–95, 101, 102, 106, 126n, 127, 132, 134, 137, 143, 147, 148, 160, 175, 187, 190, 205, 215, 220
piety, xx, xxii, 4, 5, 36, 37, 191, 193
political theology (see theology)
politics, xxii, xxiv, xxv, xxvii, 2–4, 8–10, 18, 21–27, 29, 37, 44, 46, 58, 67, 75–78, 82, 83, 93, 103, 107, 114, 118, 119, 124, 127, 128, 131, 133, 135–40, 144, 145, 151, 165, 182, 184, 194–97, 215, 216, 224
positivism, xxiv, xxvi, 91–95, 99
potentiality, 103, 136, 138, 139, 144, 159, 167
power, xxvi, 9, 21–24, 29, 34n, 43n, 47, 60, 65, 68, 71, 75, 93, 99, 105, 108, 113n, 115, 117, 120–24, 127, 132, 133, 136, 143, 152, 166–70, 174, 178, 180, 182, 185, 186, 188, 197, 203, 205, 215, 219, 220, 221
  sacrament of, 105–7, 138, 142, 143, 159, 164, 184, 185, 192, 193. 197, 204, 212, 214, 221
pragmatism, 21, 92, 93, 106, 200

Qureshi-Hurst, Emily, 177, 177n, 178n, 230

Raeder, Linda C., 126n 127n, 230.
rational, 80, 84, 86, 117, 124, 127, 140, 143, 183, 185, 190, 197, 200
  rationality, 66, 153, 183, 185, 203
Rauch, Jonathan, 11n, 215n, 216n, 230
Rausch, Thomas, 213n, 230

reason, xxv, 4, 11, 46, 50, 51, 60–63, 67, 74–80, 82–90, 94, 99–103, 106, 126, 128, 135, 137–42, 147, 150, 151, 154, 156, 168, 184, 185, 188, 190, 197, 199, 200, 202, 213, 219
religion; xxi, xxiv, xxv, 3, 4, 8–13, 16, 18, 19, 26, 29, 32, 52, 81, 85–90, 94, 102, 114, 117, 127, 132, 133, 139, 140, 141, 143, 176, 188, 194–97, 207, 208, 215–19, 221, 229
  natural religion, 85, 87, 219
  revealed religion, 87, 140, 141
res publica, 111, 130
revelation, xxi, 1, 6, 19, 25, 55, 66, 79, 80n, 83, 86, 102–107, 114, 118, 158, 168–70, 187, 190, 193, 198, 199, 201, 205, 211, 212
Revelation (book of), 3, 145, 146, 148, 231
righteousness, xxi, 24, 41, 42, 44, 58, 119, 123, 156, 166, 185, 186, 190, 193, 198
Rilke, Rainier Maria, 73, 73n, 230
Romans, Paul's Letter to the, 5, 47, 69, 70, 76, 145–48, 151, 158, 160, 168, 179, 223, 227, 228, 231
Russell, Robert John, 177n, 230

Scalia, Antonin, 95, 96, 229, 230
Schelia, Arnulf von, 8n, 230
Schmemann, Alexander 213n, 230
Schmitt, Carl, xxvi, 99, 114, 127, 130–33, 136, 143, 169, 230
Schofield, Malcolm, 77n, 94n, 230
secular, xxii, xxiv, xxvi, xxvii, 2–7, 12, 13, 18, 23, 31, 38–42, 46, 51, 53, 55, 57, 62, 73, 77, 78, 81, 90, 94, 97, 98, 112, 114–17, 127, 127n, 129, 134, 139, 146, 147, 158, 167, 168, 179, 181, 182, 188, 192, 194, 197, 199, 200, 205, 208, 209, 212, 215, 218, 221
secularism, 12, 15, 18, 27, 81n, 97, 193, 194, 196
secularity, 6, 10–12, 18, 31, 75, 80, 97, 107, 114, 127, 139, 194, 199

Sigmund, Paul E., 83n, 231
sin, xxi, 7, 22, 24, 30, 41, 44, 48, 50, 56, 61, 65–68, 70, 74–76, 78, 80, 82, 83, 90, 98, 101, 105, 105n, 118, 130, 165, 166, 186, 198, 203, 219
Smalcaldic League, 64, 115
  Wars, 63, 82, 117, 119
Snow Nancy E., 185n, 231
Solberg, Mary, 189n, 230
sovereign, 8, 34, 69, 70, 82. 91, 92, 100, 110, 112–36, 156, 183, 188, 201, 202, 217, 220; sovereignty, xxiv–xxvi, 4, 6, 14, 36, 37, 64, 69, 72–74, 77, 81, 82, 99–101, 108–15, 117–31, 134–39, 142, 143, 165, 166, 183–85, 217, 219, 220
spirit, 4, 6, 17, 24, 35, 41, 77, 89, 121, 133, 175, 182, 191, 194
  Spirit, Holy, ix, 1, 25, 30, 33, 49, 55, 60, 68, 77, 153, 200, 213, 214
spiritual authority (see authority)
spiritual kingdom, 3–6, 9, 14, 24, 27, 33–36, 52, 55, 59, 72, 73, 76, 77, 86, 96, 97, 101, 102, 116, 118, 144, 157, 179, 181–84, 195–201, 205, 207, 211–21
Spivak, Gayatri Chakravorty, 143n, 224
Springer, Carl P. E., 77n, 230
Stalin, Joseph, x, xxvi
state (see nation-state)
state of exception, 133, 148, 156, 188, 183, 195, 206, 207, 208, 220
Steigman-Gall, Richard, 230
Stout, Jeffrey, ix, 11n, 231
Stringfellow, William, 22n, 68–71, 151, 207, 231
suffering, 41n, 49, 58, 60, 65, 66, 93, 100, 101, 106–8, 125, 126, 182, 184, 186–92, 194, 197–200, 205–7, 211, 212, 216–21
Svigel, Michael J., 204, 210, 231
systematic theology (see theology)

Taylor, Charles, 12, 12n, 97, 97n, 226, 231

temporal authority (see authority)
temporality, 6, 34, 128, 140, 143–47, 152, 158, 161–64, 168–72, 176–81, 187, 197, 204, 209, 221
theology, ix–xxv, 1, 4, 5, 6,11, 12, 19, 20, 23, 25, 26, 30, 36, 56, 65, 67, 74–77, 80, 88, 114, 126–33, 139, 141–44, 160, 165, 168, 176, 189, 190, 194, 199, 208, 213, 214, 218, 228
  doctrinal, x, 20, 204n, 214
  dogmatic, xii
  systematic, xiii, 19, 20, 202n
  political, xxiv, 8, 18, 28, 36, 45, 49, 67, 76, 106, 107, 112, 114, 133, 185, 197, 221
theology of the cross (see cross)
Tillich, Paul, 231
time, as *Chronos*, 161, 163, 181, 221, 222
  as Kairos, 161, 163, 168
  as messianic, xxvi, 34, 108, 144, 146, 157, 159, 160–78, 181–83, 186, 191, 192, 197, 200, 202, 204, 209–14, 221
Tomaszewska, Anna, 87n, 231
Torvend, Samuel, 213n
transcendence, 5, 10, 103, 104, 108, 131, 137, 187, 196, 201, 211–14
two kingdoms, *passim* (see spiritual kingdom and temporal kingdom)
Tyler, Amanda, xxii, 231

utilitarian, 90, 124–26
utilitarianism, 90, 93

violence, 22, 26, 48, 50, 55, 64, 67–71, 75, 93, 137, 153, 207, 208
Vatter, Miguel, 124n, 231

Waldron, Jeremy, 83, 83n, 224, 231
Wallace, David Foster, 95n, 231
Wallnau, Lance, 28n, 208n, 227
Webster, John, 19, 20n, 231
Wengert, Timothy J., 43n, 228
Westhelle, Vitor, 29n, 57n, 67, 67n, 231

Westphalia, 3, 86n, 111–14, 119
Whitehead, Andrew, xxii, 230
Whitford, David M., 75n, 76n, 231
Wilder, Amos N., 132, 153–54, 231
Witte, John Jr., 34, 52, 56, 226, 231
Wittgenstein, Ludwig, 91n, 92n, 95n, 231
word and sacrament, 31, 39, 213, 214, 228
word and service, 31

Yoder, John Howard, 149n, 231

Žižek, Slavoj, xii, 138, 138n, 165n, 188, 189, 189n, 231

www.ingramcontent.com/pod-product-compliance
Lightning Source LLC
Chambersburg PA
CBHW031725230426
43669CB00007B/246